The Valley's Legends and Legacies III

THE VALLEY'S
Legends
& Legacies III

By Catherine Morison Rehart

Word Dancer Press

Clovis, California

Published by
Quill Driver Books/Word Dancer Press, Inc.
8386 N. Madsen
Clovis, CA 93611
559-322-5917
800-497-4909

Word Dancer Press books may be purchased for educational, fund-raising, business or promotional use. Please
contact Special Markets, Quill Driver Books/Word Dancer
Press, Inc. at the above address or phone number.

ISBN 1-884995-18-7

Rehart, Catherine Morison, 1940-
    The valley's legends & legacies III/ by Catherine Morison Rehart.
       p.   cm.
    Scripts of the KMJ radio program, The valley's legends & legacies.
    ISBN 1-884995-12-8 (pbk.)
    1. Fresno County (Calif.)--History--Anecdotes.   2. Fresno County
(Calif.)--Biography--Anecdotes. 3. San Joaquin Valley (Calif.)-
-History--Anecdotes. 4. San Joaquin Valley (Calif.)--Biography-
-Anecdotes.   I. Valley's legends and legacies (radio program)
II. Title.
F868.F8R44   1999
979.4'82--dc21

                                 CIP

First printing November 1999

Front Cover Photo: *See page 280.*
Back Cover Photos: *Descending from top, see pages: 153, 237, 92, 73, 76, 289, 171.*

To

Robert Martin Wash

With love and gratitude

———

In Memoriam

Russ & Pat Fey

Contents

Contents

Contents

Contents

Contents

Contents

Foreword

Having been born and raised in Tulare gave me great insight into what made a small town function. I remember going on house calls with my dad, Dr. Charlie Mathias, to different homes in Tulare and also to many farm houses out in the country.

Then school and sports at Tulare High School gave me another view of life in a small town. Later on, running for Congress gave me the chance to visit each and every town, large and small, in the Congressional District.

I always made a point to read about the history of the town before going there. Reading about the beginnings of a town, how it got its name, when buildings were built and why, and why it developed in the first place, was always educational but most of all it was just interesting and fun. When I got to the town and had the chance to meet with all the people who governed that town, meet with all the groups, organizations, and clubs of all types, I felt that I really knew the town and its people and really felt good about being there. All this, plus hearing many a good story about the past happenings of the town were some of the most enjoyable experiences I've ever had.

My interest in the happening, old and new, to all the Valley towns has never ceased. It makes life interesting to be aware of life and happenings around you. The what, why, when and how people do things is what really creates our fascinating history of our great Valley. That's why I've enjoyed The Valley's Legends & Legacies so much! The stories make me feel right at home!

— Bob Mathias

Preface

One of the greatest pleasures I have in writing the Legends & Legacies radio scripts for KMJ Radio is the opportunity it affords me to share my love for the Fresno community and for the Central Valley with those who listen to the broadcasts. My family pioneered in Fresno Station in 1873—my roots go deep—I joke to my friends that I am root-bound. Happily so because I could never envision living anywhere else.

From the time I was very young, I wanted to write. As I grew older my interest in local history became a passion. My dream was to write about the people, places, and events of this valley. However, I was busy raising a family, volunteering in my community, and later, finding myself a single mom, joining the workforce. The dream remained only that—a fleeting thought from time to time—in quiet moments a longing that had to remain on hold.

When I was working as Education/Information Director at the Fresno Historical Society, I received a phone call from Program Director John Broeske of KMJ Radio put the dream within reach. He told me that KMJ General Manager Al Smith had an idea for a radio program that he hoped would promote pride in our Fresno community by using history as a catalyst to tell the stories of people, places, and events. Would I like to write the scripts? That was nine years ago. In the intervening time, my dream has come true on a scale I find hard to believe.

A year and a half ago, it occurred to me that, in addition to writing the Fresno and Clovis stories, it would be interesting to include tales from other communities throughout the vast KMJ listening area. I began traveling around the Central Valley to Mariposa, Madera, Hanford, Selma, Fowler, Riverdale, Coalinga, and the foothill communities of Fresno, Mariposa, and Madera counties. I've discovered places like Wildflower and Elkhorn and Bootjack. I've met families who still live on the land their ancestors homesteaded or purchased in the 1860s and 1870s. I've met the descendents of famous 18th Spanish personages whose names—Vallejo, DeAnza, Pico—evoke the history and romance of Alta

California. Every community is unique and has its own stories to tell.

On this journey, I have discovered a special treasure—active historical societies and museums that tell the story of their respective communities, staffed by enthusiastic professionals and volunteers who are working hard to preserve the history of their communities, who are proud of their heritage, and who graciously welcome the stranger at the door who comes in search of the stories their community has to tell. Some of the stories are light-hearted, but many are not. From the creaking of the Spanish carretas carrying eloping lovers along El Camino Viejo on our Valley's west side to the coming in state of Tenaya, chief of the Yosemite tribe, to face his nemesis Major James Savage, our history is rich with drama and passion.

In addition, I have rediscovered the incredible beauty of this valley in which we live. The farmlands on the valley floor offer a unique kind of beauty. Our agricultural economy is dependent on the weather—we are all aware of it and, in a sense, it roots us to the land. The changing seasons in the vineyards and orchards are constant reminders of the cycle of life. The blossoms of spring and the gold and red leaves of fall make drives through the farmlands of our valley an unending treat.

For those who think our area is without scenic vistas, I challenge you to get in your car and drive north on Highway 41, turn east at Four Corners (Highway 145), and experience the splendor of Little Table Mountain. Or, drive east on Highway 180 through Centerville and Minker, crossing the Kings River along the way. You will take a step back in time. Often, when I take these trips, I write about them hoping that you will want to take them, too, and discover for yourself the beauty around us.

I hope you enjoy these stories about the people, places, and events that played a role in the history of our valley as much as I enjoy writing them.

Cathy Rehart

Acknowledgments

A work such as this cannot be accomplished without help from many people. To everyone who has assisted me, my gratitude is immeasurable.

First, I want to extend my thanks to Elizabeth Laval-Leyva and the Laval family for allowing me to use photos from the "Pop" Laval Collection. Their generosity and friendship is deeply appreciated. Also, thank-you to Steve Brown and Doug Stewart of Image Group Marketing Communications, Inc. for providing the Laval photographs.

I want to thank Al Smith and John Broeske of KMJ Radio. Not only do they make my words come alive on the radio every day, but, in allowing me the opportunity to work on this program, they have made my dream of writing about local history come true. They also have offered me the most incredible support. My gratitude to them both is boundless.

I have been an admirer of Bob Mathias since high school. He is one of our valley's true heroes. I am deeply honored that he so graciously agreed to write the foreword for this book.

I also wish to thank my publisher, Steve Mettee of Quill Driver Books. His skills as a graphic artist and his unfailing good taste have made my books pleasing to the eye. His ongoing support—the many telephone calls, suggestions, willingness to listen and answer questions, and his great patience—have helped beyond measure. A huge thank-you also to Josh Mettee not only for his marketing skills, but for sitting with me at book signings and lending moral support.

To my editor, Bobbye Sisk Temple, an enormous "thank-you" for your loyal friendship and your willingness to bring your editing skills to my work. Your constructive notes make me a better writer—you are a teacher as well as an editor. To Doris Hall, who always has to fine-tune the manuscript on the computer, thank you.

The Fresno County Free Library's California History Room is presided over by Linda Sitterding, local history librarian, and her staff members Mike Schimmel, Bill Secrest, Jr., Bill Secrest, Sr., and Joseph Augustino, who are unfailing sources of information. They are always available to answer questions and point me in the right direction. Thank you. To Linda, special thanks for the brainstorming sessions, the marvelous suggestions for topics, and for the good friendship we share. Gratitude also to John Kallenberg, Fresno County librarian, for his ongoing support.

Thanks also to Jan Peterson and Gail Hanson of the Fresno Bee Library for their help in providing the research materials I request. It is always such a pleasure to work in their facility.

Our Central Valley has many fine museums. Most have archival materials that are available by appointment. I want to particularly thank Muriel Powers, retired director of the Mariposa Museum & Historical Center; Pamela A. Stoddard, director/curator of the Hanford Carnegie Museum; and Helen F. Cowan, R. C. Baker Memorial Museum, for allowing me access to books and materials, for offering constructive suggestions, for answering my questions, and for checking scripts for accuracy. I am most grateful. Dwight Barnes, president of the Fresno Flats Historical Association, took me on a tour of their facility and answered numerous questions. Scott Pinkerton, Mariposa historian, provided helpful information. Thank you to them also.

What would one do without good friends? Special thanks to John Edward Powell, who has provided historical and architectural information from his files on an ongoing basis—cheerfully helping to ferret out bits of trivia that add fun and interest to the scripts; to Randy McFarland, who spent two days taking me on tours of Selma and has always been available to read scripts for accuracy or to answer questions; to Bill Coate for loaning me books from his private library, offering suggestions, and answering questions on Madera history; to Jim Oakes for loaning me books from his library that have opened up new avenues of ideas; and most special thanks to Robert Wash, my treasured friend and companion, for suggesting topics, critiquing scripts, allowing me access to his large library and newspaper files, accompanying me on trips throughout the valley, and for always being there to offer support and encouragement.

The members of three pioneer families have been of inestimable help in this project. I will never forget two marvelous afternoons at the Refuge—a place so rich in history. Thank you to Brooke Wissler for so graciously welcoming me to her ranch and for sharing the beauty of the Refuge and the rich history of the Mordecai family with me. Thank you to Brad Harlan for talking to me about his family's journey to California with the Donners, the Youngs, and the Reeds. And, thank you to Ed Kreyenhagen for sharing information about his family, suggesting topics about the West Side, and e-mailing answers to my history questions.

A special thank-you to the Reverend Bernard Guekguezian and Phil Tavlian of First Armenian Presbyterian Church for providing photos and information. Also thanks to Robert Pennell, cultural resources manager, Table Mountain Rancheria; Camille Wing of the Taoist Temple Preservation Society in Hanford; Jim Beath, community development director, City of Hanford; Vince Peterson, retired city manager, City of Hanford; and Jim Doughty, community development director, City of Huron.

I have interviewed so many people for this work—too many to mention everyone here. They are all listed in the end notes and bibliography at the end of this book. My gratitude to each one of them for graciously giving of their time to talk to me is undying. Many of these folks have allowed me to borrow photographs from their private collections. For this, too, I am deeply grateful.

Most of all I am grateful to the KMJ Radio listeners, to those who read my books, and to those I meet when I speak to local organizations. Your enthusiasm and eagerness to learn more about our Central Valley fuels this project. Al Smith's hope was that this program would promote pride in our community. If it has succeeded in doing that, then I can't ask for more.

—CMR

A Special Acknowledgment

Robert Wilson, owner of Fresno Lincoln Mercury deserves special recognition for his longtime sponsorship of *The Valley's Legends & Legacies* on KMJ Radio. His ongoing support and enthusiasm for the program is deeply appreciated.

The Valley's Legends and Legacies III

The history of the Lincoln-Mercury dealership in Fresno dates back to 1938. In that year, Ray Prior and Ted Shelton, who had become partners in 1935 when they purchased the O. W. Hunsaker Ford agency, were offered the opportunity to be the local distributors for Lincoln automobiles and to handle distribution of Mercury automobiles for the valley. They gave up the Ford dealership and hitched their star to another make of car. The business was a success.

In 1955, the dealership was sold. The new owner was a gentleman who knew the car business well. His name was Frank J. Sanders. He had just graduated from high school when he began working for Rodman Chevrolet in 1936. It was at the height of the Depression. Even though times were tough, he found he had a knack for selling cars. In the month of April 1936, alone, he sold 25 of the 70 cars the entire dealership sold that month. He worked at Rodman's for three years and then decided to go into business for himself. He bought a used car lot at 3000 E. Tulare and began to sell cars at a terrific rate—300 to 400 a month. Al Radka handled sales and promotion for the business. The promotion days were grand events. Sanders would rent a theater—the Wilson, Warnor's or Tower—for a free Saturday show for children. At Christmas, Santa would come to the lot. Families would be invited to drive by and receive a gift. Radka and his mythical sidekick "Mrs. Winterbottom" would tour Fresno in their Frank J. Sanders car— all on his Saturday radio show—capturing the imagination of all who listened. The result? Tulare Street would fill with cars.

In 1955, Sanders purchased the Lincoln-Mercury dealership. Soon he found the company needed more space so he moved from Prior and Shelton's location on Fulton Street to a large building on Tulare Street across from his used car lot. In 1973, the business moved to North Blackstone Avenue where it still is today.

On January 3, 1989, Sanders sold the dealership to Robert Wilson. Continuing Sanders' tradition of success, for the past 10 years the company has been one of the top 100 Lincoln-Mercury dealers in the nation in sales and service. In 1997, the Chairman's Award, the top award given by the Ford Motor Company, was

Fresno area families were invited to drive by the Frank J. Sanders' used car lot for a free gift each Christmas. The enthusiasm with which this was met— by everyone involved—is shown in this late-1940s photo of Sanders handing gifts through a car window.
Courtesy of Frank J. Sanders

given to the dealership. The award is based on the market share of cars they sell and on the service they give.

For more than 60 years, Fresno Lincoln-Mercury has served the people of Fresno and of the Central Valley. One of the oldest auto dealerships in Fresno, it has earned its rightful place in the legends of our Valley.

In the early years of California's statehood and just one year before Fresno County was officially created, a small settlement named Fresno City was established near the present-day city of Tranquillity. On the Fresno Slough, a branch of the Kings River that flows into the San Joaquin River, Fresno City was a stopping point for steamboats and the southern terminus of the telegraph line from San Francisco.

The Butterfield Overland Mail stage line that ran from St. Louis to San Francisco passed through Fresno City. San Francisco newspapers stationed reporters in Fresno City to intercept the eastern newspapers that were brought via the stage and to telegraph their news to their editors in San Francisco. When the telegraph line was extended south to Visalia, that much larger city became the major source of news for San Francisco.

Fresno City was founded in 1855 and lasted for about ten years. During that time, a number of buildings were constructed, including a store and hotel. Ambitious plans for a large community are evident in an old townsite map which was filed on April 25, 1860, by A. J. Downer, attorney and agent for C. A. Hawley and W. B. Cummings, the town's promoters. The map shows a proposed eighty-nine-block area that measured two and one quarter miles east and west and one mile north and south.

The proposed plans, however, never came to fruition. The building of the railroad through the San Joaquin Valley some thirty miles to the east and the development of new town sites along its route were the death knell to the small community. Fresno City faded into obscurity. Today, there is no sign that Fresno City ever existed. Not a single building or wagon track marks its site.

The original site of Fresno City was designated as a California historical landmark. In 1952, the Fresno County Historical Society dedicated a stone and bronze monument commemorating Fresno City. It stood on Whites Bridge Road near Tranquillity as a reminder that at one time there was another city named Fresno in our great Central Valley.

Unfortunately, vandals stole the bronze marker and partially destroyed the stone monument on which it was placed. Like the old town of Fresno City, it, too, has faded into oblivion.

In 1897, Dr. Warren Taylor Barr, a graduate of the Cooper Medical School which later became Stanford University Medical School, began to practice medicine in Fresno. He shared an office with Dr. Chester Rowell, whom he called "the greatest man who ever lived." One of Dr. Barr's accomplishments during his long career was that he, along with other physicians, founded the Burnett Sanitarium which today has evolved into the Community Medical Centers Fresno.

Early in his career, Dr. Barr was often called to the mountain areas to treat people who were ill or had been injured. On these trips, he left Fresno in a horse and buggy. He remembered on one trip he rode in his buggy to the top of the Tollhouse Grade to amputate the limb of a man who was hurt while working in a logging camp. He also traveled by horse and buggy to an area near the summit of the Coast Range Mountains to treat a rancher. One thing that puzzled him was that these trips usually occurred during rainstorms. Was it only when it was raining that they needed him, he wondered? These journeys usually were undertaken to treat one patient. But, by the time he reached his destination word of his planned arrival would have gotten around and there would be many people waiting who needed his services.

Dr. Barr also remembered a time when the number of malaria cases in Fresno County reached plague status. "The mosquitoes were so thick along the rivers and streams they would blind anyone walking there around sundown," he said. The disease declined when the mosquito breeding spots were cleaned up.

At the time of his death in 1955, Dr. Barr was eighty-three years old. He had seen Fresno grow from a pioneer town to a major city. He also lived to see the horse and buggy replaced by the automobile.

In the days before California's statehood, when California was part of Mexico, land was plentiful in the Central Valley. If one wished to obtain a large tract of land it was possible to petition the governor of the territory in which the land was situated. If the petition was successful the petitioner received the land in the form of a Mexican land grant.

Under Mexican law, the grant was limited to eleven square leagues (about 48,712 acres). The leagues would be divided in the following way: one would consist of irrigable soil, four would be dependent on rainfall, and six would be suitable for grazing.

After the petition was sent to the governor, the governor would ask a local officer to determine if the land was vacant. The officer's report was then sent to the governor. This was called an *informe*. Next, a copy of the petition and the report were filed with the secretary of the governor in Monterey. The original grant, with the attached papers, was then given to the petitioner as evidence of title. This was called an *expediente*. Finally, the territorial deputation either rejected or approved the grant. When the grant was finally made, the land was measured.

Using the primitive methods of the day, two horsemen with lariats 137 feet long attached to long stakes would measure the land. The first horseman would drive a stake in the ground, then gallop until he ran to the end of his rope and he would drive the second stake in the ground. The second horseman would retrieve the first stake and gallop from that point until the end of the lariat was reached once again. This would continue until they had covered approximately the number of square leagues contained in the grant. Their starting place was usually a hill, tree, or rock.

Before the Mexican period, when California was part of Spain, an individual could obtain a *concession*. For a fee and proof that land was needed on which to graze livestock, a person could obtain a parcel of land on which he could live and graze his cattle. But the land itself still belonged to the crown.

Often in speaking of California's rich past, we talk about Spanish land grants. This is a misnomer. It was only after California came under the jurisdiction of Mexico that land was granted to individuals.

The Witness Tree

At the eastern end of Elkhorn Avenue, southeast of Kingsburg, an ancient oak tree sits in a field surrounded by lesser trees. Despite the solitude of its pastoral setting, this legendary tree has its own tale to tell.

On December 7, 1843, Manuel Castro, the prefect of the Monterey District of California, which was then owned by Mexico, petitioned Governor Manuel Micheltorena for a grant of land. It was to be named the Rancho Laguna De Tache and was to comprise 48,000 acres.

Using the primitive methods of the day, the grant was surveyed and the application was approved on January 10, 1846, by Governor Don Pio Pico, then governor of California. The Mexican War began the same year. Two years later, in 1848, under the Treaty of Guadalupe Hidalgo, the United States agreed to honor all Mexican land grants approved prior to July 7, 1846.

Meanwhile, the United States government began surveying the land in the Central Valley. All surveys were based on the Mount Diablo base and meridian. In 1864, Deputy Surveyor T. J. DeWoody began his survey of the grant. His report begins, "Beginning at an oak tree thirty-six inches in diameter...on the fourth standard line south..." Today, Elkhorn Avenue runs along this fourth standard line. Based on DeWoody's survey, a patent signed in the name of President Andrew Johnson was issued to Manuel Castro and recorded in Fresno County on June 15, 1866. All of the grant lay south of Elkhorn Avenue.

Castro was destined never to live on his land. He eventually sold off portions of it and lost some to foreclosure.

Today, the Laguna De Tache grant is part of history. The towns which have been established within the perimeters of the grant—Laton, Riverdale, and Lenare, and the communities of Hub and Camden—all can trace their creation directly to the ancient oak in the field south of Kingsburg. It was from that oak that the original grant was measured. Called the Witness Tree, it witnessed the founding of one of the largest Mexican grants within the San Joaquin Valley.

It was also from this tree that the township corner of Floral and Highland avenues was measured, thus affecting the sites of Selma and Kingsburg. In 1852, the men who made the first survey of the valley placed a cup of charcoal, in addition to a stake, at the junction point of each section, or township. In 1880, a civil engineer named Caleb Davis was hired to fix the township point near the future town of Selma. He measured from the oak tree, but could not find the stake. He did, however, find remnants of the charcoal, thus verifying the original survey.

A legend of a unique kind, the Witness Tree has played its own role in the tales of our valley.

The Tragedy at Mussel Slough

The farm of Henry Brewer three and one-fourth miles north of Grangeville. This was the scene of the shooting that became known as the Mussel Slough Tragedy. Some of the bodies were laid out on the porch of Brewer's house (at the center of the photo) after the shootings took place.
Courtesy Hanford Carnegie Museum, Inc.

On the morning of May 11, in the year 1880, eight men were killed in a wheat field a few miles north of Hanford. The shots that rang out that morning sent shock waves throughout California. The resulting political crusade in some thirty years' time would wrest control of California's government from the railroad and put it back in the hands of the people.

By 1880, it was evident everywhere in the state that the bosses of the Central Pacific Railroad were in control. One of their number, Leland Stanford, was an ex-governor of California. Indeed, the railroad dominated state and federal courts and the legislative bodies as well. From the perspective of those settling the Central Valley, the railroad held all the cards.

Into this situation came the issue of land titles. A circular issued by the railroad's land office in Sacramento invited settlers to purchase land. The actual terms allowed settlers to "take up filings on the odd-numbered sections [of public land] with 'a privilege of purchase' as soon as the railway had received final patent rights." The price was set at two and a half dollars to five dollars an acre "without regard to improvements." A number of wheat ranchers near Hanford and Grangeville took the railroad up on the offer. They settled on the land, spent $400,000 improving it and, when the land was later appraised by the railroad, they were asked to pay $35 or more per acre. This was too much. The farmers protested that they were being asked to pay again for their own improvements. They brought suit in federal court against the railroad. While the suit was still pending in Washington, D.C., the Circuit Court in San Francisco issued eviction notices in favor of Walter Crow and M. J. Hart, who had purchased land from the railroad on which other farmers had already settled. The notices were to be delivered to those farmers by U.S. Marshal A. W. Poole.

Technically, the railroad had the legal right to act as it did, but, to the people of California, the railroad was wrong. The settlers became heroes.

On the morning of May 11, 1880, Marshal Poole arrived to deliver the eviction notices. He talked to the settlers and told them he felt very sorry about what he had to do. He was, he said, merely carrying out his orders.

By morning's end, eight men would be dead and the tragedy at Mussel Slough would go down in history as a turning point in ending the domination of the railroad in the life of California.

A historic marker on Road 14, just south of Excelsior Avenue, on the east side of the road, commemorates the events that took place in the wheat field at Mussel Slough.

The farmers in the area of Mussel Slough northwest of Hanford were angry with their treatment at the hands of the Central Pacific Railroad Company. They had settled on land offered by the railroad at what they deemed a fair price, made improvements and, when it was time for them to purchase that land, the railroad upped the price and sold it out from under them to other buyers. The Circuit Court in San Francisco issued eviction notices to the farmers and sent a U.S. marshal to deliver them.

The morning of May 11, 1880, saw the arrival of Marshal A. W. Poole, accompanied by W. H. Clark, in Kingsburg. They hired two horses and a carriage from Josiah Draper and headed for Mussel Slough. Two men who had bought the settler's land from the railroad, Walter Crow and M. J. Hart, were awaiting their arrival. The wheat farmers did not know the marshal was on his way. Poole met Crow and Hart and they visited the home of one wheat farmer, William Braden. Braden was not at home. Braden's furniture was carried out of his home and Hart took possession of the house. Crow and Poole rode on to the Brewer and Storer ranch and claimed it in the name of the railroad.

About this time several farmers arrived on horseback. One of them, Jim Harris, got into an argument with Crow. Harris pulled out his gun and shot at Crow, missing him. Crow grabbed a shotgun and shot Harris in the thigh and chest. Turning to Ivar Knutson, Crow shot and killed him as well. Another farmer, Dan Kelly, was the next to be shot by Crow. The marshal's bodyguard, Archibald McGregor, was downed in the next minute. John Henderson, seeing the carnage, became enraged and went after Crow, shooting at him, but he missed. In turn, Crow fired a fatal shot into Henderson's brain. Crow ran off and hid in a wheat field. Later that evening, when trying to climb a fence to get into his father-in-law's yard, he was shot and killed.

Later that day, seven settlers were arrested and taken to San Francisco for trial for resisting a United States officer. Five were convicted and sentenced to eight months in the jail in San Jose. The man who killed Crow left California under an assumed name and was never prosecuted. The residents of the Mussel Slough area

This photograph shows the five men who were convicted in the Mussel Slough Tragedy. They were, left to right, John D. Purcell, John J. Doyle, James N. Patterson, Wayman L. Pryor and William Braden. The photo was taken in San Jose in 1880 during their incarceration.
Courtesy Hanford Carnegie Museum, Inc.

treated him like a hero, offered him protection and, when it looked as if the federal government was going to come after him, helped him flee the state.

The jail situation turned into a farce. Three of the men, Wyman Pryor, John Pursell and James Patterson, brought their wives and children with them since they had no other place to go. On the first day they served time, four hundred members of Patterson's church showed up to visit. Cables and letters arrived from all over the world showing support. Indeed, the men made such a fine impression on the jailer, William Curtis, that they were soon allowed the freedom to come and go as they wished. They served their eight-month sentence in a way that made it feel like a paid vacation. One of the men, William Braden, actually married the jailer's daughter Susie.

What began as a tragedy turned into a farce—the likes of which the state of California has rarely seen.

Aunt Lil & the Gold Nugget

As often happens when one reads old newspapers, a little gem in the form of a personal story can catch one's eye. This story appeared in the August 25, 1951, issue of the *Fresno Bee*. On this day, a lady named Aunt Lil Miller was sharing her recollections with a reporter. The conversation took place in the town of O'Neals in Madera County. The town was named for Aunt Lil's father, Charles O'Neal.

According to Aunt Lil, her family arrived in the area in 1878 when she was seven years old. They settled on the Hildreth Ranch in a house built in 1861. The Hildreth Mine and the Abbey Mine were still going strong even though it was more than twenty years since the Gold Rush. She remembered that gold was so plentiful that a Wells Fargo office had been opened nearby with stages running often and on a regular schedule.

One of her memories was about the day in 1888 when a stage was robbed near Fine Gold. There was great excitement when the driver came rushing to their home to contact the sheriff. Later, that same driver was arrested for participation in the robbery.

Another memory that was fresh in her mind was the continual presence of Indians.

Later her family moved to another ranch, just across the San Joaquin River from Hamptonville, a settlement later named Pollasky and then Friant. Aunt Lil recalled the huge celebration when Marcus Pollasky's railroad reached that small town in the early 1890s. Railroad cars brought lots of people to a barbecue and accompanying festivities. There was much noise and excitement. Unfortunately, Pollasky soon left with his investors' money in his pocket.

Of all her childhood memories, one of the most vivid was of the day she was allowed to hold a gold nugget from the Hildreth Mine. She remembered how very heavy it was. And, no wonder, for it was as big as a small orange. A thrilling moment, even for a small child, as she gazed in wonder at this huge golden nugget gleaned from the earth in the foothills of our great Central Valley.

Lafayette Maynard Dixon, always known as Maynard, was born in Fresno on June 24, 1875, the son of Harry St. John Dixon and his wife, the former Constance Maynard. Harry Dixon was county clerk of Fresno County, one of the founders of the local bar association, and the first city attorney. He built a fine two-story home on the west side of Van Ness Avenue in the first block north of the present Metropolitan Museum. It was here that Maynard Dixon grew up. Harry Dixon had fought for the Confederacy in the Civil War.

At the early age of seven, Maynard showed an unusual talent for drawing. On the outskirts of the small town of Fresno he could look to the east and see the Sierra or to the west and see the more distant Coast Range Mountains. He would visit relatives at the Refuge Ranch a few miles south of Madera and observed the cowboys of the valley's west side. He seemed influenced by these sights and sought to reproduce them in his art. When he was sixteen years old he sent copies of his work to the noted artist Frederick Remington and received a reply that Maynard's work was better than his at that age and to keep painting.

The family moved to the Bay Area where Dixon began to make his living as a commercial artist. He worked for a number of publications including *The Call*, the *Examiner*, *Overland Monthly*, *Sunset* and others. His great love was, as always, landscape painting.

He had his first exhibition at the Bohemian Club in 1905; his first sale was to Mayor James D. Phelan. Dixon joined the Bohemian Club and associated with such literary elite as Frank Norris, George Sterling, Jack London, Ambrose Bierce, Edwin Markham, Kathleen Norris, and Mary Austin.

His reputation as a landscape painter grew. Among his work was a mural for the Mark Hopkins Hotel and four murals for Anita Baldwin McClaughry's mansion. He was soon recognized nationally as a landscape artist of the first rank. He fell in love with the great Southwest. Many of his greatest paintings showed its mountains and deserts.

He worked in New York for a while but soon returned to San Francisco and the Southwest. Dixon died in Tucson, Arizona, on November 14, 1946.

Dixon also loved to write poetry, but did not publish his verse during his lifetime. After his death, his widow, Edith, published his poems in a book titled *Rim-Rock and Sage.* His poetry expressed his philosophy of life and the beauty of his beloved Southwest. Those who knew him well said of him that he wrote poetry for the same reason he painted the living landscapes he loved—he had to.

Some strange stories have been told in our tales of the valley, but none stranger than this.

After the assassination of President Abraham Lincoln in 1865, it was believed that the killer, actor John Wilkes Booth, tried to escape and was tracked to the Garret Ranch in Virginia where he was shot and killed. However, many did not believe this story and rumors of his successful escape took hold of the public consciousness. Many stories circulated regarding sightings of Booth.

The most persistent advocate of Booth's escape was Finis L. Bates. In the late 1870s in Granbury, Texas, Bates met a saloon keeper named John St. Helen. During their friendship, St. Helen became seriously ill with asthma. Thinking that he was near death, he called Bates to come to his side so he could make a confession. "I am dying," he said. "My name is John Wilkes Booth and I am the assassin of Abraham Lincoln. Get a picture of myself from under the pillow. I leave it with you for future identification. Notify my brother Edwin of New York City." St. Helen got well and several days later told his story to Bates citing that Andrew Johnson had planned the president's murder and Booth's escape. Then St. Helen disappeared.

Bates traced his friend to California and, finally, to Fresno, where he lost the trail. On January 13, 1903, a man named David E. George committed suicide in Enid, Oklahoma. A woman who claimed to be a friend of his swore an affidavit that George had confessed to her that he was John Wilkes Booth, the assassin of President Lincoln. Bates, now a Tennessee lawyer, rushed to Enid. When he saw the body, he knew that David E. George, John St. Helen and John Wilkes Booth were one and the same person.

If the story is true, and there is room for reasonable doubt, where was St. Helen during those lost years between his arrival in Fresno and his death in Enid?

In another tale of our valley, the story of Mary Donleavy, the founder of Fresno's first orphanage, was told. She had been a close friend of both President Lincoln and John Wilkes Booth when she lived in Washington, D.C. She had often been Booth's dancing partner at Mary Surratt's boarding house. She also witnessed

Lincoln's assassination. She moved to Fresno in the early 1880s. She never believed that Booth was killed. How did she know that? Is it possible that John Wilkes Booth came to Fresno hoping she would help him start a new life? Are these two stories an amazing coincidence or do they lend substance to the supposition that Booth spent time in Fresno?

The controversy about Booth continues to make news. As recently as May 27, 1995, John Wilkes Booth was the subject of a newspaper report. On this day an article in the *Fresno Bee* stated that Circuit Court Judge H. H. Kaplan of Baltimore refused to allow the body of Booth to be exhumed. A group of historical revisionists had hoped to prove the body was that of someone else.

So we may ask, "Is it possible that John Wilkes Booth actually lived among the people of Fresno during the 1880s and played some role in the life of our community? Is it possible that many of the citizens of Fresno knew this man and never guessed his identity?" Strange things have happened as life has unfolded in the legends of our valley.

A Gang of Brothers

When you think of the Dalton Gang, you think of a bunch of Midwestern train and bank robbers. But did you know that the Daltons, not only the lawless brothers, but the good ones, too, lived among the people of the Central Valley?

Let us begin our story in the Midwest. Fifteen children, ten boys and five girls, were born to James Louis and Adeline Younger Dalton. James was a ne'er-do-well who concentrated his fortunes on his string of race horses. The family moved often until Adeline, using her inheritance, purchased a home in Belton, Missouri. The older boys received some discipline, but the younger group, Mason, Grat, Bob, and Emmett, were spoiled. This, coupled with a lack of guidance from their father, turned them into a pretty wild bunch.

By the 1870s, they began to travel with their father as he raced his horses on tracks in California cities, including Tulare, Fresno and Stockton. Two of the older boys, Ben and Lit, took jobs on a ranch between Goshen and Hanford. Several of the other boys followed suit, doing general work on ranches throughout the Central Valley. Mason, called Bill, married and settled on a ranch near Paso Robles. Eventually, Lit went to work as a muleskinner for Clovis Cole and his brother-in-law, Charles Owen.

Bob, Emmett and Grat returned to the Midwest. They and their brother Frank were all made deputy federal marshals in Oklahoma, then known as Indian Territory. Frank was killed in the line of duty. Soon it was rumored that the remaining brothers were engaged in cattle rustling. They headed west for Bill's ranch, trying to keep one step ahead of the law. In January of 1891, they left Bill's, carrying guns. They traveled through what is now Tranquillity and on to Malaga, where they hid out in a barn. Grat went to Clovis Cole's ranch to find Lit and ask for his help. Lit did not want any part in their plans. He drove Grat back to Malaga.

The boys then traveled south, Grat by train and Bob and Emmett on horseback. They stopped in Traver to play poker all night. This was repeated the following night in Tulare. Grat boarded the train again, followed by Bob and Emmett who, as they rode on horseback, scouted the route for a likely place to hold up the train.

On February 5, the boys were seen in Delano, drinking heavily. The next morning, they tethered their horses near the train tracks about one half mile south of Alila, just a mile from the present-day city of Earlimart, and walked back to town. As the train pulled out of the station, they jumped on board the engine. They pulled out their guns and ordered the train to stop. Shots were fired. One man was killed. The boys jumped off the train and took off on their horses.

These events led to a lawless journey that would end in the deaths of Bob and Grat and the wounding of Emmett on October 5, 1892, when they decided to rob two banks at one time in Coffeyville, Kansas.

Not everyone who knew them, however, had bad memories of them. Bob, Emmett and Grat attended a number of socials in Kingsburg and Centerville. They appeared to be handsome, polite gentlemen, and were popular dancing partners for the local young ladies.

As these tales unfold, there may be further stories of the exploits of these young men who added their own chapter to the legends of our valley.

When we hear of the Dalton brothers, we think of the notorious gang of outlaws. However, only three of the ten Dalton brothers were outlaws. Several of the others came to California, worked hard and were law-abiding, decent men. One of these was an older brother, Littleton, always called Lit. He came to the Fresno area sometime in the mid-1880s and went to work for Clovis Cole and his brother-in-law, Charles Owen, skinning mules. He also hauled lumber down the old Toll House Grade to Fresno for three years. He later worked for Clovis Cole on his huge grain ranch.

In 1890, one jump ahead of the law, brothers Bob, Grat and Emmett headed for California. They visited Lit, but he would have nothing to do with their schemes and they left. One night in January 1891, the three again turned up at Lit's bunkhouse on the Cole ranch. The next day Lit went with Grat to help him sell a lame horse. The next day the three younger Daltons left.

On the evening of February 6, Lit was in Fresno spending time with friends in the Reception Saloon. About ten o'clock word was received of a train robbery near Alila, present-day Earlimart. Lit feared that it was his brothers' doing and was sick at heart. He walked to the Grand Central Bar and was talking to friends when Grat walked in. Lit was greatly relieved, but Grat soon told him the truth. Grat, having no horse, had left the other two just before the holdup and come by train to Fresno. Lit introduced Grat to friends, calling attention to the time of night so there would be witnesses as to Grat's whereabouts at the time of the attempted holdup.

The holdup was a failure, but Bob and Emmett escaped and ultimately made their way back east. Grat was arrested as an accomplice and convicted. He made his escape from the Visalia jail, hid out on what is called Dalton Mountain, east of Wonder Valley. When flushed out by officers, he again made his escape. He did not come to Lit for help. He, too, returned east.

Lit got word that his mother was ill and he went back to her home in Missouri to be with her. He was there one night about the first of October when his three brothers, now known for their outlawry, stopped by. The next night they left for Coffeyville and their doom.

Lit came back to the valley. He continued to work for Clovis Cole. Once he and the Coles went to San Francisco on a vacation—one of the few truly enjoyable times he had. Littleton was a proud man and felt the disgrace his brothers had brought to the Dalton name. When he would go to Fresno people would point to him and stare. He finally left the Cole ranch and settled in Willows where nobody knew him. He skinned mules there for a while, then went on to Red Bluff and a job running sheep. He said the sheep did not care whether he was related to the Dalton Gang or not.

The year 1922 found him working for Miller and Lux near Firebaugh. Finally, he settled in Broderick, across the river from Sacramento. It was there that historian and author Frank Latta found him in 1938. He took a trip down through the valley with Latta visiting old scenes and friends. They visited Fresno and sat in Roeding Park for a while talking about his life. The highlight of the trip was a happy reunion with Clovis Cole, both of them now growing old. Lit, at peace with himself and the world, died in 1942 at age eighty-five.

I am sure that most of us know that we live in a city and county named for an ash tree and a valley named for Saint Joachim, the father of the Virgin Mary, but what about the name California? Where did it come from? There are numerous theories as to its origin, but only one worth pursuing and, admittedly, even that is somewhat uncertain and incomplete.

Hernando Cortez landed on the east coast of Mexico in 1519. In the next few years, after conquering the Aztecs, he divided his forces and sent them to the west. From the west coast of Mexico one can look across the gulf and see lower California. The Spanish thought it was an island. Whether it was Jiminez in 1522, Ulloa later, Cortez himself or someone else, one of them gave the name California to the supposed island. Over time the name was extended northward to include not only the entire peninsula, but upper California as well.

Where did the person who gave the name California to the supposed island get it? There is one almost certain source. About 1510, the Spanish author Ordonez de Montalvo published a romance *Las Sergas de Esplandian,* or the deeds of Esplandian. The story tells of a battle between Esplandian, his men and a troop of beautiful black Amazon women. The battle is lost by the women. They are banished to an island, said to abound in gold and precious stones, that lies at the right hand of the Indies very close to the Terrestrial Paradise. The name of the Amazon queen was Calafia; the island was called California. This book was widely ready by the Spanish and no doubt Cortez and his men were familiar with it. They were hoping to find riches in the supposed island they saw. Whoever gave it the name California undoubtedly had Montalvo's story in mind.

Where did Montalvo get the name for his island? One intriguing idea is this: when Charlemagne was defeated in southern Europe and had to retreat, Roland was in command of his rear guard. Roland and all his men were killed. This inspired the French epic *Chanson de Roland* or the song of Roland. It describes an island in the sea abounding in riches and called *Califerne.* Who knows, perhaps Montalvo was familiar with this French ballad.

Whatever the source and meaning of the name California, an unarguable fact is that for people all over the world, the state of California is regarded as the land of promise and wealth. For settlers to the state as diverse as the Forty-niners of the Gold Rush era, the pioneers who crossed the prairies in covered wagons, the Southerners who came west after the defeat of the Confederacy and, more recently, the immigrants from war-torn southeast Asia, California has beckoned as a place to begin life again. It is the land of hope and prosperity—just what the Spaniards had in mind when they bestowed the name California on their "island" in the early years of the sixteenth century.

One the first jobs the legislature of the brand new state of California tackled in 1850 was to create counties—twenty-seven in all. The largest of these new counties was Mariposa. It covered one-fifth of the area of the entire state. It reached from Tuolumne County on the north to San Diego and Los Angeles counties on the south, and from the top of the Coast Range Mountains on the west to the state line of the territory of Nevada on the east side of the Sierra. The little community of Agua Fria was chosen as the county seat. A year and a half later, the selection of a permanent county seat was put to the voters. As a result of this election, the county seat was moved to the town of Mariposa.

This large county was to become known as the "Mother of Counties." In 1852 Tulare County and a portion of Los Angeles County were formed out of Mariposa County. In 1855 Merced County and a portion of San Bernardino County were formed. In 1856, Fresno County was created. During the next forty-three years, six other counties, Madera, Kings, Kern, and portions of Mono, Inyo, and San Benito, came into existence. All eleven of these counties had once been part of Mariposa County.

All the inhabitants of these areas looked to Mariposa as the seat of county government in 1851. In 1854, the Mariposa County Courthouse was built. It has the distinction of being the oldest courthouse west of the Rockies still in use today.

An interesting sidelight to the story of the "Mother of Counties" took place over one hundred years later. In 1957, Superior Court Judge Thomas Coakley, following authorization from the Mariposa County Board of Supervisors, was made a committee of one charged with acquiring furniture for the Mariposa Courthouse's law library and Superior Court judge's chamber. He contacted every county that had once been part of Mariposa County and asked them to donate usable antique furniture.

Seven of the counties responded: Mono County donated chandeliers for the courthouse and the historical society museum; Merced sent a large table and swivel chair that had once been used in the courthouse at its first county seat, Snelling; Kings sent three oak chairs; Fresno is represented by a large wall clock from its historic courthouse; Tulare gave one highboy walnut bookcase, one large double judge's walnut desk, two walnut tables from its auditor's office, and one double pedestal walnut desk; Madera sent an oak desk that had been used by its county clerk; and Los Angeles donated six chairs from the California Supreme Court, one chair and two dictionary stands.

As a result, the historic Mariposa Courthouse now holds permanent gifts that, in a sense, bring its legacy full circle. Not only do they add to the history of the building, but they also enrich the stories of both the counties that gave them and the Mother of Counties that provided the beginning to the history of them all.

At the time of the Mariposa County Courthouse Centennial Celebration in 1954, the man who was called upon to chair the event had lived in this mountain community for only one year. A genial man of Irish-American ancestry, Thomas Coakley not only presided over this extremely successful event with gusto, but went on to become one of the most influential and important citizens of Mariposa.

Born in Oakland, California, in 1905, he worked his way through the University of California at Berkeley and its law school, Boalt Hall, by being a hotel band leader. During the decade of the 1930s, he played at the Athens Club in Oakland, at the Hollywood Roosevelt Hotel, and at the Palace Hotel and St. Francis Hotel in San Francisco. Occasionally his band would be heard on the radio. In later years, he would use his talent as a drummer in Mariposa's Lions Club Follies.

After passing the bar, Coakley opened a law practice in San Francisco. From 1939 until 1942, he served as a California deputy attorney general. Over the years he also served as president of the San Francisco Bar Association, a director of the San Francisco Chamber of Commerce, a member of the Board of Governors of the State Bar of California, a trustee of the California Historical Society, and a member of Rotary International.

In 1953, Governor Earl Warren appointed Coakley to be the Superior Court judge for Mariposa. Coakley and his wife, Katherine, and their children moved to this mountain community. In 1957, he was asked to help form the local historical society. Its first museum was established in the downstairs portion of the Masonic Hall.

Eleven years later, in 1968, Tom Coakley and his wife donated the land on Jessie Street which became the site for a permanent museum and county library. Coakley chaired the fund-raising drive for the building that was completed and dedicated on May 23, 1971. Today, the Mariposa Museum and History Center stands as a reminder of Coakley's dedication and tireless efforts for his community.

Tom Coakley had a keen sense of humor to go along with his

love of California history. In 1954, when Mariposa celebrated the centennial of its courthouse, he was the Grand Noble Humbug of the Matuca Chapter of the Ancient and Honorable Order of E Clampus Vitus. As Humbug, he presided over the initiation of new members including several from Fresno—Sidney Cruff, chairman of the board of supervisors, County Counsel Robert Wash, Charles Palmer of Pacific Gas & Electric Company, and John Cooper of Cooper's Department Store.

Thomas Coakley died in May of 1995. His list of community accomplishments will be long remembered by the people of Mariposa. So will his good-nature and broad smile. A true legend of our valley and the mountain areas to the east, Thomas Coakley served the people of his county well.

The Butterfly

A trip into the Sierra foothills is a treat at any time of the year, but in autumn, when the trees turn crimson and gold, the trip becomes a feast for the eyes. When the journey takes the traveler into the gold country, he will travel through areas of California that are relatively unchanged.

To visit one of the oldest cities in the central part of California you must drive on Highway 99 to Merced and turn east on Highway 140, or you may choose to take the Le Grand exit just north of Chowchilla. When you reach the town of Le Grand, you will turn on the road to Mariposa and follow it until you reach Highway 140. Soon after you have turned onto that road, the valley begins its ascent into the foothills. Civilization suddenly seems far away as the road curves and dips into Catheys Valley. Oak trees dot the hillsides where in spring wild Mariposa lilies blanket the hills with yellow and white dashes of color. The road climbs into the mountains. The oak trees are taller and fuller and, as the road curves and winds, breathtaking views are afforded you.

All at once the road curves once more and you have reached Mariposa, the seat of government for Mariposa County. This small community, like the other towns in Mariposa County, has never been incorporated. It is governed by its board of supervisors. Situated on hills with streets that dip and wind through the town, it has a special kind of charm. The main street retains many historic buildings and a feeling that at any moment gold miners and other characters of the Gold Rush-era might reappear.

The main streets of the town are named for the family of John Charles Fremont, whose Mariposa Grant included the site of the present-day town. Charles Street is the main thoroughfare. Jessie Street, named for Mrs. Fremont, runs parallel to it. Bullion Street is named for her father, Thomas Hart Benton, who was given the nickname "Old Bullion" because he advocated the free coinage of gold. Jones Street was named after Jessie's brother-in-law, Cary Jones, a lawyer who helped Fremont establish permanent title to his Mariposa Grant.

The name Mariposa was given by Gabriel Moraga who, when leading an expedition into the vast Central Valley in 1806, saw swarms of yellow butterflies—in Spanish, *mariposas*.

Mariposa offers the traveler a chance to visit the historic 1854 courthouse, the Mariposa Museum and History Center, and the California State Mining and Mineral Museum. Antique shops abound as well.

If you wish to see Yosemite, you continue on Highway 140. If you want to return to Fresno, a special treat is in store. Turning onto Highway 49, you will embark on the final link of this road that is popularly called the Golden Chain. It takes you through the historic town of Bootjack and through the towns of Nipinna-wasee, which means the home of the deer, and Ahwahnee. Breath-taking vistas of the Sierra await you at each turn of the road. All too soon, you will reach Oakhurst. This is the end of the Golden Chain. A turn onto Highway 41 brings you on the road back to Fresno.

A worthwhile trip at any time of the year, in the spring and autumn it is a soul-satisfying experience.

The Mariposa County Courthouse, built in 1854, once served the area that is today Fresno County. The building is the oldest county courthouse west of the Rockies that has been in continuous use.
The Image Group from the Laval Historical Collection.

A highlight of any visit to Mariposa is a visit to the oldest county courthouse west of the Rockies still in use—the Mariposa County Courthouse. Built in 1854, this structure is set in a small park located on Bullion Street. The visitor's first impression of the building is one of stately grandeur, yet with a simplicity—a spareness of design—that speaks clearly of the building's pioneer heritage. Its puritan whiteness is reminiscent of a New England meeting house. The front facade is of Greek-revival styling with a pilaster at each end that is flush with the building. The front double doors are each flanked by a window; three windows on the second floor are set in perfect proportion. A classical pediment fills the gable line above the second floor. The edifice is topped by a cupola that contains a clock. This was added in 1866.

The structure is built of white (sugar) pine that grew less than a mile away. It was hand-planed at the building site. According to the pamphlet that is given to visitors, "No nails were used in the supporting structure. The beams are held together with pine pegs and are strengthened by mortise and tenon joints." Ponderosa and sugar pine were used throughout the interior.

When one enters the building, one is immediately aware of its history. There are display cabinets in the long hallway and pictures on the walls that honor the judges who have served in its courtroom and show how eleven other counties were carved out of Mariposa County. The courthouse was constructed during 1854 and was accepted by the Court of Sessions on February 12, 1885. It might be said that for a short time it was the courthouse for all the valley floor including the future site of Fresno until Merced County was created on April 19, 1855. It did serve as the courthouse for all the foothill and mountain areas of present Fresno and Madera counties until Fresno County was created on April 19, 1856.

Upstairs is the Superior Court. All the original furnishings are still in place. The spectators benches, counsel tables, jury box, and judges bench all were handmade and still show evidence of the use of the carpenter's plane. The original nine-foot long judges bench is long enough to seat the three judges who preside during a Court of Sessions. The simplicity of the room belies the important cases that have been argued there. The courthouse was accepted in the National Register of Historic Places in part because famous and notable civil, mining, and water cases were argued in this courtroom. Two of these are the Biddle Boggs vs. Merced Mining Company and the Fremont land grant title.

In 1891, a vault was constructed at the north side of the building. The courthouse, itself, has undergone two major renovations. Careful consideration has been given to maintain the historic integrity of the structure. As a result the Mariposa County Courthouse continues not only to serve the citizens of its area, but also stands as a reminder of the rich, colorful history of that area—a true legacy of our valley and the mountain areas to the east.

A Museum in the Mountains

A visit to the mountain community of Mariposa is not complete without spending time at the Mariposa Museum and History Center on Jessie Street.

The museum is encircled by outdoor exhibits that capture the imagination and lead the visitor through the early history of the area. Two Umacha Indian cedar bark dwellings, a Tca-pu-ya Indian sweat house and several grinding stones represent the area's earliest inhabitants. The Gold Rush period is captured with a series of implements used in gold mining that bear colorful names—windlass, used for hoisting gold-bearing ore from the mine shaft; a rocker, which was used for washing gold-bearing gravel; an arrastra, which pulverized gold ore that had been placed in a rock-lined pit by dragging large stones pulled round and round by donkeys; and many other such pieces of equipment. The final outdoor exhibit is a huge five-stamp mill that was used to crush ore into fine particles of sand, releasing the gold from the quartz.

On entering the museum, the visitor truly steps back in time. A counter and shelves filled with goods of a hundred years ago give the feeling of a general store. Just to the right of the front door, however, the fun begins. A gold mining exhibit introduces you to a self-guided tour. The number "1" painted on the floor in front of the exhibit case tells the visitor that this is the place to start. Following the numbers through the next room, you will visit one exhibit after another chronicling the rich history of Mariposa from the Indian period, through the Spanish and Mexican eras of California's past, the Chinese influences, John C. Fremont and his Mariposa Land Grant, the story of the bandit Joaquin Murietta, and the Mariposa Courthouse.

Along the way, you will visit an assay office, a typical parlor and kitchen of one hundred years ago, a drug store, a milliner and ladies' dress shop, a newspaper office, and a schoolroom, and see an exhibit of children's toys and apparel. All of these exhibits are filled with marvelous authentic items, including Jessie Fremont's punch bowl and lace collar.

By the time you are ready to leave, you will feel as if you have truly taken a walk through the history of the Mariposa area.

It has long been fashionable to celebrate wedding anniversaries. Indeed, when couples have attained the twenty-five- or fifty-year mark, it is an occasion to celebrate. Silver and gold anniversaries are very special times for families and friends to gather round and salute the fortunate couple. But, have you ever heard of anyone hosting a party for a paper anniversary? Do you know what a paper anniversary is?

The community of Oleander, located around Adams and Cedar avenues, was the site for just such a celebration. On Thursday evening, December 21, 1899, Mr. and Mrs. A. J. Ruby invited fifty close friends to join them for a party on their first anniversary, traditionally symbolized by paper. In keeping with the theme of the event, the invitation asked each guest to represent a book, magazine or newspaper by some item in their dress.

When the guests arrived at the party, each was assigned a number from one to fifty. Each guest was also given a card with the numbers one to fifty listed down one side. Opposite each number was blank space in which to write the holder's guess of what book or periodical the person bearing the corresponding number intended to represent. The person who received the most correct answers would win a prize.

Not only were the guests arriving in most interesting attire, but the room was also buzzing with comments as the mingling party-goers try to figure out the correct answers. A great deal of levity accompanied the search.

Finally, the answers were given. Mrs. Nicholson won the prize for having the most correct answers. Another prize was given for the person who gave the most unique representation of a book or magazine. E. A. Roach, whose theme was the *Pickwick Papers*, wore a badge made of toothpicks, a lamp wick and a number of strips of paper. Another notable work, titled *Essay on Man,* was depicted by the letters S A worn on Asa Wilkins' lapel.

The evening continued with recitations and songs by the guests. At midnight the guests retired to the garden, where a sumptuous supper was served under a tent adjoining the house. A good time was had by all.

For those who travel along Fresno Street and turn onto Kearney Boulevard, an interesting sight greets their eyes. On either side of the boulevard are two huge modernistic pylons that create a gateway to this lovely, historic roadway. Did you ever wonder who placed them there?

On the evening of June 1, 1933, hundreds of Fresnans gathered at the entrance to Kearney Boulevard. They had come to celebrate the completion of the new gateway and to dedicate it to the memory of M. Theo Kearney, who had given the landscaped roadway to Fresno County in the mid-1890s.

Gerald H. Catania, a West Fresno attorney, was master of ceremonies for the evening. He introduced Mike Bruce, John Mazzeo, and Ralph Tote—all members of the American Progressive Association—who were the three who made the project a reality. Several other speakers praised the project and those involved.

Excitement was in the air as Mayor Zeke Leymel spoke to the crowd praising the West Fresno organizations who were responsible for initiating and completing this project. The city had appropriated the money to pay for the gateway.

Then all eyes turned to the large illuminated pylons inscribed with the words "Kearney Boulevard." A hush fell over the crowd as Josephine Giordano, the young daughter of Ralph Giordano, better known as Young Corbett III, stepped forward and cut the ribbon linking the two pylons. The Edison Technical High School band began to play and everyone cheered.

The Kearney pylons were designed by architect Charles Franklin who would, in 1941, with partner Ernest J. Kump, Jr., create the plans for Fresno's modern city hall. This building was given national recognition in 1942 when the architect's renderings were displayed in the Museum of Modern Art in New York as one of the forty-seven most advanced works of architecture during the years 1932-1942.

In the late 1970s, the integrity of the pylons was threatened by a decision to change the configuration of the entrance to the boulevard to make access to Fresno Street safer for motorists. The addition of signal lights near the base of these gateways was a major concern. Happily, a meeting of members of the department of public works and the Historic Preservation Commission for the City of Fresno worked out a solution. Today, the historic Kearney gateway is still intact and adds another piece of history to its neighborhood.

South and slightly west of downtown Fresno, there is a community that bears the name of an evergreen shrub that produces white and red double blossoms. So hardy is this shrub that it thrives through the heat of a valley summer and the occasional drought of a valley winter. The land on which this community is located was originally called the Easton Colony. Although people began to settle there in 1880, its official beginning dates to January 10, 1881, when a post office was established near the corner of Cedar and Adams avenues. The promoters decided to change the name to the Washington Colony. They wrote to Washington, D.C., for approval.

One morning in 1881, Judge J.W. North, the developer of the Easton Colony, set out for Fresno in his wagon to see if a letter granting this request was in the day's mail. The back of his wagon was loaded with oleander cuttings that he intended to plant later in the day. He arrived at the post office only to find that the letter had not arrived. It did, however, arrive the next day. The postmaster opened the letter and read that the request for the name change was denied. Evidently, there were too many communities named Washington. He knew that the judge would not return for another week and wondered what to do about the situation. Remembering Judge North's wagon full of oleander cuttings, he submitted the name Oleander to the postal authorities in Washington. It was approved and the new community became officially known as Oleander.

Another version of this story is that the judge's daughter suggested the name.

In 1883, the Oleander School District was formed. The first classes were held in a private home. By 1884, thirty houses had been built in the settlement. The Valley Railroad laid tracks through Oleander in 1897, causing more people to move to the area. A number of raisin and fruit packing companies were constructed on the east side of the railroad.

As the community grew, a railroad depot, general merchandise store, blacksmith shop, service station, and Oleander Hall were built. A Fresno County Library branch opened at Cedar and Adams avenues. The Congregational Church and Danish Mission Church served the spiritual needs of the residents.

The community of Oleander, founded on a portion of a well-traveled trail that originally extended from Laguna de Tache and Kingston to Millerton, is still recognizable at the corner of Cedar and Adams avenues. Even though the post office and library are gone, a number of homes and a school attest to the fact that this is still an active community. And, as is true of many other valley areas, the descendants of some of the early pioneers still live there.

A Master Architect

One of Fresno's premier architects of the early to middle twentieth century was H. Rafael Lake. Born in San Rafael, California, on February 9, 1894, Lake studied architecture at the University of California and then transferred to the Massachusetts Institute of Technology, graduating from that institution in 1916. He served in the armed forces during World War I. He then served a five-year apprenticeship under Cass Gilbert in New York City.

In 1923, Lake moved to Fresno when he was commissioned to design the Hotel Californian. Later that year, he became a staff architect for the Trewhitt-Shields Company. A year later, he became a partner, and the firm's name became Shields, Fisher and Lake. In 1925, the firm's name was changed again, to Fisher, Lake and Traver. Lake ran the company's Fresno office; Fisher and Traver headed the office in Los Angeles. Among their projects in Southern California was the Hollywood Roosevelt Hotel.

In addition to the Hotel Californian, Lake designed a number of commercial buildings including the L. C. Wesley Super Garage and the Blue Cross Veterinary Hospital. During the Depression years of the 1930s, Lake joined Allied Architects to design the Fresno County Hall of Records and the Memorial Auditorium.

Among the residences to his credit are the Arthur Bernhauer home on Van Ness Boulevard in Old Fig Garden and the Harry W. Shields and Ralph Merritt homes on Huntington Boulevard. He designed and built his own home on the northeast corner of Butler and Clovis avenues in 1925.

Lake's home is built in the style of a Spanish farmhouse, giving the visitor a feeling of a rural setting. Built to suit the climate and life-style of the Central Valley, the home has thick walls constructed of hollow tile covered with stucco. The living areas of the home are on four levels, giving the feeling of rambling spaciousness. The differing levels and varied roof lines are beautifully woven together to create a charming structure that makes the visitor feel transported to a romantic spot like the French Riviera. The craftsmanship throughout is outstanding as befits the home of a master architect. It is a unique Fresno residence.

In 1948 Lake and his partner, William Hastrup, designed the clubhouse for the Sunnyside Country Club. It replaced the historic Oothout Home that was destroyed by fire in 1941.

H. Rafael Lake died in Fresno in 1958, leaving behind an important architectural legacy. He derived his skill in adapting varied architectural styles from his training in the European or Beaux-Arts tradition. The period revival styles reflected in his buildings have added a richness to the architecture of the Fresno community.

Fresno State Normal School under construction in September, 1915.
The Image Group from the Laval Historical Collection.

In 1908, a group of Fresno's leading citizens, including C. L. McLane, superintendent of Fresno Unified Schools, met to discuss the possibility of establishing a teacher training institute in Fresno. The ultimate result of their efforts was the signing of a bill by Governor Hiram Johnson that appropriated $35,000 for operating expenses and the purchase of property for the future school. On September 11, 1911, Fresno State Normal School was born.

The first classes were held at Fresno High School, then located at O and Stanislaus streets. Fresno Normal School's purpose was "to train teachers for the area and to provide quality education for practicing teachers in the valley." C. L. McLane was appointed the first president of the new college. He was joined by a faculty of twelve and a student body of one hundred and seventy. Two years later, in 1913, the school moved to temporary buildings on a ten-acre parcel of land at University and Van Ness avenues. The school's enrollment continued to grow and the school did as well. In fact, the students watched as the red brick Administration Building was being constructed in 1915.

A special feature at the new site was the campus training school. One of the few laboratory elementary schools in the United States and the first such facility at a state normal school, this school was a place for students to observe and to teach on their own campus—an innovative program for student teachers at that time. This training school eventually became known as the Laboratory School and was an important part of the educational program for teachers until 1970.

As the normal school grew, extracurricular activities were developed. The Drama Club was the first group formed. It was joined by the Tea Club, the Glee Club, the Debate Club, the Men's Club and a branch of the Young Women's Christian Association.

The school was acquiring an identity and a more spirited student body. The administration, always aware of the need to set a proper example, decided to prepare a list of guidelines, a ten commandments of sorts, that would allow students to maintain a certain standard of propriety and decorum. The list reads as follows: "Do not drive tacks in the plaster. No sliding down the banister. Keep off the grass and do not pick the flowers. Never run for a streetcar. No dancing in the auditorium at noontime. No flirting from the third-story window. No cuttings except in agriculture. Do not eat lunches in the hall. No cramming allowed except in physiology. Playgrounds are for seniors only."

The school that would eventually become Fresno State College and then California State University, Fresno was duly launched and on its way to greatness.

A Red Cross Surgical Squad working in a class-room of the Fresno State Normal School in 1917. *The Image Group from the Laval Historical Collection.*

There is an avenue in southern Fresno County that has a name so rich with the flavor of another era that its story must be told.

In August of 1856, John Barker left his ranch near Kingston and, with three other young men, saddled up his horse and embarked on an elk hunting trip on the Fresno plain. The area was filled with wild antelope and elk. The men loaded their large ox-drawn wagon with provisions. They set up camp midway between the Kings and San Joaquin rivers. Water was available for the horses, but it was putrid and unfit for the men to drink.

Noticing a large bowl-shaped indentation in the plain that had a depth of about twenty feet, Barker decided to dig at its deepest point. While the others hunted, he undertook this task. Sure enough, he struck clean, pure water. Soon the bowl had become a small lake. Looking around, Barker noticed hundreds of elk horns. With his horse and riata, he gathered up as many horns as he could and piled them until the stack was eight feet tall. This would serve as a marker so he could find the water hole again. The men continued their hunt, taking their kill to Fort Miller, where they sold the meat to miners and Indians.

Barker returned to his large pile of elk horns. Here he started a new ranching operation, the first settlement on the Fresno plain, calling it his Elkhorn property. Soon, the Butterfield Overland Mail Company established a new route from San Francisco to Saint Louis with a station called Elkhorn Springs on Barker's property. In 1858, a telegraph line and operator also were located there.

In 1860, Cuthbert Burrel purchased the 20,000-acre Elkhorn Ranch. Some years later a small village, called Burrel, began to develop just a quarter mile northwest of the old Elkhorn Station.

Today, the huge herds of elk and the colorful stagecoaches are gone. But Elkhorn Avenue remains, stretching across the map of Fresno County, reminding us of a huge pile of elk horns marking the spot where clean water was available, allowing people to live on the land called the Fresno Plain.

A Farm Show in Tulare

In 1966, three men in ag-related businesses, Bill Huvall, Neil Huffsmith, and Kent Koe, traveled from the Tulare area to Colusa, California, to see an orchard show. Several months later they sat down in Huvall's garage with a bottle of Scotch to discuss all they had seen. They asked Bill Wolf to join them. They were all active members of the Tulare Chamber of Commerce, and as they talked, one of them had an idea. "If those guys in Colusa could put on a farm show, why, we could do it, too!" Out of that discussion came a major event that has brought people from all over the world to Tulare every February for thirty-two years.

Known the first year as the Farm and Row Crop Show, the name Tulare was added during the second or third year. It was first sponsored by the Tulare Chamber of Commerce and a resolute group of volunteers including, among others, Kent Koe, Bill Wolf, Frank Lagomarsino, George Serpa, Clyde Stagner, and Neil Huffsmith. Many people came that first year and were impressed by all they saw.

The show got bigger each year and, in 1976, a nonprofit entity called the International Agri-Center, Inc. was formed by the volunteers. Governed by an eighteen-member board of directors, the International Agri-Center, Inc. has nine full-time employees and six hundred volunteers. They work year round to prepare for the event that is now called the California Farm Equipment Show and International Exhibition. They also produce the California Antique Farm Equipment Show and the Western Dairy Expo that are held in April and October, respectively.

The event includes more than just a chance to look at farm equipment. Seminars on a wide range of subjects are offered. These seminars are led by experts and researchers in their respective fields and provide all sorts of practical information for those in the ag industry. Special events are held for women such as cooking demonstrations, craft demonstrations, and fashion shows. As the show grew, so did the need for more space. In 1982, the event was moved to its current 160-acre site on Laspina Avenue in Tulare.

One special feature of the farm show is the International Business Center, where all sorts of services, such as interpreters and guided tours, are offered to those who visit the show from all over the world. Coming from as far away as New Zealand, Australia, Russia, and Germany, these visitors are not only offered the opportunity to see the latest farm equipment and inventions, but they are given the chance to place orders for these goods to be shipped to their countries.

Visitors from almost every state in the Union come to Tulare for this show, too. They see a showcase for all the best and newest that is available for their farms. For the farmer, who has to live his life by the seasons, the show has become a tradition. Plant in spring, harvest in fall, and go the Tulare farm show in the winter.

Today, in its thirty-second year, the California Farm Equipment Show and International Exhibition—Tulare Farm Show for short—is the largest event of its kind in the world. Who would have thought that all this could come out of a visit four men had over a bottle of Scotch? Well, it did and, as a result, on three days in February the hotels in cities as far away as Bakersfield and Fresno will be filled with guests who have come to our great Central Valley to see all the latest farm products and get the cutting-edge information that they need for their farms and businesses.

In 1983, the sixteenth year of the Tulare Farm Show, an event of such magnitude occurred that folks are still talking about it. The show is always held on the second Tuesday of February. Planning begins much earlier than that and, in this year, things were proceeding nicely.

On the Monday evening before the farm show, the grounds crews were checking everything to make sure all was in readiness for the event. All at once, about 11 p.m., a freak windstorm hit. As the crews watched in horror, the hurricane force wind puffed up three of the largest exhibit tents, pulled the stakes that held them out of the ground and toppled them over. For the next hour huge gusts of wind tore through the exhibit grounds. Then the wind stopped as quickly as it had begun.

The chairman of the event, Hildreth Van Helten, who was recovering from heart surgery, was called. Because he could not come out to help, Richard Rogers, who had chaired the event the previous year, stepped in to assist. All the board members were called and came out immediately. By 2 a.m. on Tuesday morning, they had assessed the damage. Seventy percent of the inside exhibit spaces had been damaged. They made a very difficult decision. The event would have to be postponed until Wednesday. They all got busy calling farmers and exhibitors to let them know. The media helped by getting word out to the community so that people would not arrive in a few hours expecting to visit the farm show.

Then they faced the daunting task of cleaning up the mess. They decided to go home and get a little sleep and to meet again at day break.

When they got back to the exhibit grounds they could not believe what they saw. An army of volunteers had arrived to help. Not only farmers, but members of the city staff. Indeed, there was representation from a whole cross-section of the Tulare community. Farmers from as far away as Lindsay not only came to help, but brought their workers and trucks with them. City clean-up crews arrived. Some people volunteered to serve coffee and sandwiches to keep everyone's energy up. It was as though the entire community had turned out to lend assistance to make sure that the Tulare Farm Show would open after all.

By 2 p.m. Tuesday afternoon the clean-up effort was completed. The Tulare Farm Show opened on Wednesday morning. Attendance was good. Important as that was, even more important was the feeling of good will that was generated by all those who pulled together to help. All those volunteers came because they believed in their community. Their efforts meant the show would truly go on. And, go on it did, to become the largest event of its kind in the world. They left an enduring legacy to their community and are certainly worth remembering in the tales of our valley.

The Legendary Man of Badger Pass

Seventy-one years ago, in the Laurentian Mountains north of Montreal, Canada, Nicolas (Nic) Fiore put on his first pair of skis. He was six years old. In his own words, "It was love at first sight."

Born in Montreal, Nic Fiore loved the out-of-doors. He not only was a skier, but an ice skater and bicycle racer as well. He became a certified ski instructor in Canada in 1946 and taught full-time at the St. Adele Lodge in the Laurentian Mountains. In the winter he served as a ski instructor and in the summer he was the sports director.

The ski school director invited Nic and three other Canadians to come to Yosemite with him for a visit. The director recommended Fiore to the Yosemite Park and Curry Company. After the group returned to Canada, Fiore received a letter from the Curry Company asking him to come to Yosemite for a winter to teach. Because Fiore spoke only French and wanted to learn English, he felt this would be a good opportunity to accomplish his goal. He said yes. He arrived in 1948 for a four-month stay. He has been in Yosemite ever since.

In November of 1956, he began teaching the Dry Ski School in Fresno, sponsored by the *Fresno Bee*. The classes were held on four consecutive Tuesdays on the lawn of the Holmes Playground. According to Fiore, eight hundred to nine hundred people would show up for each of the first three classes. The final class, which was held at Badger Pass, drew between seven hundred and eight hundred people. These classes were held each year for over thirty years.

Fiore's job does not end when the snow melts. In the summer he is director of the High Sierra Camps. The year-round beauty of Yosemite is truly part of his daily life.

It is the snow season that still brings him the most enjoyment. He loves Badger Pass because it is a family place. "The weather and the slopes are gentle here," he says. His favorite part of the job is twofold. Watching someone learn to ski—taking him through each step from the very beginning until he can ski down a hill—and making that experience an enjoyable one gives Fiore a real sense of accomplishment. He also savors the friendships that he has made with people who come to Badger Pass year after year. Some of the families he has taught are now bringing their fourth generation to him so he can teach them to ski also.

As he celebrates fifty years of teaching skiing at Badger Pass, he still loves his work. He lives one day at a time with no plans to retire. For many of those who treasure the mountains around Yosemite in both summer and winter, Nic Fiore is a man who has made their mountain experiences more memorable. He certainly takes his place among the legends of our valley.

A Mardi Gras in the Tower District

When KMJ General Manager Al Smith moved to Fresno, one of the things he missed most about leaving his native New Orleans was the yearly celebration called Mardi Gras. After living in Fresno for a few years, he began to see that the Tower District would be a perfect place to begin a local celebration of this event.

The Tower District, which is the center for much of the theater, arts and fine dining in Fresno, had another appealing feature—just like the neighborhood in New Orleans where Mardi Gras is held, it is an area that is conducive to walking. An event of this kind would bring people into the neighborhood—an idea that appealed to KMJ Radio which, at that time, was located in the heart of the Tower District.

In 1994 KMJ had lent its support to a Mardi Gras concert at the Wild Blue night club in the Tower District that had been arranged by the Fresno Free College Foundation. Concert organizers were so pleased with the response that they decided to approach the local merchants to ask for their support in organizing a Tower District-wide Mardi Gras event.

The merchants of the Tower District Marketing Committee had already been considering just such an event, and working with local musician Evo Bluestein, organized the first official Tower District Mardi Gras celebration called, "Fat Tuesday in the Tower."

With the cooperative efforts of the local merchants, Evo and the KMJ team, the 1995 "Fat Tuesday in the Tower" was a success with over a thousand attendees. The 1996 event attracted two thousand people. By 1997 "Fat Tuesday in the Tower" had officially been adopted as the new Fresno holiday. Six thousand visitors attended that year, prompting the streets to be closed to accommodate the crowds.

With such a phenomenal growth rate, the 1998 Tower District Mardi Gras Celebration was expanded to three days of floats, feast and frolic. The first ever Tower District Mardi Gras Grande Parade was held. Thanks to a grant from the Gundelfinger Foundation, Evo Bluestein and the Tower District Preservation Association brought the Grammy Award-winning artist Queen Ida and her Zydeco Band to the Tower Theater for a concert that opened with the Bad Boys Zydeco.

The celebration was be launched with the parade on Sunday, February 22, bringing the rich sights of Mardi Gras to Fresno. On Monday, the smell of Cajun cooking filled the air as New Orleans-style dishes were prepared by Tower District chefs. Each restaurant featured its own version of Cajun/Creole cooking. The three-day celebration reached a crescendo on Fat Tuesday as the neighborhood vibrated with the sounds of Mardi Gras. About twenty bands played throughout the Tower District, including concerts on four outdoor performance areas.

What began with a longing for home has turned into a celebration that has added another tradition to Fresno's rich texture and has added another chapter in the tales of our valley.

Bulldog Backers

In 1933 a group of men formed a support group whose pur-pose was to raise money for scholarships for athletes at Fresno State College. They hoped to recruit six hundred members who would make donations to the Bulldog program, hence they called their group the 600 Club.

In 1950, a decision was made to incorporate the group as a nonprofit fund raising organization. The name was changed to the Bulldog Foundation. The average amount of money they raised each year was about twenty thousand dollars. One hundred male student athletes each year benefited from their efforts. Jess Rodman, Ray Harris, Phil Ellithorpe, Ed Ricks, Bob Greelis, and Lee Terzian were some of the men who served as president during the 1950s.

During the 1960s, the foundation continued to grow, totaling seven hundred members by the end of the decade. With the growth came the ability to help more student athletes with scholarships.

In 1972, a permanent staff was hired to handle the annual fund-raising drive. The first executive director, Lynn Eilefson, introduced a team concept—one hundred members made up the team and sought to recruit memberships during the five week effort. Ticket benefits also were offered with memberships at certain levels. In the first year of using these new concepts, donations doubled. By the end of the 1960s, the Bulldog Foundation could boast twenty-eight hundred members.

The 1980s saw the foundation grow to an astounding degree. During this ten-year period over twenty-six million dollars was raised which helped more than four hundred fifty student athletes. Four thousand people could call themselves members of the Foundation.

In 1990, thirteen new scholarships were added, making a total of 244 full grants in eighteen NCAA sports offered each year. This gave each recipient $5,000 for room and board, fees, and books. Now as the new millennium approaches, twenty sports are supported and more than four hundred fifty young men and women receive some portion of a scholarship now valued at $7,400.

The latest annual fund raising record is $6.8 million during the year 1998-99. The pledged amount for 1999-2000 is over $7.1 million. For the fourteenth straight year, the Bulldog Foundation has the distinction of being the number one volunteer fund raising team in the country. As important as the dollar amounts are to support the athletic scholarship programs, many Bulldog Foundation members also support other programs within the university. They feel that the university's eight academic schools are benefitted by the students within their schools who are there because of their athletic scholarships.

As the foundation enters its sixty-seventh year, the goal is still "to be the best." Integrating the best athletic program possible with a superior academic program gives their scholarship recipients the opportunity to score both in the classroom and in their chosen sport.

The goal of the Bulldog Foundation members reaches beyond the university experience of these young people, however. They hope that after graduation, these young athletes will go on to become leaders and good citizens of their communities.

A number of stories have been told about the early chairmen of the Fresno Board of Trustees, who were in essence the early mayors of Fresno. However, none has been told about one notable member of that illustrious group, Columbus Joel Craycroft.

Born at Cape Girardeau, Missouri, on December 13, 1845, C. J. Craycroft was the youngest of four sons of Benjamin and Elizabeth Craycroft. The couple also had two daughters. The family moved to Springfield, Illinois, and then to Macon County, in another part of that state. In 1853, when C. J. was eight years old, his father contracted black diphtheria during an epidemic and died. From that time until the Civil War began, C. J. worked first on a farm and then in a brick plant, to help support his family.

On June 20, 1861, he enlisted for three years in the Union Army, serving first in the 68th Illinois Regiment and then transferring to the 70th Regiment. He was ordered to Washington, D.C. where he became ill with typhoid fever. Later that year, he enlisted for three years in Company F 62nd Illinois Volunteers. When the war ended, he was at Monticello. In 1866, he was mustered out of the service.

He married Rebecca Grable in October 1866. Three children were born to the couple, but only one, Arlie, lived to adulthood. He died of lockjaw in 1888, at age twenty-two. Rebecca died in 1872. Two years later, C. J. married Frances Baldridge of Walnut Hills, Illinois. Once again, three children were born, but two died in infancy. Only their son, Frank Joel Craycroft, lived to adulthood.

In 1879, C. J. moved his family to California—first to Warm Springs and then to Panoche, where he engaged in sheep ranching. After Frances' death in 1886, he moved to Fresno. He initially worked as a contractor and, in 1887, opened a brick plant. As the city of Fresno grew, so did the need for brick in the construction of homes and buildings. Craycroft's business grew and in several years the name of the firm became C. J. Craycroft and Son.

In 1892, Craycroft was elected to serve the city of Fresno as a member of the board of trustees. In 1893, one rather famous meeting of this august body took place. Joseph Spinney was elected president of the board, made a speech thanking the members for electing him, resigned his post, and nominated C. J. Craycroft for the position. The whole thing took just ten minutes. Craycroft was elected president of that board and, as such, was the mayor of Fresno, serving for eight years.

On November 17, 1915, after a fall from the roof of one of his business properties, C. J. Craycroft died.

An Olympic Athlete Extraordinaire

August 28, 1948, was one of the proudest days in the history of the cities of Tulare and Visalia. It was on this day that Bob Mathias came home as the triumphant decathlon champion of the 1948 Olympic Games.

Three weeks before, when news of his victory reached Tulare, every whistle and siren in the city had blared simultaneously for forty-five seconds. Hundreds of cars had filled the streets of the city forming a giant parade that, for nearly three hours, blocked not only the main street of town, but the state highway as well.

A crowd of twenty-five hundred people awaited Mathias at the Visalia airport. The seventeen-year-old hero walked down the steps of the plane, grinning and carrying an Irish shillelagh. His Tulare High School classmates reached him first. They lifted Mathias onto their shoulders and started through the excited hometown throng. The crowd surged forward. Mathias dropped to the ground and into the arms of his waiting parents, Dr. and Mrs. C. M. Mathias. The music of the Tulare High School band was almost impossible to hear through the screams of the crowd.

From Visalia, Mathias and his family were escorted by a three hundred-car caravan south on Highway 99 to Tulare. When the procession entered K Street in downtown Tulare, all the fire department and factory whistles were blowing. Banners hung across the street. Store windows were filled with posters reading, "Welcome Bob." Thousands lined the streets, waving and shouting to the young man who had made them all so proud. When they reached the Tulare City Hall, Mathias was given the key to the city by Mayor Elmo Zumwalt.

Two days later, on August 30, Mathias was praised by Governor Earl Warren at a dinner given in his honor in Tulare. The next day three thousand Fresnans filled Ratcliffe Stadium and Mathias was presented with a trophy from the people of Fresno.

Four years later, at the 1952 Olympics in Helsinki, Finland, Bob Mathias once again won the gold medal in the decathlon. He set both an Olympic and a world record for this event. Later he entered politics and in 1966 was elected to the Congress of the

United States, serving his constituents in the valley with distinction until 1974.

For the people of Tulare and all the Central Valley, August of 1948 was etched in their memory forever. For it was then that a fine young man, one of their own, endured the most grueling athletic event of the Olympic games, conquered it and stood tall, bearing his gold medal before the world with dignity and grace. An extraordinary legend of our valley is Bob Mathias.

Two-time Olympic gold medalist, Bob Mathias was also a football star at Stanford, played in the Rose Bowl, was drafted by the Washington Redskins, served in the Marine Corps, starred in *The Bob Mathias Story* (Allied Artist's story of his life), *China Doll*, and *The Minotaur*, co-starred with Keenan Wynn in NBC-TV's *The Troubleshooters* (1959-1960) and served four terms as U.S. congressman.
Photo courtesy of Bob Mathias

Tidbits from 1885

Just six short weeks after the city of Fresno was incorporated, the Local News page of the *Fresno Evening Democrat* offered several interesting tidbits for its readers. Under the title "Ought to be Horsewhipped," a few of the men of our fair city were scolded for spitting their chewing tobacco in the close vicinity of several young ladies who were attending a reception for the Modesto Guard. The gentlemen's uncouth actions resulted in numerous tobacco stains on the ladies' lovely dresses. The editor suggested that in the future the police patrol the sidewalk during receptions at the Opera House so that situations like this would not occur again.

Another article told the story of a wagon loaded with whiskey and bacon. It seems that the wagon drew up in front of Hud Burleigh's house in the northern part of town minus the driver. Not all of the whiskey could be accounted for, however, which is probably why the driver was missing. It was assumed that he was more interested in the whiskey than the bacon—and loaded himself up with the whiskey and took off for parts unknown.

The final article described a meeting of the Women's Christian Temperance Union at the Opera House. The meeting opened with songs and scripture readings. The main address, which was given by the Rev. DeWitt of Salt Lake City, was described as "spicy and interesting." He exhorted the multitude present to "awake from their selfishness and feel the duty they owe to their fellow man." He said that much could be accomplished by encouragement. Immediately following the speech, one Mr. Ward entertained the group with a fine rendition of the song, "Have Courage, My Boy, to Say No." He was followed by Mrs. Skelton, who regaled the group with the topic, "Is the late incorporated City of Fresno going to spoil her records by supporting corner groceries¿" She advocated Temperance Grocery Stores in their stead.

Thus were the activities of some of the people of the new City of Fresno in the year 1885—a year of great importance in the tales of our valley.

On April 19, 1856, the California legislature passed an act creating the County of Fresno. The new county was carved out of the counties of Mariposa, Merced and Tulare. Ninety-nine years later, in 1955, the board of supervisors appointed a committee to plan and carry out a centennial celebration in 1956.

As the year began, events were planned not only in Fresno, but also in other towns and communities throughout Fresno County. Soon most men were growing whiskers for a whiskerino contest and many women began wearing period dresses. A campaign to raise funds to rebuild the old Millerton Courthouse was started with an appropriate ceremony held on its proposed site. A book titled *The Fresno County Centennial Almanac*, on the history of the county, was published.

The climax of the centennial celebration was a giant parade on Saturday, April 21, led by Governor Goodwin J. Knight and his wife, followed by Sade Elizabeth Smith, "Fresno County's Pioneer Queen," and Helen Zorilla, "Miss Century of Progress." Hopalong Cassidy on his horse Topper, many notables, beautiful floats, and numerous bands were cheered by thousands of Fresno County citizens who jammed the sidewalks. Many others watched from the windows of office buildings, thrilling to the passing parade. Events continued throughout 1956, especially during the Fresno Fair.

When the board of supervisors decided to hold a centennial celebration they said in their resolution that the purpose shall be…"that the pioneer living and dead might be honored as we pause for this brief time to salute those whose sacrifice and toil laid the firm foundations for the growth and prosperity of our county; that those in the fruitful years of life may, for a moment reflect on the richness of the heritage bequeathed us by those pioneers and recognize that the temple of today was built upon the pillars of the past, and that to fully know and love this warm, quiet, lovely place that is our home on the earth we must know of its youth; and finally that our children may be impressed that today is only the harvest of all the days that have gone before and will be handed on to them and their children and their children's children in trust that those who will be here one hundred years from now may give thanks as heartily as we do for the privilege of living in this the best of all possible places."

Whether it was a board member, their clerk, the county counsel or someone else who composed that poetic expression for the board is unknown. What is known is that the heartfelt hope of the board as expressed was truly realized and that the event remains as one of the most memorable in the tales of our valley.

A Commemorative Communion Service

On October 21, 1955, just one hundred years after the first recorded religious ceremony took place at Fort Miller, an outdoor communion service was held at Millerton Lake to commemorate that event. This celebration was the first in a series of events that would usher in the one hundredth anniversary of the formation of Fresno County in 1856.

On that long ago day in October of 1855, a large group of people gathered in a hastily cleared room in the officers' quarters at the fort to witness the baptism of Mary Carroll, the first white child born at Millerton. Officiating at the service was the Right Reverend William Ingraham Kip, the Episcopal Bishop of California.

The bishop arrived from Los Angeles after a long, harrowing stagecoach journey of two weeks. He was not pleased with the conditions that prevailed on his arrival. He arrived on a Sunday only to find that the populace of Millerton was not exactly keeping the Sabbath in a way that a religious leader would condone. As he wrote in his book, *Early Days of My Episcopate,* "It (Millerton) consists of some 20 houses, most of them of canvas, two or three being shops and the majority of the rest drinking saloons and billiard rooms. The population on this day seemed to be given up entirely to dissipation." His displeasure was conveyed to some of the officers who quickly saw to it that a room was made ready for the religious service.

Bishop Kip's family came to America with Henry Hudson aboard the ship *Half Moon* in 1609. Of French descent, his ancestors were forced to flee France and settle in Holland during religious wars in the sixteenth century. The bishop was born in New York, studied law at Yale, and was graduated from the General Theological Seminary in New York in 1835. He was ordained soon after. After serving as a pastor in three churches in the East, he was consecrated a bishop in 1853 and journeyed by boat to California where he served his church for almost forty years. During this time, he received a doctor of law degree from Yale and a Ph.D. in sacred theology from Columbia. He was the author of several books and articles. He died at the age of eighty-one in 1893.

One of the highlights of the service that was held at Millerton

Lake on Sunday morning, October 21, 1955, was that the celebrant of the communion service used the same silver chalice that Bishop Kip had used one hundred years before in the communion service in that primitive barracks in Fort Miller. During the intervening years, it had been in the possession of Bishop Kip's family in San Francisco. Mrs. Carroll Peeke, Kip's great-granddaughter, personally brought it to Fresno for this special occasion.

A Farm Boy from Caruthers

In 1946, George Peter Hammond was given the post of director of the Bancroft Library, the University of California at Berkeley's prestigious library of California history. What was significant about this appointment was that this gifted scholar was a son of the great Central Valley, a farm boy from Caruthers.

The road to the Bancroft Library had not always been easy. Hammond's parents were Danish immigrants who farmed in Minnesota and North Dakota before moving to California. Hammond, the second son in a family of three boys and four girls, was thirteen years old in 1909 when his father bought a piece of raw land near the small village of Caruthers.

Like farm boys of that time, Hammond worked hard in the fields helping his family make a living. When Hammond graduated from the small Caruthers Elementary School, the nearest high school was Washington Union in Easton. He rode his bicycle sixteen miles to school each day. The principal, Mervyn F. Thompson, who recognized in this young man the avid desire to learn that is the mark of the truly gifted student, took a special interest in him. He introduced Hammond to the study of history and awoke in him the desire to get a good education.

After graduating from Washington Union High School, Hammond entered the University of California at Berkeley in 1916, graduated in 1920 and went on to obtain his master's and doctor's degrees, concentrating on early California history. In 1922, with a fellowship from the Native Sons of the Golden West, he spent a year in Spain researching in the archives in Seville. In 1923, he began his teaching career at the University of North Dakota. In 1925 he went to the University of Arizona and in 1927 to the University of Southern California, where he remained until 1946 when the call came inviting him to the post at the Bancroft Library. The new position included a professorship in history. During all these years Hammond had authored many articles and several books on the history of California and the Southwest. He became one of the foremost authorities on the history of the American Southwest.

Hammond did not forget his roots. In 1963, he was master of

ceremonies at a reunion of the first thirty classes of the Washington Union High School. His proud mentor, Mervyn Thompson, was present on that occasion.

Dr. George Peter Hammond retired from the University of California at Berkeley in 1965.

On November 20, 1969, he came to Fresno and gave an inspirational talk to the California Artists and Writers of the San Joaquin Valley. Many of Hammond's friends and relatives from Caruthers attended this meeting.

Now, the Caruthers farm boy and noted historian rests in the Washington Colony cemetery very close to the high school where he began his journey on the road to greatness. The story of the life of George P. Hammond, from his humble farm boy beginnings through all of his accomplishments, is an inspiration to students and teachers alike, adding another proud chapter in the tales of our valley.

Jim Savage's Monument

One spring afternoon, when the wildflowers were covering the hillsides with a lush tapestry of colors, our traveler set out on a journey through the rolling foothills of Fresno and Madera counties. This drive was not a whim; he had an aim in view. He was in search of the monument that Dr. Lewis Leach erected to mark the burial spot of Jim Savage, one of the earliest pioneers of the Central Valley.

Driving north on Highway 41, our traveler crossed the San Joaquin River. On this particular day, the grass that carpeted the hills and fields was a resplendent green—a reminder of the many storms the valley had endured through the winter and early spring months. Popcorn flowers, golden poppies and blue lupine swept across the landscape, standing out in contrast to the verdant background. Mother Nature had truly blessed the valley this spring.

At Four Corners, a left turn brought the traveler onto Highway 145. From there he took a right turn on Road 27 and soon another right turn on Road 400. In a few minutes he arrived at his destination, Hensley Lake. He turned left at the Buck Ridge entrance and followed the road until he arrived at a parking lot overlooking the lake. Just north of this spot, high on a hill, he could see the Jim Savage monument—etched against the blue sky.

Leaving his car, the traveler climbed the hill. There, at his feet, four bronze plaques told the story of Major James Savage, who was a pioneer miner, trader and the discoverer of Yosemite Valley. During the Gold Rush, Savage had operated a trading post three miles upstream from this spot, at a place called Fresno Crossing.

The plaques also tell of his death at the hands of Walter Harvey. Savage was only twenty-nine years old. This event occurred many miles away at Poole's Ferry near the Kings River. Savage was buried nearby.

Several years later, Dr. Lewis Leach, who had been Savage's business partner, had Savage's remains moved to a site on the Fresno River. He ordered a granite monument in Connecticut and had it brought to California to mark the site. There it stood for many years until the construction of the Hidden Dam on the Fresno River began. When the dam was completed, the marker would be covered by the waters of the newly created Hensley Lake. So, on Sunday, August 15, 1971, Savage's remains were moved yet again— this time to the site high above Hensley Lake. The marker was moved there also.

On May 19, 1974, the Jim Savage Chapter 1852 of E Clampus Vitus placed near the monument four bronze plaques telling the story of Jim Savage. A fifth plaque at the base of the monument commemorates this event.

Leaving Hensley Lake, our traveler drove north on Road 400, journeying through the rolling hills to Coarsegold. Then he turned on Highway 41 south to Fresno. In a few minutes he could see Little Table Mountain rising in all its majesty from the valley floor, looking like an incredible ship looming high above the fields of grass.

Crossing the San Joaquin River he noticed that the berms on each side of the freeway had been planted with blue lupine. I wonder, he thought, if someday, one hundred years from now as development continues north, this will be the only reminder of how the valley looked in spring. A sobering thought, indeed.

Mr. Bulldog

Fresno can boast many organizations that could not exist without their volunteer base. One such group, the Bulldog Foundation, has been the top volunteer athletic fund raising organization in the United States for fourteen consecutive years. This has been accomplished by the hard work of a legion of volunteers—nearly five thousand of them!

Each year when the five-week fund drive begins, 330 Bulldog Foundation members sign on as "players." Their job is twofold: to approach members about renewing their memberships and to sign up new members. At the end of five weeks, the top fund raiser is determined and is given the designation of "Mr. Bulldog."

In 1981, the first year this honor was given, Robert Duncan won the title. For sixteen succeeding years Dennis Woods earned the designation. When the numbers were tallied in 1999 no one was surprised when, for the eighteenth time, Dennis Woods was again named Mr. Bulldog.

Woods is a native of Fresno and a graduate of Roosevelt High School and Fresno State College. His first dream was to be an English teacher. He majored in English and completed his student teaching, but after graduation became a co-owner of Hestbeck's Market instead. After twenty-three years, he sold his interest in the store and in 1993 became the founding chairman of the United Security Bank. His title now is bank president.

In 1997, Woods was named the National Athletic Fund Raising Volunteer of the Year by the National Association of Athletic Development Directors. When asked why he works on the Bulldog fund drive, Woods replied, "I have always appreciated the education I received from Fresno State. My fund drive efforts are my way of paying back the university and giving an opportunity to other students."

Woods' involvement with local organizations is not limited to the Bulldog Foundation. He also works with the Lions Club and is one of the founders of the Lions Eye and Tissue Bank of the San Joaquin Valley.

In working as a volunteer for many years, Woods has witnessed the leaders of our community giving not only from their pocketbooks, but giving of their time as well. He considers Bob Duncan his mentor and from him learned the joy of giving something back to his community.

In Woods' twenty-three years of working on the foundation's fund drive, he has reported $2,742,000 in membership pledges, which translates into scholarships for student-athletes at California State University, Fresno. A true legend of the valley, Dennis Woods has certainly earned the title of "Mr. Bulldog."

Second Street in downtown Selma on October 26, 1914.
Courtesy of The Selma Enterprise.

When the traveler leaves Fresno to travel south on Highway 99, he reaches three towns in rapid succession—Fowler, Selma, and Kingsburg. Each is a unique community unto itself. The focus of this story will be on Selma.

Unlike other Central Valley towns along the railroad's path, Selma was not a creation of the railroad. It actually began with the founding of the Valley View School District on May 6, 1878. Leading the way in this endeavor were Monroe Snyder and George B. Otis, two early settlers in the area. The first teacher, Frances Sargeant, taught her class of thirteen students in a room of the George Church home. Soon after, Snyder and Otis gave land to the district and a school house was constructed.

Two years later, in mid-April of 1880, a town site was laid out on the railroad five miles north of Kingsburg. Snyder and Otis had promoted a town site near their property. Then Jacob Emory Whitson and Egbert H. Tucker proposed a town site just a half mile north. The railroad refused to accept two town sites so close together and preferred the Whitson site. Realizing that it made economic sense to band together, the four became partners in the town site development project. Each took an undivided one-quarter interest in the forty-acre town site that was carved out of Whitson's land.

Thus was Selma established. The task of laying out the town followed. A civil engineer named Caleb Davis had been elected county surveyor in 1876. Starting at the Witness Tree near Kingsburg that had been used to measure the Laguna de Tache Grant, he "chained the necessary distance west on what is now Elkhorn Avenue and then north on the alignment of Highland Avenue. From there, streets were laid out."

The city of Selma was incorporated in March of 1893, the second city in Fresno County to attain this status.

Selma can make a unique claim. The first building that was ever constructed on the land that would become Selma is still standing and in use. Called the Section House, it was built in July or August of 1872. It was the only building for miles around and housed the Chinese section crew which was building the railroad and their leader, an Irishman named Pat Reardon. Seventy years ago, the house was moved. Now a private residence, it stands at the corner of Park and Sheridan streets.

Today, Selma's central business district is filled with restored historic buildings. Rather than being laid out in a grid pattern, the streets curve and flow into one another, creating a feeling of friendliness and charm. The downtown ambiance is so inviting that the traveler wants to stop and explore its restaurants and shops. Always a pleasant place to visit, Selma has carved out its own place in the history of our valley.

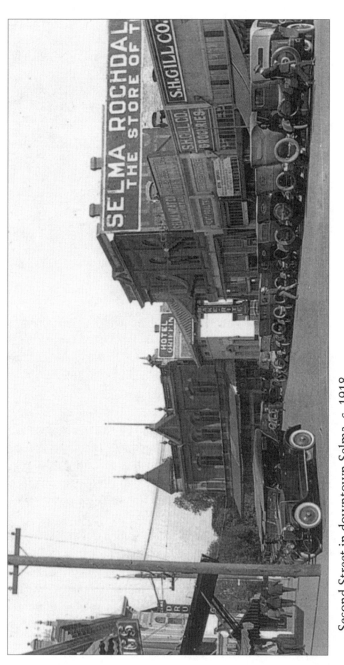

Second Street in downtown Selma, c. 1918.
Courtesy of The Selma Enterprise.

Mrs. Selma Michelsen
Kingsbury Latimer, the
lady for whom the city of
Selma is named.
*Courtesy of Selma Branch of
the Fresno County Free Library.*

M ost cities receive their names in a rather straightforward manner. However, the city of Selma was named three times before a permanent name was chosen, and, even then, the person for whom Selma was named was a matter of some dispute for a long time. Indeed, the truth is still a matter of conjecture.

First, the name of the man who donated the land for the new town, Whitson, was submitted to the Central Pacific Railroad authorities. They already had a town named Whitney and vetoed this selection. Next, the name Irwin, which would honor the governor of California, was given. This, too, was disqualified by the railroad. The third choice was Crocker, in honor of one of the owners of the railroad. This was rejected, too.

Finally, A. N. Towne, general superintendent of the railroad, offered the following suggestions: Dalton, Weymouth, Sandwich, and Selma. George B. Otis, one of the four partners of the town site land, made the selection. He chose Selma because it "was a very fondly used name in Switzerland for a beautiful, amiable, sweet-tempered maiden." He submitted this name to Towne, who approved it.

Only one problem remained. No one bothered to ask Towne which fair maiden named Selma was being honored. As a result two ladies named Selma believed that Selma was named in their honor.

Selma Gruenberg Lewis firmly believed that her father, who she claimed was a close associate of Leland Stanford, president of the Central Pacific Railroad, showed her photo to Stanford, who promptly named the new town for her. There is no documentary evidence to back up this claim, but she called herself the "Godmother of Selma." Her life was spent in the East and in Europe. As the goddaughter of Jennie Jerome, Winston Churchill's mother, she hobnobbed with society figures during the early part of the twentieth century. Her world was one far removed from life as it was lived in Selma, California. Even though she never lived there during her lifetime, her ashes were interred at Selma's Floral Memorial Park on July 3, 1944, five months after her death.

The other Selma's name was Selma Michelsen Kingsbury Latimer. She was born on board a ship moored at the foot of Taylor Street in San Francisco in 1853. Selma married Sanford Kingsbury, an assistant of Towne's. Kingsbury died four years after the marriage took place. The young widow later remarried, lived to the age of sixty and is buried in Sonoma County. Photos show that she was a beautiful young woman, and she is generally accepted by historians as the person for whom Selma is named.

Jacob Emory Whitson, whose intended wheat field became Selma's townsite, served as Fresno County treasurer. *Courtesy of The Selma Enterprise.*

"Sandlapper" was a derisive name probably given by cattle men to those men who came to the Central Valley in the 1870s to plant wheat and tend the land. One of their number provided the land for Selma's townsite. His name was Jacob Emory Whitson.

Whitson was born on January 17, 1838, in Grant County, Indiana. His father died when he was six. His mother remarried and moved the family to Iowa, where Whitson spent a good part of his boyhood helping to support his family. He married Mary Ann Patterson in 1861. The Civil War had begun and in November of that year he enlisted in the 13th Regiment Iowa Infantry and went off to serve in the Union Army. He fought under General Sherman for three years, seeing duty at Shiloh, Corinth, Vicksburg, and the burning of Atlanta. He returned home to Mary Ann and their son, Bill, in 1864. The couple went into farming and had three more children.

Two of Whitson's uncles, Silas and Elias Draper, had moved to the Central Valley and had played a prominent role in establishing the town of Kingsburg. In the summer of 1876, Whitson decided he wanted to move west. Mary Ann did not want to leave. So adamant was she that they did the unthinkable at that time—

they separated. Whitson left his family and moved to California. Two years later, Mary Ann filed for divorce.

Whitson first went to Laramie, Wyoming, then to Salt Lake City and San Francisco, where he got a job as a Bible salesman. In 1877, he headed into the San Joaquin Valley and stayed at his uncle's Temperance Hotel in Kingsburg. When he was mustered out of the Army, he received a soldier's land warrant. Using this, he purchased 160 acres of land bisected by the Central Pacific Railroad five miles north of Kingsburg. It was too late in the season to plant wheat as he had hoped, and, since it was a drought year, he had to wait until the next spring to plant his crop. For one dollar and seventy-five cents, he built a six- by nine-foot cabin made of mountain shakes on the highest point of his land. From this vantage point he could see all his property and guard it. This was necessary, because until he worked his land, someone else could file a claim on it.

With the exception of Pat Reardon and his Chinese crew at the railroad's section house nearby, his only companions that first summer were desert owls, coyotes, tarantulas, and scorpions. It was a rather lonely beginning and he often walked to Kingsburg for entertainment and company.

However, soon other forces would intervene. And, as we will learn in another tale of our valley, Whitson's homestead was to have a much more lasting and important purpose than a wheat field. It would become the site of the city of Selma.

Selma, in its long history, has had not just one, but three opera houses named for Charles Frederick Unger. Unger was a farmer, house mover and drayman. Interestingly enough, none of the three Unger opera houses began life in a building intended for that purpose.

The first Unger Opera House was started by Mr. Unger himself, in 1888. He purchased a public hall and moved it to Whitson Street, between Second and Third streets. He remodeled it, adding on to the building to make room for a large stage. On the evening of November 28, 1888, a grand ball and supper were held to mark the beginning of the first season. On December 19 of that year, the first play was presented. Titled *The World*, this drama was the first of many productions. Indeed, it could be said that over the years some of the best talent on Broadway appeared on the stage of the Unger. Edwin Booth, the famed Shakespearean actor and brother of Lincoln's assassin, performed on the Unger's stage on May 25, 1889. After the turn of the century, attendance began to decline. A new theater was needed—one that was more sophisticated and with better facilities. The first Unger Opera House closed in 1904.

In 1906, Charles Frederick Unger purchased the old Valley View School building. He moved it to a parcel of land on Second Street, just east of Whitson Street. This building had a well-equipped stage, a balcony and room for more seating. Unger developed portable flooring that allowed gradually elevated seating for stage shows. It could be removed when a flat floor was needed for other events. This Unger Opera House showed motion pictures, a form of entertainment that was gaining in popularity. The second Unger Opera House closed on May 1, 1920. Mr. Unger died in 1926.

For the next sixty-five years, Selma was without an Unger Opera House. Then, in 1985, a group of volunteers formed the Raisin' Cain Arts Organization Committee and focused its efforts on a building that had been moved to Selma's Pioneer Village. Built in 1918 as a temporary classroom for Garfield School and later used for the same purpose for Roosevelt School, this building had

Charles Frederick Unger, who was the premier purveyor of
entertainment in Selma for 35 years, was a man of many trades
in his younger days, including bookseller.
Courtesy of The Selma Enterprise.

a stage and enough room for a sizable audience. It also bore a striking resemblance to the first Unger Opera House.

Although the building was just a shell, these volunteers went to work and created a theater and a home for the arts in this part of Fresno County. On March 14, 1986, the houselights were dimmed as Selma High School's Fantasy Company presented its production of *Up the Down Staircase*. For ten years, until July 13, 1996, the stage of the Unger saw many spirited productions by the Raisin' Cain Players. By then, time had taken its toll on the old building. The players had to find a new home. Happily, they did.

Thanks to the Selma Hospital District, the building that once housed the St. Andrew Presbyterian Church was offered to the city and is now called the Selma Cultural Arts Center. February of 1997 saw the houselights go up in the new C. F. Unger Hall, which houses the center's theater. Once again, the Raisin' Cain Players and other local thespians can present lively entertainment for the citizens of our great Central Valley.

The Final Curtain

On July 13, 1996, an evening of nostalgic memories began to unfold at the Pioneer Village in Selma. Sitting under the trees waiting for dinner to be served, people remarked how sad it was that the third of Selma's Unger Opera Houses was about to close. Yes, of course, it was good that a new cultural center would eventually be available for the Raisin' Cain Players' productions, but there was something about the old building that was irreplaceable. Maybe it was because so many people had poured their hearts and souls into creating the theater out of the shell of the old building—they had literally crafted it with their bare hands—that made this closing so hard to face. For both actors and audience this was going to be an evening of memories and tears.

At 8:40 the curtain went up. Master of Ceremonies Randy McFarland welcomed the audience and introduced the director, Dennis Adkins. Then Gary Gould and the Raisin' Cain Chorus sang "Thanks for the Memory," which had new words befitting the occasion. This was followed with selections from a number of the shows presented by the company including, among others, *Fiddler On the Roof, Oklahoma, Bye Bye Birdie, Peter Pan, Harvey,* and *The Wizard of Oz.* The thespians sang, danced, and acted their hearts out for three hours and twenty minutes, making this the longest show on record. The audience responded enthusiastically to each number, remembering, perhaps, the evening they first saw it performed.

Then the entire company gathered on stage for the Finale Ultimo. As they sang "The Party's Over," tears began to flow. After the final line of the song was sung the lights over the stage began to go out one by one. The hall was dark except for a lone spotlight that shone on a picture of Charles Frederick Unger which had presided over the evening from a set at stage right. Unger's image slowly faded to black as the spotlight went out. A hushed silence broken only by muffled sobs filled the opera house. Then the house lights came on dimly to allow the audience to leave. The final curtain had come down on the third Unger Opera House.

And what about Mr. Unger himself? Although he died in 1926, the thespians who trod the boards of this theater just knew that his spirit was there. They could feel it. Indeed, on several occasions he seemed to appear at the end of a show. It was puzzling that director Dennis Adkins was never on hand to meet Mr. Unger at any of these sightings, but, nonetheless, others thought they saw him.

On this last night a couple of strange things happened. Lights kept going out and odd noises could be heard. Perhaps Unger, too, was sad. A year later, when the crew was setting up for a production of *Peter Pan* in the new C. F. Unger Hall, they kept hearing noises and were sure that Mr. Unger's spirit had moved to the new facility. One might hope that this is so.

The Boys & Girls Clubs of Fresno County had a humble beginning. On March 30, 1949, twelve men met at the home of Philip Jenkins to organize the West Fresno Boys Club. They wanted to provide a positive and safe recreational facility for boys to come to after school and on Saturdays. The first club opened at 1219 Tulare Street. The membership grew, and in 1959 the West Fresno Boys Club moved to its current, larger quarters at 930 Tulare Street.

In 1962, the East Fresno Boys Club was formed. Soon after this, the people in Pinedale wanted to start a club. In 1966, after a few failed attempts, the Optimists Club got involved. With their ongoing support, the Pinedale Club opened and continues to provide the young people of their neighborhood with a safe haven where they can meet positive role models and find creative ways to spend their free time.

In its fifty-year history, the Boys & Girls Clubs of Fresno County has only had two executive directors, Don Stevenson and Ken Quenzer. In the late 1960s, Ken asked his wife Muriel to help one day a week. She said she would if girls could be allowed into the club one day a week. This was arranged. Soon, girls were allowed in two days a week. Now, they hold equal membership with boys and are allowed to participate during all the hours the clubs are open.

Today, there are seventeen clubs serving almost thirteen thousand young people throughout Fresno County. Two thousand children a day visit the clubs. A staff of eighty trained youth development professionals provide guidance, supervision and act as role models. An army of volunteers helps in many areas, including tutoring, mentoring, health services, and foster grandparenting.

A visit to the Zimmerman Club on Belmont Avenue is an uplifting experience. The huge activity room, with its soaring white walls and skylights, is filled with light. Here young people can play all sorts of table and board games, but are also exposed to other activities. Opening off this room is a library, computer center, fine arts room, and a room with two pianos and musical instruments. The emphasis on the educational programs is equal to, if not greater than, the sports programs. The goal is to show young people a better future and how they can get there by staying in school and working hard.

A gym, with a weight room and exercise room, is close by. A separate room for teens is just down the hall. A health care facility serves not only the children, but neighborhood families. More than two hundred fifty young people a day flock to this club. Every child has to fill out a one-page membership form and pay five dollars a year or forty-nine cents a month so that he or she can come as often as they want and use all the facilities. The aim is to make them feel they own this club and are part of the group. Gang members are welcome, but they must leave their gang affiliation at the door. While they are inside, they are members of the club. Helping them feel a sense of belonging and offering them a positive alternative has made many leave their gangs for good.

As the Boys & Girls Clubs of Fresno County began their fiftieth year of service to our young people, they can look back at their history in Fresno with pride and look to the future with hope. In the words of Ken Quenzer, "This is an exciting time. The community is beginning to see the effects of not paying enough attention to our kids...not investing in youth development like we should. We're becoming a little more willing to do that."

Coats in the Courtroom

Fresno's historic courthouse, which was torn down in 1966, saw many remarkable people pass through its portals. From the pioneer lawyers who helped to tame the wild frontier town of Fresno Station to the more sophisticated attorneys of the early 1960s, each generation added another layer of history and tradition to the fabled structure.

During the 1920s, the courtroom of Superior Court Judge Campbell E. Beaumont could be found in Department 2. The judge was highly respected for his fairness and judicial competency. He was also a meticulous person and expected the lawyers in his court to behave according to proper etiquette and to dress in a respectful manner. Through all the years he served, Judge Beaumont never lessened his expectations in this regard. Near the end of his career, he called a young attorney into his chambers at the end of a day's court session and gave him a proper dressing down because he had not stood up when he addressed the court. The judge's admonition was never forgotten.

One hot July day, a lawyer named Melvin Gibbs was scheduled to try a case in Judge Beaumont's courtroom. The old courthouse was not air-conditioned and the courtroom was extremely hot and uncomfortable. Because of the heat Gibbs decided to forgo his coat. Judge Beaumont was appalled and told Gibbs to leave and not to come back until he was properly attired.

Melvin Gibbs happened to be a man of small stature. He left Beaumont's courtroom. The first person he saw was attorney Jim Campbell, a good friend who not only weighed about three hundred pounds, but stood six feet tall. In Gibbs' haste to find a coat this did not seem to matter—all he could think of was pleasing the judge and getting back in the courtroom with his client. He asked Campbell if he could borrow his coat. Campbell said yes. Gibbs grabbed it, put it on and ran into the courtroom.

When he stood to speak, Campbell's coat hung down to Gibbs' knees, the sleeves practically hit the floor, and the shoulders of the coat settled at Gibbs' elbows. Gibbs was quite literally engulfed by Campbell's coat. He presented such a vision of the ridiculous that the courtroom spectators and other attorneys had a hard time keeping a straight face. In fact, the only person who failed to see the humor in the situation was Judge Beaumont, who said nothing. It was a moment in the life of the old courthouse that those who were present will never forget and one that adds a touch of the humor and whimsy of another time in the history of our valley.

A Walk through the Park

The Anna Woodward Memorial Fountain shown at its original location in Courthouse Park in 1921. It was erected by Oscar J. Woodward in memory of his wife.
The Image Group from the Laval Historical Collection.

Any day is a good day to take a walk in Courthouse Park. Not only is it filled with lovely shade trees and squirrels, but it is also the heart of our city and as such provides a little something more than beauty. It was here that our county government was established, thereby turning the little railroad stop called Fresno Station into something more than just another Wild West town—it was now destined to become the major city in the Central Valley.

The best place to start your walk is just in back of the courthouse on the M Street side. Here you will see the Fresno plaque that is fixed to a large piece of granite. Read what it has to say. Imagine how this area looked before the railroad came when wild elk and antelope swept across the open plains.

Then walk to M Street and stand before the statue of the Brotherhood of Man. This sculpture by Clement Renzi depicts three clergymen, Monsignor James Dowling, Rabbi David L. Greenberg and Dean James M. Malloch, who had a radio program on KMJ for many years. They discussed religious and social issues and, many feel, helped to launch the ecumenical movement.

Walking south toward the corner of Tulare and M streets, where you will come to a huge sculpture of Armenian folk hero David of Sassoon by Varaz Samuelian.

Turning west on Tulare Street you will soon see a round granite structure supported by Ionic columns. This is the Anna Woodward Memorial Fountain. Installed in 1923, it honors the memory of the wife of Oscar J. Woodward, pioneer Fresno banker. Across from the Woodward memorial stands Atante de Tula, a large replica of a Toltec sculpture from A.D. 900. Donated by the people of the government of the State of Hidalgo, Mexico, in October 1980, it is a gift to the Mexican American community of the San Joaquin Valley and to the County and the City of Fresno.

At the corner of Tulare and Van Ness a marker memorializes author and native Fresnan William Saroyan. It faces the corner where he sold newspapers as a young man. Just to the left of this marker stands the oak tree planted on July 4, 1976, to commemorate our nation's bicentennial. As you read about the oak tree and look up at it, you will notice a bronze statue of a man seated in a chair. This is Dr. Chester Rowell, a pioneer doctor, state senator, member of the board of regents of the University of California, and mayor of Fresno. His statue faces the corner where his home stood. Today, the Rowell Building occupies that site.

Walking along the path you can see another statue, a bust of Martin Luther King, Jr., the great Civil Rights leader, created by artists Jame Zarl Smith and Larry deWitt. A wide variety of community organizations donated funds so this work could be commissioned and placed at this site.

Next, walk to the planting area in front of the courthouse and read the plaque that was placed there by the Jim Savage Chapter 1852 of E Clampus Vitus on September 28, 1974. It tells about the rough board building that housed the first county offices and the laying of the cornerstone for the historic courthouse.

It seems fitting that this park bears the generic name Courthouse Park for it truly exists for all the people. Within it are many memorials to individuals and peoples who played an important role in the life of our community. This park provides a touchstone to the past. A walk through this lovely park reminds us of our history.

This wooden octagonal building was the home of the First Armenian Presbyterian Church of Fresno. Built in 1902, it was located at 515 Fulton Street. By the time the building was gutted by fire on October 30, 1985, it was the last wooden church building in the city.
Courtesy of First Armenian Presbyterian Church.

On September 6 and 7, 1997, the members of Fresno's First Armenian Presbyterian Church gathered to begin a year-long celebration of their church's one hundreth birthday. The roots of their church go back to the 1870s with the arrival of Jacob Seropian, the first Armenian to settle in Fresno. This was the beginning of a migration of Armenian immigrants to the Fresno area.

Because of the presence of Congregational and Presbyterian missionaries in their homeland, many Armenians were Protestant. Many of the new immigrants worshipped at the First Congregational Church. The year was 1893. Because their appearance and language were different and the use of garlic in their diet caused some to complain, the newcomers were asked to sit apart from the rest of the congregation. Such discrimination caused other Fresno churches to reach out and welcome them to their congregations. However, discrimination continued well into the 1920s.

On July 25, 1897, forty Armenian settlers met in a small room in Nicholl's Hall at 1151 I Street (now Broadway). After hearing a sermon delivered in Armenian by the Reverend Lysander Tower

Burbank, they enrolled as charter members of a new Presbyterian church: the First Armenian Presbyterian Church of Fresno. The new congregation elected and installed three charter elders: Avedis Vartanian, Khachig Michaelian, and Hagop Azhderian. The Reverend Burbank was installed as their minister. Edgerly Hall, the DeWitt Building, and the Armenian Hall were among the places where worship services were held.

In 1901, the members voted to build a church. They bought property at 515 Fulton Street from Dr. Thomas Meux and others for $1,650 in gold coin. During construction, members contributed their labor. Arsha Peters brought his team of mules to dig the basement. In April 1902, the three-story wooden, octagonal-shaped church was completed. It was here that William Saroyan worshipped as a child. This building served the congregation until 1941 when a new California mission-style edifice was built on First Street at Huntington Boulevard.

Thirty years later, a need for new facilities existed. In 1975, ground was broken for a new sanctuary on this site. Completed and dedicated in 1976, it is built in a style reminiscent of the historic church on Fulton Street. Inside, the soaring beamed ceilings lead upward to the heavens. The stained glass windows are filled with Christian symbols and tell the story of Christianity in Armenia. A walk in Centennial Hall takes a visitor on a journey that tells the story of the church. Above the wainscoting, scores of pictures tell not only about the church, but of the families who have been involved in its life. In Fellowship Hall, stained glass panels from the 1941 sanctuary have been restored and are displayed as a memorial to the late Paul Melikian.

For a hundred years this church has served as a gateway for Fresno's Armenian community. The Armenian families who came to Fresno in the 1890s looked to the church for guidance and assistance in their new country. The members of the First Armenian Presbyterian Church of Fresno, the oldest Armenian congregation in California, look forward to continued growth and service to God and their community.

The Reverend Lysander Tower Burbank

The first minister of the First Armenian Presbyterian Church of Fresno was originally from New England. Although not of Armenian ancestry, he spoke the Armenian language fluently and had close ties to the Armenian community. It happened in this way.

Lysander Tower Burbank was born in Fitzwilliam, New Hampshire, on November 24, 1828. His ancestors had arrived in America in the mid-1600s. His father was a farmer who chopped wood for the local school and provided its teacher with room and board. When he was twenty-eight years old, Burbank entered Williams College, a small liberal arts institution in Williamstown, Massachusetts. A year later, he enrolled in Union Theological Seminary in New York City. On completion of his studies three years later, he became a licensed Presbyterian minister. He married Sarah Van Vleck and returned to his hometown of Fitzwilliam where he was ordained as a Congregational minister.

Two weeks later, the couple boarded a ship called the *Smyrniote* and sailed to Armenia where they intended to serve as missionaries for the American Board of Commissioners for Foreign Missions. They arrived in Bitlis on October 13, 1860. Their mission was to convert souls to the Protestant Christian faith.

During their ten years in Armenia, five children were born to the couple. In 1870, they returned to the United States. The Reverend Burbank served as pastor of a number of churches stretching from Virginia to Nebraska to Colorado and finally to Fresno, where he was called to be the organizing minister for the First Armenian Presbyterian Church of Fresno.

The Reverend and Mrs. Lysander Burbank served this congregation for two years before moving to Oregon to engage in evangelistic work there. A few years later they retired to Hanford where the Reverend Burbank died in 1912. Among his relatives was the noted horticulturist Luther Burbank of Santa Rosa, California.

Reverend Lysander Tower Burbank and his wife, Sarah, taken on May 16, 1910, on their Golden Wedding Anniversary. *Courtesy of Laurie McGaw, Rev. Burbank's great-grandson and the First Armenian Presbyterian Church.*

The Raisin Drive

Early in this century M. Theo Kearney and others had attempted to organize raisin growers into a cooperative to give them bargaining power. In 1912, the California Associated Raisin Company was formed, marketing raisins under the Sun-Maid label. The company was not a true grower cooperative, having participating capital stock, but it could control the market if it had a large number of growers contracting exclusively with the company.

On September 8, 1920, a suit was brought by the United States to dissolve the California Associated Raisin Company, claiming that Sun-Maid was engaged in unlawful restraint of trade. The case dragged on. In 1922 the federal Capper Volstead Act was passed regulating grower cooperatives.

In early 1923, a plan was adopted to legalize Sun-Maid as a true grower cooperative. Preferred stock in the amount of $2.5 million would be issued, bearing interest at 7 percent, with control in the hands of the grower members. Funds received would pay off the old stockholders. New grower contracts would be obtained covering 85 percent of all raisin acreage. If the sale of stock did not go well or if 85 percent of the growers failed to sign on, the whole project would be abandoned and the company dissolved. The government approved. A campaign was set.

Kickoff day was April 2, 1923. April 26 was Fresno's traditional Raisin Day. The 25th was set for completion of the drive. The 25th arrived. The stock sale was completed, but the required 85 percent goal for new contracts was not reached. The next day three thousand people attended a meeting in Courthouse Park. They decided to extend the deadline for ten days.

As we will learn in our next tale of the valley this set the stage for the most violent, lawless ten days the valley has ever witnessed.

In our last tale of the valley, a drive was launched to obtain new grower contracts covering 85 percent of all raisin acreage. These would be signed exclusively with Sun-Maid Raisin Company. The drive deadline came. The 85 percent goal was not reached. Three thousand people met in Courthouse Park and decided to extend the deadline by ten days. It was April 26, 1923—the beginning of the most violent, lawless ten days in the history of the Central Valley.

All over the raisin growing areas, gangs set out determined to use any means to secure contracts. Violence and coercion were considered justified. Night riders, many with guns, roamed the region. If a grower refused to sign he was beaten. Some were thrown into canals. Vines were cut down and property was destroyed. One gang, the Biola Bunch, never failed to get signatures—at gun point, if necessary. Law enforcement ceased to exist. It was said that if the sheriff was called for help, the only reply would be, "Sign up." As the deadline approached, any grower not signing was held in public contempt. People were convinced the entire area would suffer financial disaster if Sun-Maid dissolved.

"SUN-MAID DRIVE LEAPS FORWARD—VICTORY IN SIGHT," touted a May 5 headline. The next day, five bombs exploded in Courthouse Park—a prearranged signal. Newspaper headlines proclaimed "MAGNIFICENT VICTORY." There was joy in Fresno. Sirens shrieked, bells pealed, and bands played. People poured into town from all the farming communities nearby.

Sun-Maid was reorganized as a legal grower cooperative. Now, of course, all is changed. Membership in Sun-Maid is purely voluntary. It may be instructive to note, it is a much more successful business now than in those early years that are now only a distant memory in the tales of the valley.

Judge J. W. North

The man who developed the farming community named Oleander, Judge J. W. North, was a native of New York.

After graduating from Wesleyan University in 1842, he practiced law in Syracuse, New York. Eight years later, he moved his family to the new territory of Minnesota. For several years they lived in a log cabin on an island in the Mississippi River. Today, that island is part of the city of Minneapolis.

North continued to practice law until 1856. Then he built a grist mill, sawmill and a hotel at a small crossroads area that later was named Northfield in his honor. Many years later Northfield was where some of the most bloody and futile escapades of Jesse James and his gang of bank robbers took place.

In 1860, North was a delegate to the Republican convention in Chicago that nominated Abraham Lincoln for president. He also was one of the group who personally went to Lincoln to tell him that he was the nominee of his party.

A year later, North was sent as surveyor general to the Territory of Nevada. In August of 1863, President Lincoln appointed him as a justice to that territory's supreme court. A year later, North tried to resign, but Lincoln ignored his resignation, forcing North to stay in his job until Nevada became a state in December 1864.

After the Civil War, North sold his law practice. He bought an iron foundry in Knoxville, Tennessee, and moved his family there.

By 1870, however, the West began to beckon him. He moved his family to Los Angeles and played a major part in developing what is now the city of Riverside.

Soon, he was eager to move again. This time he decided to move north into the San Joaquin Valley, where land was just becoming available. He became the developer of the area that would be called Oleander. He purchased forty acres of land for himself at Adams and Cedar avenues, later buying more land and donating a parcel of it as a site for the Oleander School.

Judge J. W. North died in Oleander on February 22, 1890. Not only had he seen his dream of colonizing this rich area into farms, but he had also become one of the most respected and influential men in this section of California.

The Alabama Colony

In 1868, William Chapman and Isaac Friedlander of San Francisco invested in land in an austere spot called the Fresno Plains. That same year three plantation owners from Mississippi and Alabama, Judge Samuel Holmes, Major C. A. Reading, and Levin A. Sledge, came to California to purchase land. They represented a group of Southerners eager to escape the aftermath of the Civil War. The Confederate loss robbed them of their economic and social positions; they wanted to begin a new life. They looked at property southwest of the present-day city of Madera. Impressed by the fertility of the land, they bought a large parcel for two and a half dollars an acre. They called their land the Alabama Colony and wrote glowing reports to their friends urging them to come west.

Among the settlers who arrived in November of 1868 were Dr. Joseph Borden and family, the Henry Pickens family, and brothers James P. and Harry St. John Dixon. Thomas P. Devereux and George Washington Mordecai had settled on land nearby three months before, but were not part of the Alabama Colony. Millerton, the nearest settlement, was twenty miles away. All their goods had to be brought by wagon from Stockton. Life was austere and hard, but they had a sense of humor that helped them deal with their new situation. For instance, the Pickenses named their spartan home the Cradle of Innocence, and one of the bachelors lived in a tent he called Hell's Half Acre. Harry St. John Dixon named his Refuge, indicating a haven from past misfortunes.

They began farming their land—the first group to do so in this section of the Fresno Plains. They worked hard, but a series of problems plagued them. Three years of drought were not conducive to producing bumper crops, roving bands of wild horses and cattle were a constant threat to what did grow, and most of the settlers had been plantation owners in the South and dependent on slaves and servants. They were not used to doing hard work. By 1875, most of the settlers left—many went to the new town of Fresno Station. Today, the Alabama Colony is only a distant memory in the tales of our valley.

A trip into southern Madera County brings the traveler to a place with a unique history in the annals of our valley. Driving along a stretch of road that is unremarkable in the vistas it offers, the traveler comes to a wide curve. He notices a lush forest of trees to the west as he negotiates the curve. It makes him wonder what is hidden away in that beautiful spot that stands out so charmingly from the rest of the countryside.

Turning his car into a long driveway, he drives down a lane lined with eucalyptus trees. A herd of cattle can be seen in the distance. Another curve brings him to a charming home nestled among tall trees and plantings. The traveler has arrived at Refuge—the ranch and home for 130 years of the family of Harry St. John Dixon and George Washington Mordecai.

Harry Dixon named his ranch Refuge because, as a Southerner recently arrived from Mississippi in 1868, this land offered him a haven from the horrors of Reconstruction following the Civil War. A few years later Dixon left. Mordecai, who had married Dixon's sister, Louise, purchased the Refuge from Dixon for six dollars. Mordecai eked out his living on this desolate section of the Fresno Plains by raising sheep and cattle and engaging in grain production. He worked hard and made the land profitable.

Today, the ranch is in many ways a time capsule. In one corner of the property the Mordecai family cemetery sits shrouded in trees and foliage. Another part of the ranch contains outbuildings that the family continues to restore. The dairy, tank house, cook's cabin, blacksmith shop, outhouse, and two barns stand in silent testimony to the busy farming operation that was conducted here. Scores of trees create the feeling of a Southern plantation. This is underscored by the gracious reception given the traveler by the three generations of the Mordecai family who live on the ranch.

Unique among the pioneer homes of our valley, the Refuge is still a haven of sorts—a place of beauty and tranquillity—and represents continuous ownership by the family who established it 130 years ago—a true legacy by any standard.

The Founder of Madera County

George Washington Mordecai, who was to be remembered as the founder of Madera County, was born on his family's farm near Richmond, Virginia, in 1844. His father died when he was three years old, leaving his mother with four children. Just one month after his seventeenth birthday, in 1861, Virginia seceded from the Union. He and his brothers, William and John, enlisted in the Second Company of Richmond Howitzers. Serving under General Robert E. Lee until the end, they were surrendered at Appomattox Courthouse on April 9, 1865. Weary and depressed, they returned home.

Virginia, in the throes of Reconstruction, was not a place to begin again. Financed by his uncle and in the company of his cousin, Thomas P. Devereux, he left for California. They purchased land in a desolate area known as the Fresno Plains which at least offered them the chance for a new start. It was August of 1868.

Three months later other setters arrived in this area south and west of the present-day city of Madera. Two of them, James and Harry Dixon, had a sister, Louise. She and Mordecai fell in love and were married on October 26, 1876. The Dixons decided, like the other settlers, that the land was too difficult to farm and they wanted to leave. Mordecai bought their ranch called Refuge for six dollars. He and Louise moved to the ranch and raised their family.

Over the years, in addition to farming their land, Mordecai became involved in politics. He was elected to a term in the State Assembly in 1890. In 1892, he was reelected. It was during this term of office that he introduced Bill A.B. 154 that would create Madera County. The bill passed and the voters concurred at a meeting held in Fresno on January 28, 1893.

In later years, George Washington Mordecai retired to his ranch. On a June day in 1920, he decided to ride over his property. On this ride, he suddenly died. He is buried in the family cemetery on his beloved Refuge—now at one with the land he loved.

Due to the propensity of our valley to suffer from floods in the years when heavy rains and snow bring extra water, several dams have been built to harness this water so it can stored. A by-product of these dams is the creation of lakes that can be used for recreational purposes. One of these dams, located on the Fresno River in Madera County, is the subject of our story.

The Fresno River was the boundary between two major Indian nations, the Miwoks on the north and the Yokuts on the south. The river was important in the history of the Gold Rush era. Miners flocked to the river and the areas around it—soon mining camps with colorful names like Coarse Gold Gulch and Grub Gulch dotted the map.

It was on the Fresno River that James Savage and Dr. Lewis Leach opened their trading post, offering supplies for the miners and others in the area. It was on the banks of the Fresno River that John Jackson Hensley began a ranching operation in 1861.

Hensley mined for gold in Calaveras County. He then lived in Tulare County where he raised cattle. In 1861, he and his wife, Margaret, settled on government land just two miles down the river from Savage's store and began a farming and cattle ranching operation. Hensley was elected a justice of the peace in 1862 and was elected to the county board of supervisors in 1876.

Hensley descendants continued working the land until the United States government purchased it to begin construction of Hidden Dam in 1972. The project took six years. In 1978, Hidden Dam and its newly created lake and park, which cover a combined area of 3,000 acres, were opened to the public. The earth and rock-fill dam, built at a cost of $32 million, is 5,730 feet long and 162 feet high. It is estimated that without this dam, the city of Madera would have been flooded several times during the last twenty years.

The newly created Hensley Lake, which offers all sorts of recreational possibilities for visitors, has been named for the family that farmed the land now covered by its waters—a reminder of the rich history of our valley.

As we celebrate the Sesquicentennial, the one hundred and fiftieth anniversary of the discovery of gold in California and the events leading up to statehood, it is illuminating to take a look at some of the centers of population in the foothills of Fresno and Madera counties. These communities were beehives of gold mining and logging activity and bore names that evoke that era— Coarse Gold Gulch, Fine Gold, Grub Gulch, Narbo, Zebra, Hildreth, String Town, and Poison Switch—to name a few. Two of them will be the subject of our story.

In the foothills of Madera County, due west of present-day Oakhurst, was a settlement called String Town. In 1881, a post office was established there and the name was changed to Gertrude in honor of the wife of John Haley, the owner of the Enterprise Mine. The town had enough residents by 1888 to support its own school. A man named Mike Baker was the discoverer of the Enterprise Mine. He sold it to Judge J. E. Grant for the sum of twenty thousand dollars. Legend has it that the judge received his money back in the space of just six weeks. By 1900, the gold mine had ceased to produce enough to keep people interested in staying in Gertrude. Everyone left and the town ceased to exist.

A crossroads just outside Gertrude acquired the interesting name of Poison Switch. The first business located there was a saloon. This little settlement was located alongside the Madera Flume. It was a major stopping point for the wagons that brought lumber down the mountains from the Miami Mill. The lumber was unloaded at Poison Switch and emptied into the flume to be floated down to Madera. After the teamsters unloaded their wagons, they would "switch" over to the saloon for a refreshing drink or two or three. Noting this, their superintendent called the crossroads Poison Switch.

Although these two communities cease to exist, they earned their place in history by adding to the local lore of a most colorful time in the history of Fresno and Madera counties.

The Gambetta Mine in 1913. Marge Angelo stands on the
left; an unidentified miner is on the right.
Courtesy of Philip and Gay Wright.

In the foothills of Madera County, south and west of the
towns of Ahwahnee and Nipinnawasee, is a site so peaceful
and empty that its very appearance belies the fact that it once
was home to over a thousand people. Located on the old stage
road to Yosemite, a town once stood here that had "two hotels,
two general stores, eight saloons, one school, a Chinese laundry,"
and numerous homes. In the nearby hills, several gold mines, including the Enterprise, the Gambetta, the Crystal Springs, the Cale-
donia, the Rex, the Josephine, and the Mammoth, were the basis
for the economy of the town.

In 1851, placer miners set up camps along the Fresno River.
Early in the 1880s, a member of the J. B. Gullemin family found a
gold nugget as large as a man's thumb along a creek. Digging, he
found the main vein that was eight inches wide. This strike became known as the Gambetta Mine. Other mines were found soon
after. The discovery of these mines brought scores of people to the
area. A new town was born. It was named Grub Gulch because it
was said that "miners could always get enough gold from the river
to grubstake themselves into better times."

The town's Morrison Hotel and Thomas Hotel had many fa-

One of the hotels at Grub Gulch in 1913. The Morrison and the Thomas hotels hosted two United States presidents—Theodore Roosevelt and William Howard Taft.
Courtesy of Philip and Gay Wright.

mous guests, including presidents Theodore Roosevelt and William Howard Taft. The streets of Grub Gulch were often lined with expensive carriages owned by the rich who were passing through on their way to Yosemite. People from the other mining settlements—Fine Gold, Poison Switch, and Fresno Flats—came on horseback to attend the dances that were held here on Saturday nights. By 1906, the last mine petered out. A new railroad to Yosemite was completed, ending the era of stage travel. In 1910, the last saloon closed.

Today, Grub Gulch is gone. Only a marker dedicated by E Clampus Vitus remains to mark the spot where gold was once king; where whiskey was sometimes used instead of water to fight fires; and where the raucous voices of miners could be heard above the thundering hoof beats which heralded the arrival of a stagecoach bound for Yosemite.

A Community on the Flats

It started out as Fresno Flats. It was so named because it was located along the Fresno River and was in a mountain meadow that is referred to as a "flats." The area had been home to local Indians as far back as time could be counted. In 1850, Fresno Flats owed its existence to nearby gold camps and then to the lumber industry because the mining operations needed such things as sluice boxes and flumes. Many of the early mills were located in Crane Valley (today the Bass Lake area).

In 1865, Robert Nichols and his family moved to Fresno Flats from Millerton. They were soon followed by other settlers. Following the Civil War, a number of people were moving into the central San Joaquin Valley and engaging in cattle raising. The demand for timber products was increasing. More people began to move into the Flats. Many of these new arrivals were farmers. A real community was beginning to develop.

With the advent of the railroad through the valley and the founding of Fresno Station and Madera, the need for lumber to build homes and businesses increased even more. The community grew in response to this need. A large sawmill was built with a flume that would link it with the railroad. Despite a downturn in the economic climate in 1877, two years later a new stage road opened from Madera to Wawona. It went right through Fresno Flats and brought visitors into the town. In 1881, the village had, among other buildings, two general stores, a hotel, restaurant, saloon and a post office.

Today, Fresno Flats has another name—Oakhurst. As one drives on Highway 41, an unparalleled experience awaits. After making a long climb suddenly the road curves and a long descent begins into the quiet valley where Oakhurst is located. As the road twists and turns, the panoramic view of the mountains takes one's breath away. For the residents of this thriving mountain community, it is all part of their daily life. For the visitor, it provides an unforgettable reminder of the majesty and beauty of our Sierra Nevada mountains.

Once there was a village called Fresno Flats. Located in a picturesque valley in the Sierra, it was a peaceful, productive mountain town. Its residents were farmers and lumbermen. One day in 1885, two local men, Charley Meyers and his brother-in-law Billy Prescott, robbed a stagecoach. Charley was later acquitted of the crime, but, for many, memories were long and such events were not forgotten.

Charley and his wife, Hattie, left Fresno Flats and moved to Portland, Oregon. They later divorced and, in 1899, Charley married a young lady named Kitty Whittle. They moved back to Fresno Flats to the homestead his father had left him. Charley was ready to face the embarrassing questions that were bound to come up and he more than proved himself to the local townspeople by becoming a well-respected member of the community. His bride, however, grew tired of people saying such things as, "You live in Fresno Flats? Isn't that where Charley Meyers robbed the stage?"

In 1912, she obtained a petition to change the name of the town to Oakhurst. Only the newer residents would sign it, but she got enough signatures and sent it to Sacramento. The petition then went on to Washington, D.C., where it was speeded along with help of the local congressman. The first person who heard the news that the name of the community had been changed was the postmaster. It was a shock to the older members of the town and created a lot of unhappy feelings. It took until 1925 for the name Oakhurst to come into common usage.

One tradition remains unchanged. Just as the old village of Fresno Flats was located on the stage road from Madera to Wawona, so, too, is the new town of Oakhurst located on a main road. When Highway 41 was completed west of the old town in 1936, the town moved its location to the new highway.

The 1870s Laramore-Lyman House is open to visitors to
Fresno Flats Historic Park and contains exhibits relating to life
in Oakhurst in the latter part of the 19th century.
Author's photo.

A trip into the mountains on Highway 41 from Fresno
brings the traveler to Oakhurst. A right turn on to Road
426, then a left turn on Road 427 brings the traveler to the Fresno
Flats Historical Park. Here, in a charming setting nestled in the
trees, the traveler can quite literally step back in time and enjoy
buildings that played a role in the history of this community and
its surrounding area.

The first stop is the museum. Here, one can see an overview
of the history of Fresno Flats. There are many exhibits that invite
lingering. A self-guided tour is possible because everything is carefully labeled and explained. A library and research center is adjacent to the museum.

Then the traveler can choose a guided tour or choose to start
at the kiosk with its map and listen to an audio explanation of the
buildings and exhibits and proceed on his own. The first building
is the two-story yellow framed Laramore-Lyman House built in
the 1870s by pioneer merchant Robert Laramore. An exhibit be-

hind the house contains large agricultural implements and a section of the Sugar Pine Flume. The Dupzyk Barn contains an exhibit about the mountain timber industry. Next is the Raymond Jail, a small, rather grim, reminder of the need to stay on the right side of the law. A restored blacksmith shop and barn filled with tack equipment are viewed next. A wagon shed contains several horse-drawn vehicles.

Next the visitor comes to the restored 1869 Taylor Log House, a typical Sierra home in the mid to late 1800s. Built of sugar pine logs, it contains two rooms separated by an open area called a "dog trot." One of the rooms was used for cooking and living, the other was the parents' bedroom. The children slept in a loft above. It is said to be the last structure of its kind in California. Two one-room schoolhouses and the old Fresno Flats jail round out the tour. The traveler leaves feeling he has learned a lot about the history of this fascinating corner of Madera County.

Coarse Gold Gulch

Coarse gold nuggets were found in the placers of the first miners who came to Coarse Gold Gulch, hence its name. In 1851, Messrs. Roney and Thornburg opened the first business in the area. Charles Michael bought their business several years later. In spite of the name given the settlement by the miners, early maps show the name of the village as Michaels. In 1878, the first post office was established and was called Coarse Gold Gulch. The name was shortened to Gold Gulch and then, in 1899, the present name of Coarsegold was officially designated.

As placer mining petered out in 1866, Coarsegold became important as a stagecoach stop for travelers going into the mountains. By 1876, when the wagon road to Yosemite was finished, several stages made regular stops here everyday. In 1880, the Khron family built the St. Charles Hotel. This facility continued to operate until 1927 when a fire destroyed it. The Coarsegold Inn, a granite building, replaced it and was a landmark for travelers until 1958 when it, too, was burned. Another inn was built and opened in 1959. Ironically, it suffered the fate of the other two hostelries in 1989 when it also was destroyed by fire.

One feature of the town can be remembered by many valley residents. A town well, with the date 1852 inscribed on it, sat right in the middle of the main road. It gave the town a sort of Biblical flavor to travelers passing through. The well was moved twice, in 1935 and in 1975. There are plans to place it permanently near Highway 41.

Today, many tourists pass through Coarsegold on their way to Yosemite. People still look for gold in the streams that wend their way through the area. Sometimes they find specks of gold gleaming among the bits of sand. There is still some gold in the foothills of our great Central Valley.

Coarse
Gold Gulch
as it looked
in 1889.
*The Image
Group from
the Laval
Historical
Collection.*

Baseball has held a place in the hearts of Fresnans since the first ball club was formed in 1883. Fresno has produced many players who went on to the major leagues. But, did you know that very possibly the finest high school baseball team this nation has ever seen was the Fresno High School Warriors team of 1958? Not only did it dominate all its competition, but it broke all national high school records—and, as of this writing, those records still stand.

The team's three extraordinary pitchers, Jim Maloney, Dick Ellsworth, and Lynn Rube, all signed professional contracts, Rube with the St. Louis Cardinals, Maloney with the Cincinnati Reds, and Ellsworth with the Chicago Cubs.

Within five years after graduation Maloney and Ellsworth became major league twenty-game winners—ironically, receiving this distinction on the same day. The catcher, Pat Corrales, also went on to the majors, playing for nine seasons. Rounding out the team were the late Blair Pollard, Jim Albracht, Tom Jacobson, Jerry Martinez, Chuck Smith, Fred Tuttle, Glenn Schmidt, and the late Jack Reinold. This phenomenal group of young men was coached by Ollie Bidwell, who called it "the finest team I ever coached."

The team amassed a 25-1 record that included 18-0 against prep competition. They played not only all the high school varsity teams, but also the Stanford, UC Berkeley, and Fresno State freshman teams. They beat them all. The only game they lost was to the Fresno State frosh, but they beat that team three other times. One of their records, which still stands, is fifteen shutouts—an all-time record for California. Dick Ellsworth, in a game against Merced, struck out twenty batters. He went on to pitch a 6-0 no-hitter against Roosevelt High, striking out sixteen players. Jim Maloney struck out twenty-five in a game against Visalia's Mount Whitney High School. The team's offensive talents were just as incredible. They scored 288 runs that year. That translates into an average of over eleven runs per game.

Surely, these Fresno High Warriors were a team for all seasons—unsurpassed in the annals of high school baseball. They certainly established their own place in the legends of our valley.

Fresno High School varsity baseball team of 1958. Front row: Blair Pollard, Jim Albracht, Pat Corrales, Chuck Smith, Jerry Martinez, Dennis Schneider, Fred Tuttle. Back row: Glenn Schmidt, Jack Reinold, Jim Maloney, Dick Ellsworth, Tom Jacobsen, Lynn Rube.
Fresno High School Owl of 1958, author's collection.

Dick Ellsworth   Pat Corrales   Jim Maloney

Ollie Bidwell, coach of the Fresno High School varsity baseball team of 1958.
Fresno High School Owl *of 1958, author's collection.*

What makes a phenomenally successful baseball team? Is it talented players? Is it a good coach? Is it something more? The 1958 baseball season at Fresno High School was unlike any other. Take an extremely talented group of ballplayers, add a tough coach, mix in high standards and discipline, and the results are there for all to see—they established an all-time national high school record, that, more than forty years later still stands.

Coach Ollie Bidwell not only taught baseball, he taught a work ethic. On the first day of practice, the boys were told what the standards were: everyone would have a short haircut, everyone would be a good citizen on and off the school grounds, everyone would work hard and adhere to the rules. He taught the boys that no one is better than anyone else, but that each one must strive to do the best he is capable of doing—he demanded that. He believed that the more the boys knew about the fundamentals, the better they would play the game. He organized spring training drills just like the major leagues. The boys trained for hours, drilling each skill over and over until they were ready to drop. They learned what baseball was all about—they learned another lesson as well—that you polish each skill until you become the best that you can be. They learned confidence. These were lessons that carried over to the classroom and that prepared them for life.

Jim Maloney remembers going to Berkeley to play pre-season game against the Cal frosh and the Stanford frosh. Several parents drove the team. Marjorie Maloney, Jim's mother, was driving a group in her nine-passenger station wagon. In the back seat Chuck

Smith, Gary Gostanian (team manager) and Jim were playing nickel-ante poker to pass the time. When they returned home Coach Ollie Bidwell found out about the poker game and suspended all three for one or two games. Even though the offense happened outside the ballpark, the coach didn't care. His standards had been broken, so a price had to be paid.

Dick Ellsworth remembers that when he entered the major leagues the year after graduation, his pitching coach was amazed that he instinctively knew the procedures for spring training. He had already trained this way at Fresno High. Ellsworth reflects, "How fortunate that we all came together at the same time. Each one was the best in the league at the position he played. When you are in high school, you feel there is no tomorrow. Ollie Bidwell made us believe in a tomorrow."

They all reached for the stars and scaled heights that no other high school baseball team ever attained before or since—a legendary record in the tales of our valley.

Some twelve miles south of downtown Fresno and eight miles west of Kingsburg, Fowler Avenue crosses Clarkson Avenue and heads south toward the town of Laton. This crossroads is just north of Elkhorn Avenue, the northern boundary of the area that once comprised the Laguna de Tache Mexican land grant.

In the early 1860s, this area was barren land, home only to horned toads, tarantulas, and wild antelope. In November of 1875, B. M. Stone, newly arrived from Louisiana with his family, was the first settler in the area. His brother-in-law, C. Joplin, and the Joseph Prather family joined him. In 1876, several other families moved to the area.

Their first need was water to irrigate any crops they wished to plant. So they set about building a ditch, which was called the Emigrant Irrigation Ditch. In 1878, Stone harvested his first crop of grain. By 1882, his 320-acre ranch was producing wheat, alfalfa, and fruit. In spring, the fields became a mass of wildflowers—so high that they tickled the underbellies of horses riding through the fields. For this reason the area was called Wildflower. On June 21, 1878, a post office was established here, officially giving the community its name. Exactly twenty years later on June 21, 1898, the post office was closed. The farming operations continued.

Over the years, other families have moved to Wildflower. Mart Raven came to live here about 1932. He first lived on the McCord Ranch, a dairy on the east side of Fowler Avenue. In 1937, he became the first person to raise cotton in the area. Today, he lives on the west side of Fowler Avenue running a ranching operation that includes 1,400 acres of peaches.

Today, the only indication of this community's name is the sign on the lone store on the southwest corner of Clarkson and Fowler. Established by the Aparkian family many years ago, the Wildflower Superette, which has had three owners, is still open for business, serving this tiny community in a quiet corner of Fresno County.

In the stories of our valley, we have told the sad tale of Dr. Vincent, who, in 1890, murdered his wife, Annie, in an alcholic fit. Three years later Dr. Vincent was executed in Courthouse Park, in the only legal hanging in Fresno County. Formal invitations were issued to leading citizens of the community. Six hundred people attended.

The day before the event, the area of Courthouse Park just outside the jail was a beehive of activity. The scaffold, which was on loan from Sheriff R. H. Broughton of Santa Barbara, was put in place. Five men had been hanged from its crossbeam, two for killing their wives.

Inside the jail, there was an almost festive air. A large number of men, women, and children filed through the cell block to see Dr. Vincent, who greeted them all with great politeness. He had been a man of lavish tastes who appreciated fine cigars, gourmet dinners, and excellent wine until alcohol and drugs took hold on his life. On this, his last day, he conducted himself with dignity and told his jailers that he was enjoying his visitors. Indeed, he joked that his powers of conversation were being taxed because he tried not to repeat the same conversation with each person. He felt this would be boring for Henry Scott who was guarding him.

So many people asked to see the scaffold that jailer Manly estimated he must have walked thirty miles that day conducting tours. He complained that he wore out a pair of six-dollar kangaroo leather shoes. Adding to the carnival-like atmosphere were two Salvation Army women who stood inside the jail office loudly singing "Beulah Land" to a group of men in a holding tank. Several others fled to their cells as the women began their performance.

The next day Courthouse Park was filled with people from all over the Central Valley. Many families came with their children and picnic baskets. Just before noon Dr. Vincent, with a cigar in his mouth, climbed the scaffold, finished his cigar, and met his fate. Afterward, the Rev. J. H. Collins of the First Congregational Church said, "I've officiated at nine executions, but this was the best conducted I've seen." And so ended another chapter in the tales of our valley.

George Dunlap Moss

A ride east on Highway 180 is pleasant at any time of the year. In the spring and fall is it especially so. After passing through the towns of Centerville and Minkler, the ascent into the mountains begins. The vistas change rapidly and eventually the traveler finds he has reached a colorful spot called Clingan's Junction. Here, a right turn can be made and, in a few miles, the traveler will arrive at one of Fresno County's oldest communities, Dunlap.

Located in a foothill valley, originally called Shipe's Valley for 1868 settler John Shipe, Dunlap was first called Mill Creek. As the community grew, a school district was established on May 3, 1875. In the fall of 1881, George Dunlap Moss moved to the small settlement to become the master of the Mill Creek School. He felt the area was too isolated and applied to the United States government requesting that a post office be established in Mill Creek. They rejected his request because at that time California had many communities with similar names and well over a hundred streams that bore the name Mill Creek. Instead of being discouraged, Moss applied again, this time submitting his middle name, Dunlap. This time he met with a favorable response. On November 13, 1882, the Dunlap post office opened. Interestingly enough, the post office was located in the school house and Moss had to do double duty, serving the school and acting as postmaster. Moss moved away in 1883.

The community began to grow in the 1890s. Today, the Mill Creek School is known as the Dunlap School and is part of the Kings Canyon Unified School District. The miners are long gone from this quiet valley. They have been replaced by farmers tending their orchards—apples are an important crop. The tiny village once known as Mill Creek is still tucked away in this corner of Fresno County. It bears the name Dunlap—a reminder of a teacher named George Dunlap Moss who wanted to open a window to the outside world.

Millwood

The foothills of our Sierra Nevada Mountains are filled with areas that once were thriving towns and now are only meadows—one could drive right past and never know they had existed. Indeed, they exist only in written records. One such place was called Millwood.

Millwood was a 1890s lumber town. It was located near Sequoia Lake, which was formed to provide water for the Sanger Lumber Company's flume that sent logs from Millwood to Sanger. Millwood grew quickly and had a number of businesses—including the undertaker, who advertised that he was available day or night. It developed a rather riotous reputation, due in part to its thriving red light district that actually was a separate village of its own about a mile south.

Millwood became something of a summer resort for folks from the hot valley. Two hotels accommodated guests who first had to endure the grueling stagecoach ride. The ride began in Sanger at six o'clock in the morning. Travelers went by way of Centerville, Minkler, Clarks Valley, and then, at Streets Station, the stage stopped for a change of horses. From there it was on to Squaw Valley and Dunlap for another change of horses and lunch. Then the stage continued on to Millwood, arriving at about five o'clock in the evening.

Passengers on the stagecoach were divided into classes. First class travelers rode all the way. Second class passengers paid a lower fee and had to disembark on steep grades and help push the stage up the mountain—not much fun on a rainy day. The return trip was even more fun. The driver would stop at the top of a steep road and cut down a tree. Everyone got to help. The tree was tied on the back of the stage to act as a supplemental brake. Otherwise the stage and its passengers would overtake the horse teams, and disaster would result.

A depression in 1909 caused the lumber operations in the Millwood area to go bankrupt. People left and Millwood was consigned to history and the mists of time in our legends of the :valley.

High above our great Central Valley, tucked away in an area of the Sierra Nevada Mountains called the Silver Divide, are several bodies of water that have been given the collective name of the Graveyard Lakes. They are all tributaries of the South Fork of the San Joaquin River and are located just three and a half miles from Edison Lake in the northeasternmost corner of Fresno County. The term Graveyard comes from a nearby peak and meadow where many years ago two sheepmen were murdered and buried. Graveyard Peak rises 11,520-plus feet above sea level. It is a salt and pepper granite mountain—the material that is popular for tombstones—hence, another reason for its name.

Each of these ten lakes has an individual name. Even though they are in one of the most beautiful lake basins in the High Sierra, their names conjure up ominous images and horrible deeds. They are: Funeral Lake; Ghost Lake; Graveyard Lake, Lower; Graveyard Lake, Upper; Headstone Lake; Murder Lake; Phantom Lake; Pumice Lake; Spook Lake; and Vengeance Lake.

All but one of the names were given to conform with the collective name of Graveyard by William A. Dill of the California Department of Fish and Game in August of 1949. Pumice Lake derives its name from the pumice that can be found nearby. The only lake Dill did not name was Funeral Lake, named by Charles Fisher, a fisheries biologist for the department.

Headstone Lake was so named because of its position in the group at the head of the canyon and just below Graveyard Peak. William Dill thought it also resembled a head or a headstone. Vengeance Lake was so named by Dill because it was V-shaped and the word *vengeance* was appropriate to the theme.

Today the lakes are all stocked with trout and enjoyed by those who journey to the high country. Their names, however, are more likely to evoke visions of Halloween with ghosts and goblins frolicking about rather than thoughts of a relaxing vacation.

Irrigation has allowed our great valley to bloom in many ways. It is water that provides the life blood for agriculture, for cities and for people. It is water, and the canals and rivers that bring that water to the land, that has allowed our desert to become a civilized place. Indeed, even the most unlikely places in our valley are growing the most unlikely crops.

A case in point is the small community of Wasco, located on Highway 46, just a few miles due west of Highway 99. Wasco was incorporated in 1945. The main crops of the area were cotton and potatoes. Then an amazing thing happened! In the mid-1950s, rose companies began looking for a rural area with an appropriate climate, proper soil, available water, and an accessible labor force. In 1908, Perkins Rose Farms had established itself in nearby McFarland. It later left, but now other companies remembered the area and began to return. They made a good decision, because today the area around Wasco, McFarland and Shafter that once was desert is covered with fields of roses in every stage of production. It has become the largest rose bush producing area in the nation. Sixty-five to 75 percent of all the roses grown in the United States come from this area.

In 1968, a group of people in Wasco decided to hold a Rose Festival. It has grown steadily each year and now includes a Rose Pageant with a queen who presides over the four-day event. She is crowned on Thursday evening in the Wasco High School auditorium. The next day a tennis tournament and carnival begin. Saturday starts with a pancake breakfast and the Junior Women's Club Fun Run. A parade; barbecue; art show; rose show; rose field tours; a mini Rose Bowl, featuring the Packers football team; golf, tennis, and basketball tournaments; and Wasco museum tours are offered on Saturday and Sunday.

The theme for Wasco's thirtieth Festival of Roses was "Let the Good Times Grow." The event offers something for everyone plus a look at a unique and beautiful part of the agriculture of our great valley.

A Prize-winning Vintner

For Andrew Mattei, the journey from a modest farm in Switzerland to ownership of one of the largest and most productive vineyards and wineries in Fresno County was an amazing one. His father was a teacher, and Andrew received a good education. In 1874, at age eighteen, he decided to immigrate to Nevada, where he worked in the timber industry for two years. He then worked in the dairy business in Modesto, San Jose, and, finally, in Los Angeles, where he went into business for himself.

In 1887, he visited Fresno County. So impressed was he with the areas agricultural potential, he purchased the William Wilkinsen ranch. Three years later he bought an adjoining grain field. The property was on a parcel that is today the southwest corner of Fowler and Central avenues. He planted a row of palm trees extending out to Central Avenue. He began planting vineyards and buying more property. By 1900, his holdings had increased to 1,070 acres.

In 1892, he made his first wine. Ten years later he was making wine and brandy and continuing to expand his operations. He had produced wine primarily for the local market, but, in 1913, began to ship his wine and brandy to eastern markets as well. The quality of his product was recognized at the 1915 Panama Pacific Exposition in San Francisco, where he was awarded twenty-two prizes for his wines, including the Medal of Honor. By 1919, he was the largest individual vineyardist and vintner in the United States.

Later, Mattei built several properties in downtown Fresno. One of his most lasting contributions is the Mattei Building, later the Guarantee Savings Building, at the southwest corner of Fresno Street and the Fulton Mall. He also built the Andella Market at Belmont and Van Ness avenues. The name was a combination of his first name and his wife's name, Eleanor.

For the traveler heading east on Central Avenue, a cluster of palm trees in the middle of the section at the southwest corner at Fowler Avenue still stands as a reminder that here some of the finest wines in the country were once produced by the talented and hardworking vintner Andrew Mattei.

The Andella Market under construction in 1929. Built by vintner Andrew Mattei, it was one of Fresno's first drive-in markets. Decades later it would house the popular New Rendezvous restaurant.
The Image Group from the Laval Historical Collection.

The Honorable Charles A. Hart

The story of Fresno County's first judge is one of determination, hard work, and success. He was born into an old New York family. His father was a banker and state senator and saw to it that his son received a fine education. After graduation from college, the young man worked for a time as a civil engineer, but soon turned to the study of law. He was admitted to law practice in New York state. At this point, his desire for adventure outweighed his interest in law. He joined a group of men from New England who wanted to head west. They went by steamer to Mexico and then traveled by land to Los Angeles and up the coast as far north as San Francisco. They turned inland and arrived in Merced County on August 7, 1849. The Gold Rush was in full sway. They met a man named Captain Cutler who gave them sage advice about placer mining. For two years they worked in the diggings and found large quantities of gold—often as much as sixteen ounces a day.

In 1854, the young man from New York, Charles A. Hart, journeyed south to Millerton. Here he opened a law office. When Fresno County was created in 1856, he was appointed the first county judge. He served for one term and then returned to his law practice. In 1863, the government closed Fort Miller. Hart purchased, at government auction, the land on which Fort Miller was located. He turned one of the old buildings of the fort into his private home.

In 1865, Hart married Ann McKenzie, the widow of James McKenzie, a sergeant with the U.S. Army who had been stationed at Fort Miller. She had three children. She and Hart had one child, Truman.

After the county seat was moved to Fresno in 1874, the Harts and McKenzies purchased the old site of Millerton and acquired other adjacent land. Hart died in 1903.

In 1939, the McKenzie family sold their property back to the government when the Friant Dam project began. Today, Millerton Lake covers the 12,000-acre ranch of Judge Charles A. Hart and the McKenzie family.

Although many of our valley towns came into being because of the railroad, one did not—it was established because of the need to bring lumber out of the mountains and into the valley by way of what would become the world's longest flume.

In 1874, the California Lumber Company was organized. Two years later the company decided to build a flume that would carry timber from the mountains to the valley floor. But where would its terminus be? The company's owners were approached by Issac Friedlander and William S. Chapman, who offered them a large tract of land provided they would end the flume on this property. The land was barren—completely devoid of habitation or vegetation, but the offer was accepted. The flume was built. A town site was laid out. A town was born. The name Madera was given to the new community because it is the Spanish word for lumber. In September 1876, lots were offered at an auction sale. Captain Russel Perry Mace bought the first lot and built Mace's Hotel. Several homes were built for employees of the lumber company. The first store was built by H. S. Williams in 1877. On April 26, 1877, the Madera Post Office opened its doors with E. Moore as the postmaster.

Madera continued to grow in spite of a series of fires that wiped out a number of businesses. In 1888, the Madera Fire Department was established, boasting forty volunteers and all the latest equipment for fighting fires.

Like many other valley towns, the new community had its share of saloons, gambling dens, and shady ladies. It also had an active chamber of commerce and a good public school system. It was not until 1907 that the city of Madera finally voted to incorporate. By that time it was already the county seat of Madera County and boasted a fine courthouse. Madera had come a long way from its humble beginnings as the terminus of a flume.

Captain Russel Perry Mace

The first man to purchase land in the new town site to be called Madera was an adventurer who hunted buffalo with the legendary Kit Carson.

He was born in Boston in 1820. His father manufactured carpenter's tools. In his teens, he decided that life offered more opportunities for adventure than the classroom. He boarded a steamer bound for New Orleans, signing on as a cabin boy. When the boat arrived at its first port, he left and went to work for a French trader who did business with the Comanche Indians. He rode on a wagon train filled with shotguns, blankets, and other goods. They were bound for Bent's Fort on the Arkansas River. These goods were traded with the Indians for skins and hides. He then went to work for the American Fur Company, where he met Kit Carson, working with him for the next two years. At one point, they killed four hundred buffalo that were used to feed the company's men. In 1844, he returned to New Orleans, where he worked for a wine distribution company. When the Mexican-American War broke out, he volunteered, and was severely wounded. While convalescing, he raised a group of volunteer troops and became its captain, a title he carried thereafter. His first lieutenant died of yellow fever. He married the man's widow, Elizabeth. In 1849, they, along with her young son, headed for California. They engaged in mining first in Yuba County and, finally, near Millerton. Elizabeth died in 1864. In 1866, he married Jennie Gilmore and moved to the foothill area that today is O'Neals. In 1874, they moved to Borden.

When the first land in the new townsite of Madera was offered at an auction sale, Captain Russel Perry Mace was on hand to buy the first piece of land, staking his belief in Madera's future. On this land he built a hotel and tapped in on the new tourist market as more and more people discovered the beauties of Yosemite Valley. Mace, an avid horseman, weighed 350 pounds and had to have a special saddle built to handle his frame. A big man in every sense, Captain Russel Perry Mace has earned his place in the history of Madera County.

The naming of cities is a fascinating subject. Many people know the origin of the name of Modesto, one of the largest of our Central Valley cities. For those who don't, it is as follows. As the four owners of the Central Pacific Railroad, Mark Hopkins, Leland Stanford, Charles Crocker, and Collis P. Huntington, built their railroad down the valley, they decided to establish a town on the Tuolumne River. They had as their chief financier William C. Ralston. One day, during a visit Ralston made to the site, they told him they would name this town for him. He replied, "Oh, no. I do not want you to name the town for me." A Mexican railhand standing nearby said, "El senor is muy modesto," which means, "The man is very modest." Whereupon Leland Stanford said, "We'll just call the town Modesto, reflecting your modesty."

A short-lived town in Fresno County had a name for which no one has been able to account. It was located fourteen miles southwest of Huron. A post office opened there in August of 1890 with Thomas B. Pettypool as postmaster. It closed on May 15, 1895. The name of the town was Last. L-A-S-T. It's a mystery why someone would give a town such a name. Was it the last hope, the last chance, or the last straw? Perhaps it was dead last. Since no one wrote it down, we may never know.

It is a source of some debate as to how the small town of Famosa, in the southern part of our valley, received its name. This story may be apocryphal, but because it is of long standing, it will be repeated here. It so happened that when the railhead reached this point all the Big Four of the railroad were present. It was a hot summer day and they were sitting down enjoying a cool drink. Crocker said, "Well, Leland, since we're going to have a town here, what should we name it?" Just at that moment the waiter appeared and noticing their four glasses were empty said in his Southern drawl, "Mistah Stanfod, how about fo mo, suh?" Whereupon Stanford said, "That's what we'll name it—Famosa."

The Eisen Brothers

One of the earliest ranches in the Fresno area belonged to Francis T. Eisen. Bounded by the present-day streets of Kings Canyon, Fowler, Belmont, and Clovis avenues, this ranch was established in 1873 on land Eisen purchased from the German Syndicate for ten dollars an acre. In that same year Eisen planted wine grapes in what would be remembered as the first commercial vineyard in the valley.

As he prepared to harvest his first crop, he asked his brother, Professor Gustav Eisen, a wine expert, to come to Fresno. In 1875, they built the first winery and distillery in the area and produced two hundred gallons of wine. Over the years they enlarged these facilities as their business grew. They not only grew many varieties of grapes on their ranch, but bought grapes from other ranches as well. By 1881, they were producing 80,000 gallons of wine a year including Riesling, Zinfandel Claret, Zinfandel Port, Sweet Malaga, and Dry Sherry. In 1892, the brothers won a gold medal at the Dublin Exposition for their wines. When Francis Eisen died four years later, in 1896, the brothers were producing 300,000 gallons of wine per year and had gained a worldwide reputation for their wines.

The Eisen Winery operated until Prohibition forced it to close. After the repeal of Prohibition, it began operation again. Several years later it closed permanently.

Francis Eisen is called the father of the raisin industry. As we have told in another tale of our valley, some of his grapes dried on the vine and were marketed in San Francisco as a "Peruvian importation."

For their contributions to the wine and raisin industry of our great valley, the Eisen brothers, Francis T. and Gustav, will long be remembered in the legends of our valley.

Professor Gustav Eisen

Francis Eisen, asked his brother, Gustav, to come to Fresno to help him start a winery. Gustav Eisen was a professor of natural science in Sweden. When Gustav arrived in Fresno in November 1873, he noted that there were sixteen buildings in the new town, which included everything that had a roof.

In 1883, after the winery was established, Frederick Roeding made Gustav Eisen the manager of his Fancher Creek Nursery, located just east of the Eisen Vineyards. Roeding was a good businessman, but Eisen was an educated horticulturist. In 1885, White Adriatic figs were being grown in Fresno County. However, no one had been able to successfully produce a mature Smyrna fig. In examining some old documents Eisen discovered that the Smyrna fig would not produce unless the pollen from a Capri fig was introduced into a Smyrna fig by a tiny Blastophaga wasp, an insect not found in Fresno County. In 1887, he presented this finding to a group of Fresno horticulturists and was laughed at. Later, George Roeding, Frederick's son, received Capri figs that contained the Blastophaga wasps from an agent of the U.S. Agriculture Department. The wasps pollinated the Smyrna fig. The result was the Calimyrna fig and the real beginning of the fig industry in our valley. While Roeding got the credit for this achievement, the idea undoubtedly came from Eisen.

Gustav Eisen, a nature lover, toured much of the Sierra with Frank Dusy and appreciated its beauty. He was especially moved by the grandeur of the big trees. In 1890, as a member of the California Academy of Sciences, he testified in support of redwood conservation before a congressional committee. His testimony persuaded the legislators to preserve the redwoods rather than allowing the lumber interests a free hand in all the big tree ranges from Yosemite to Tulare County. In doing this, he made a major contribution toward saving one of California's most important treasures.

The Reunion That Never Ends

W hen the first signs of autumn come to our valley, one's thoughts might turn to football and memories of school days past. For many, fall means homecoming parties and class reunions.

The graduates of Parlier High School have found a way to make their class reunions more meaningful than most—they go on indefinitely! How do they manage this, one might ask? It happened in this manner.

In April of 1987, Laverne O'Bryant and Mary Jo Tolleson decided to meet for lunch. They had been planning a reunion for the Parlier High School classes of 1936-1942 over the phone and thought it would be a lot more fun to do this in person. However, by the time they arrived at the restaurant word had gotten around, and they were joined by seven other classmates. Everyone had a good time reminiscing and planning the reunion party. They met often before the reunion and then met again afterward. They decided they had had such a good time seeing each other that they would meet on the first Wednesday of each month at 1 p.m. to have lunch and visit.

And so they have for the last twelve years. Many other Parlier High grads have joined the group, swelling their numbers considerably. What do they talk about? The old days, of course—about the old brick high school that was torn down in 1967; the basketball team of 1938, which many of their group view as the finest the school ever produced; the years of World War II and the impact it had on them all; the big home of pioneer vineyardist I. N. Parlier, for whom Parlier is named; and the world's largest fig tree, which was planted by Mr. Parlier in 1886 and stood until it collapsed in 1940.

Many of their number call their monthly lunch gatherings the longest running class reunion in our Central Valley. It very well may be. It certainly sounds like one of the most enjoyable.

In the days before settlers came into the great Central Valley, antelope and elk roamed the land. The antelope are gone now, but, for a brief time, their presence was immortalized by the naming of a town for this wild animal.

In 1872, as the railroad was being built through the Central Valley, a store and hotel were built at the newest train stop just north of present-day Madera. Seeing so many herds running free, the Central Pacific Railroad Company named the new community Berendo, a misspelling of the Spanish word for antelope. Eventually, the "o" was replaced by an "a" and the town became Berenda. On February 12, 1873, a post office was opened in the new town.

With more settlers coming into the area, Berenda became a shipping center for wheat and barley crops. The town grew quickly. Hotels were built along with blacksmith shops, general stores and, of course, saloons. Soon there was a crying need for a school. Since Berenda was located on land owned by cattle baron Henry Miller, he built a schoolhouse and donated it, along with five acres of land, to the town.

Berenda was a transfer point for the booming tourist business to Yosemite. Travelers would leave the train, stay overnight, and then board a stage the next morning for the journey that would take them to see the wonders of Half Dome and the big trees. In 1886, the railroad built a branch line from Berenda to Raymond, making that town the main transfer point for travelers. Gradually business in Berenda diminished. People moved to Madera. In 1935, the post office closed.

Today, Berenda is only a spot on the map. No structures stand to mark its place. Like the antelope for which it was named, Berenda has passed into oblivion—a mere memory in the tales of our valley.

During its long history, Fresno has embraced newcomers from all over the world. Immigrants from some of the most ancient cultures in the world have found a new home in our city. This was the case at the turn of the century when a group of new arrivals came from the birthplace of democracy—Greece.

The newcomers were mostly single men who came to seek their fortune in our Central Valley. They founded businesses in West Fresno. Soon they were able to bring their wives and brides-to-be to their new home. With their families established, there was a pressing need for a church. Weddings and baptisms could take place only when a Greek Orthodox priest happened to be traveling through town. More important, they needed a spiritual home to comfort and sustain them in their new land.

On May 6, 1923, the Greek Community of Fresno was organized. Anastasios K. Pinoris was elected the first president. A twelve-member board of trustees was put in place. Articles of incorporation were drawn up and submitted to the archdiocese in New York for approval.

The first Divine Liturgy was celebrated on November 27, 1923, at Holy Trinity Armenian Apostolic Church. The Rev. Father Karavelas traveled from San Francisco to officiate. Nine months later, in August of 1924, the Rev. Father Michael Mandillas arrived in Fresno and became the first priest for the community. Later that month, the board of trustees met in the home of Gus Spiropulos to consider the possibility of building a church. They picked a site at 740 Fresno Street and voted a construction budget of $5,000. A donation of $1,500 was offered by George Ballas for the privilege of naming the new church for Saint George—his patron saint.

Contributions came from members of the Greek community who lived throughout the Central Valley. On October 27, 1924, the small white church was dedicated. This was a milestone in the history of Fresno's Greek community.

A Church for St. George

May 9, 1954, was a proud day for Fresno's Greek community. On this day a ground breaking ceremony for the new St. George Greek Orthodox Church was held at Orchard and Yale avenues. The bishop of the IV Diocese of the Greek Orthodox Church, His Grace Athenagoras Kokinakis, officiated.

The architect of St. Sophia Cathedral in Los Angeles, Gus W. Kalionzes, of the A. R. Walker, Gus W. Kalionzes, C. A. Klingerman Architectural Firm of Los Angeles, was selected to design the new structure. Renowned iconographer William Tzavales and his assistant, Innencenzo Daraio, were commissioned to paint the icons inside the church.

For nine long months the congregation waited to see the completion of their new church building. Then, on Sunday, February 27, 1955, the sacred articles were brought in a motorcade from the old church at 740 Fresno Street to the new church. Divine Liturgy was celebrated for the first time in the new building.

Today, a modern Sunday school building and a social hall serve the parishioners.

The annual Greek Food Festival embraces everyone in our Central Valley community who wishes to attend. During this weekend, the opportunity to taste the best in Greek food and to experience the music, dancing, language, and culture of the Greek people is available to all. It is also possible to tour the sanctuary and to view the beautiful icons that were created in 1954. The first time one enters the sanctuary and sees the incredibly beautiful icon of the Blessed Virgin holding the Christ Child, one cannot help but gaze in awe. It is an unforgettable moment.

In 1999, St. George Greek Orthodox Church celebrated seventy-five years of service to the Greek community of Fresno. From their humble beginnings early in this century until the dawning of the new millennium, the members of Fresno's Greek community have made invaluable contributions to life in our valley. Like other cultural groups who have settled here, they have added a beautiful piece to the mosaic of cultures that make up our Central Valley community.

On July 1, 1875, a post office was established in a southwestern part of Fresno County with Thomas Thompson as postmaster. Named Liberty Settlement, the area was not exactly a settler's dream. It was filled with swamps, tules, sloughs, trees, and underbrush. Added to this were wild antelope, elk, horses, hogs, and horned toads. Because the swamp around Liberty was called a river, the post office was renamed Riverdale in the early 1880s.

The post office was moved to James Powell's ranch and then to the Elisha Harlan ranch in 1883. Lucy Harlan became the postmaster. At first the mail was brought by a rider on horseback every other week. Eventually, it was delivered once a week and, then, twice weekly. Lucy would sort the mail on her dining table. Delivery day became a social event—everyone dropped by to pick up mail, have refreshments, and catch up on all the local news.

In 1898, the San Joaquin Ice Company established a milk skimming plant on the east side of present-day Valentine Avenue just north of the Burrel ditch. It was the first business in Riverdale. William Henson was the operator. Henson decided this would be a good site for a general store, so he built one next to the milk skimming plant. He soon bought land on the northeast corner of Valentine and Mt. Whitney avenues and moved his store there. He resigned from the plant and devoted his time to running the store. Henson's customers were offered a whole range of items from hardware and shoes to notions and fancy goods. In 1901, the post office was moved to Henson's store and he became the postmaster.

The town of Riverdale dates its beginning to the establishment of the milk skimming plant in 1898. In 1998, the citizens of Riverdale celebrated their centennial.

The Cream City

In the 1890s, canals and levees were built to control the flood waters of the Kings River. The resulting reclaimed land became lush pasture land. In the Riverdale area, many farmers began to raise dairy cattle. Each farmer would go through a process of hand skimming the cream off the milk. In 1898, a milk skimming plant was built. An invention called the De Laval separator made the skimming process more efficient. Now the farmers could bring their milk to the plant where the work of separating the cream from the milk would take place. The cream was made into butter. The skimmed milk was fed to hogs and calves. The increased demand for butter coupled with more profitable milk production and processing caused the dairy business to grow rapidly.

The farmers decided to unite their efforts. In 1909, the Riverdale Cooperative Creamery was formed. Managed by J. H. Jorgenson, it merged with Danish Creamery in 1930 and remained an important milk and cream processing plant until 1960, when the plant was closed. It had become more cost effective to transport the whole milk directly to the Danish Creamery plant in Fresno. This is still done today.

In 1911, several members of the Riverdale Cooperative joined with the Dairymen's Cooperative Creamery of Tulare. They organized Challenge Butter Cooperative and distributed and sold butter to the Los Angeles area.

At the time the first dairy cooperative was formed in 1909, the Cream City Celebration was launched. This annual festival included a parade, a carnival, games, and a host of other events. Today, the Cream City Celebration has become the Riverdale Spring Festival. One of the special features is the free ice cream provided by local dairy farmers.

Although the Riverdale plant is now silent, the milk that is produced in the Riverdale area today and sent to Fresno for processing far exceeds production of an earlier era. Today it is a significant part of the total dairy industry of the number one dairy state, California. Riverdale is still the Cream City.

The Harlans of Riverdale

The story of the Harlan family begins with the birth of Elisha Harlan on August 3, 1838, in Berrien County, Michigan. His father, George, a wagon master, decided to bring his family to California. They left Michigan in 1845 and traveled to Lexington, Missouri, where they spent the winter.

In the spring of 1846 they began their trek across the plains. Elisha was eight years old. He spent most of the journey on horseback because it was his job to herd the extra oxen. The Harlans joined a wagon train whose members included the Reed, the Young, and the Donner families. When they arrived at the Hastings' cutoff, the Harlan-Young party went on ahead. They arrived at Sutter's Fort on October 8, their wagons having been the last to make it over the Sierra before the great snowfall hit. The Donners waited while Jake Reed searched for a better route. This delayed them. They met their tragic fate in the winter snow. Members of the Harlan party went with the first rescue teams to bring out the surviving Donners.

The family located first at Santa Clara, then Mission San Jose, and Yerba Buena, which would become San Francisco. In 1848, George tried his luck in the gold fields, but soon returned to the San Francisco area. He died in Mission San Jose in 1850. Elisha's mother had died four years earlier. Elisha, now twelve, went to live with his brother, Joel, who had been cattle ranching in the San Ramon area and was now running a butcher shop in Yerba Buena. Elisha attended public school and learned the cattle business from his brother.

In 1860, Elisha set out on his own, buying land near Kingston. In 1868, he moved to Liberty, now known as Riverdale, where he homesteaded 160 acres of land. He added to his holdings. By 1905, his extensive ranching and dairy operation totaled 700 acres. Eventually, the Harlan homestead passed out of the family, but the present generations of Harlans live nearby on land Elisha purchased from Turbacio Madril in 1865. They are still in the ranching business. One of the family's treasures is a reminder of their deep roots in the Riverdale area. It is a deed to their property dated in 1875 and signed by President Ulysses S. Grant.

A Courthouse for Madera

In 1893, after the citizens of the area of Fresno County north of the San Joaquin River voted to separate and form their own county of Madera, they had to decide where their new government offices would be located. The first meeting of their board of supervisors was held in the Masonic Hall at 126 East Yosemite Avenue in the city of Madera, the new county seat. For the next few years the offices and court were scattered around town. It was obvious that a courthouse was sorely needed.

Seven years later, a lot in the Hughes Addition was offered to the county for one dollar. The land adjacent to it was purchased for $3,500. Now that there was a site for a courthouse, the bidding process opened. Architects were invited to submit plans for a building that, the supervisors decided, should be fireproof, built of granite, and not cost more than $60,000. A bid of $59,963 was accepted, but then the supervisors had the problem of furnishing the building, buying fixtures and adding all the extras that such projects require. The actual cost of the building would amount to almost $100,000.

October 29, 1900, was an exciting day for Madera County residents. A barbecue, horse races, and games accompanied the laying of the cornerstone. A time capsule, containing a number of historical items such as an 1882 wanted poster for Black Bart, over a hundred copper coins from Chinatown, the architectural drawings for the building, and William Hughes' silver mounted rabbit's foot, was placed in the cornerstone. Two years later the building was finished.

In 1906, the building caught fire. The cause was never determined, but the top floor, the roof, and the clock tower were burned. Reconstruction work cost $48,853.

Unlike Fresno's historic courthouse, the historic granite building still stands. It houses the museum and offices of the Madera County Historical Society and welcomes all who come up its steps to learn the history of the area.

Night Doesn't Become a Naked Lady

During the 1930s, the P Street neighborhood in downtown Fresno had undergone a few changes. The W. P. Millers moved north, their home was torn down, and the lot was vacant. Just north of their former property was a home that was a rental. The tenants were a married couple.

It was rumored in the neighborhood that when the husband had to work nights, the wife often had gentleman visitors. It was noted that they usually were roomers from the nearby Santa Fe Hotel. On the evening on which our story takes place, the wife was entertaining a gentleman. It was late, so late that the owners of the house just south of the vacant lot, Mr. and Mrs. J. R. McKay, had gone to bed. All at once their slumbers were brought to an abrupt end as loud screams, accompanied by frantic calls for help, ended their peaceful dreams. A loud banging on the front door sent Mr. McKay running down the hall. He opened the door and was horrified to find a totally naked woman standing on his front porch.

Rubbing the sleep from his eyes, he called the police, who arrived immediately. One of the policemen asked him to get a sheet. He called to his wife, Belle, who yanked a sheet off their bed and rushed to the front door. The policeman wrapped the woman in it and escorted her to the police car. He told Mr. McKay that her husband had come home and surprised her and her gentleman caller. McKay replied that all he cared was that his name would not appear in the paper.

The next day brought good news and bad news to the McKay household. The good news was that the sheet was returned laundered and pressed. The bad news was that, although McKay's name was omitted from the front-page article that appeared in the newspaper the next day, the lead sentence began, "At 1022 P Street..." In the small town of Fresno, everyone knew whose house that was, and Mr. McKay was never allowed to live it down.

A Stagecoach & Two Robbers

Aside from the normal rigors of stagecoach travel, there was another reason to approach an upcoming trip with apprehension—the ever-present possibility of being robbed. For one group of travelers leaving Yosemite bound for Madera, the possibility became a reality. The stage rounded a hairpin turn and there stood two masked men dressed in black. They pointed their guns at the drivers and ordered them to lie on the ground. They had the passengers disembark, line up on the road, put all their cash in the dirt, and place their jewelry beside it. None of this was unusual— just a normal, everyday robbery on the stage road. All at once things changed. The robbers told the group to remove their clothing. They politely said good-bye to the thoroughly humiliated group of travelers and told the drivers to continue on their journey, calling them by name! When the group returned to Madera, the sheriff was alerted and began a search for the armed men, but he failed to find them.

The reporter from the *Fresno Expositor* had better luck. He came to Madera and interviewed the travelers, who were still in shock over their frightening experience. Not only did they regale him with grand tales of their exploits, but he found that some of the other guests at the hotel where they were all staying were rather amused with the goings-on. It all made marvelous fodder for his newspaper article.

Some of the guests who were going to be boarding the stage in a day or so were not quite as amused. In fact, they began taking some precautions for their trip. One gentleman purchased an ivory handled pistol that he proudly showed the reporter. The other gentlemen scheduled for the trip were rather frightened. The ladies, however, were not. One woman kept asking the reporter if he thought they might be robbed. The hotel manager, Mr. Badager, overhearing this question, rather loudly proclaimed, "Of course not!" The young lady, hearing this, was rather downcast. She had so hoped they would—which showed a certain courage and sense of romance among the so-called weaker sex in Fresno County in the 1870s.

The Soldiers & the Barley Sack

The word "laughable" is rarely used to describe a robbery, but, on a summer day in 1902, no other word could be better suited to describe what took place on a trip involving the Yosemite Stage and Turnpike Company's Cannonball Stage.

On the day our story took place, the stage had left Raymond on its way to Yosemite. The passengers included several workers from the granite quarry. About a mile and a half before they reached Grub Gulch, a man with a barley sack over his head and holding a gun stepped out of the shadows and ordered the driver to stop. He told everyone to get out of the stage and line up on the side of the road. They did, and he took all their valuables. As he did this, two wagons filled with wood approached. The bandit ordered the drivers to stop, get out and hand over their valuables. Now, a stage, two wagons and about twelve people were blocking the road.

Two unarmed cavalry soldiers appeared on horseback. They were outriders for a group of soldiers who were following at some distance. They, too, were ordered to stop. Three more stages and a wagon carrying mail drove up. The drivers and passengers joined the ranks of the others along the side of the road. By this time, the gunman's bag was getting rather full. However, he was still in control, holding all of these people at gun point.

Next two troops of cavalrymen came along. None of them was armed. They, too, were ordered to dismount and join the large party of people along the side of the road. Now the robber was holding a major, two captains, two first lieutenants, two second lieutenants, several soldiers, four stages, one mail wagon, two private wagons, many horses and several private citizens, and keeping them at bay with his gun. He decided that he had better quit while he was ahead. So, he backed up a hill telling the assemblage to stay where they were. As soon as he disappeared, the soldiers took off after him. All they ever found was his barley sack. He managed to make off with all the loot.

Not long after the Alabama Colony was established in December of 1868, there was a movement to name it Arcola after the name of one of the colonist's ranches. Many of those who lived in the colony did not accept the name. In April of 1872, less than a month after the Central Pacific Railroad arrived at the Alabama Colony, Leland Stanford came to personally view the progress of the construction of the rail line. When he arrived at the switch near Cottonwood Creek, Dr. Joseph Borden met him and took him to his home for dinner. After an evening of Southern hospitality and genial conversation, Stanford named the new town site Borden, for his host.

Two general stores and a hotel were built in the new town located near present-day Highway 99 where it intersects with Avenue 12 just south of Madera. Saloons, barber shops, and other businesses also were established. The town grew rapidly—so rapidly, in fact, that when an election was held in 1874 to determine the new county seat for Fresno County, Borden was on the ballot and received several votes.

The California Lumber Company decided to build a V-shaped flume from its sawmill in the mountains to the valley floor. It would have its terminus near the railroad. The people of Borden were elated. They were sure it would end in their town. Then they could build a planing mill and their town would be assured of continual growth.

Then something happened. Issac Friedlander owned a large parcel of land north of Borden. He offered to donate enough land for a planing mill and the terminus of the flume to the California Lumber Company. Since Borden's unsuccessful negotiations with the company had come to a halt over the price of land, the company took Friedlander up on his offer. The result was the founding of Madera. Within a few years, Borden faded away. Today, the once promising town is a dim memory tucked away in the history of our valley.

One of the most fascinating of the gold mining towns of the former Fresno County, now Madera County, was named Narbo. It was located not far from Coarse Gold Gulch. Its story began in this way. In 1883, a man by the name of DeFries was part owner of a mine that was not producing very well. He loaded his shotgun with placer gold and shot it into the opening of the mine shaft. After "salting" his claim in this way, he was able to sell the mine to a Frenchman named Marcellin Fache.

Fache didn't know much about gold mining, but he had grandiose ideas. He incorporated the mine under the name Quartz Mountain Mill Company. By selling shares of stock in his company to people in France, he raised a great deal of money. He built a huge chateau for himself and his executive staff atop a high peak. The chateau boasted so many windows it was called "the house of glass." Only the finest furniture and accessories were bought for the chateau.

All of this activity and the hopes for profit from the mine brought settlers, many of them French, to Narbo. Saloons, stores, and a French bakery soon served the town.

Fache built a very expensive sixty-stamp mill. It would be used to extract gold by crushing the gold bearing quartz. Since the machinery was operated by a huge water wheel, it was necessary to have a source of running water to power the wheel. He hired Chinese labor to build a twenty-five mile ditch from Crane Valley to bring water to the mill. The ditch was completed, but Henry Miller of Miller & Lux successfully fought to deny Fache water rights. So Fache purchased a $15,000 engine to power his mill. When he finally got it running, the amount of gold extracted by the operation was such a small amount that, after only six days, the engines were turned off. Except for bringing cultured manners and fine food to the rough world of mining, the French experiment was a failure. It did, however, leave us with a moral to ponder—all that glitters like gold on the surface may have very little substance underneath.

As we continue to celebrate California's Sesquicentennial our thoughts turn to another of the old gold mining towns in the foothills of the Sierra. Located on the old stage road from Millerton to O'Neals, the town got its start when Tom Hildreth opened a mine and a store in the late 1870s. The opening of other mines brought settlers who came seeking wealth. Others came and opened stores. Soon the town of Hildreth was booming—some said at its height the population reached three thousand. On April 16, 1886, a post office opened with Jonathan Hildreth as the postmaster.

The Hanover, Hildreth, Abbey, and Basinet mines were the four largest mines in the area. It required many men to work these mines and, for a brief time, Chinese laborers were brought in to help. The other miners objected, and the Chinese laborers were run out of the area.

The veins of gold were rich in the Hildreth area. It has been estimated that the quartz mines yielded $14 million in gold. The placer mines, too, were credited with a wealthy return. In nearby Long Gulch, it was said that one company's area worked by nine men produced a ten-pound pail full of gold each day. The men were paid every evening with one ounce of gold.

As most good things must come to an end, so did the seemingly endless flow of gold. By 1893, the veins began to run out. The people left for greener pastures and, in 1896, the post office closed.

Today, the mines stand silent. The old stage road is deserted. The sounds of horses and wagons are gone. Mother Nature has reclaimed this quiet corner of the foothills. Where miners once worked, lizards doze lazily in the sun. Only a rock wall remains to mark the spot where the old hotel and a town once stood—a town that is now only a memory in the tales of our valley.

The Lost Horde of Gold

Our tales of the valley have told of a number of stagecoach robberies, but one that occurred in the 1860s was probably one of the most costly. One day a four-horse stage carrying ten thousand dollars in gold bullion from the Abbey Mine in Hildreth was making its way through the foothills of the Sierra. The cargo was destined for the U.S. Mint in San Francisco. About a mile outside Hildreth, a gunman, dressed like a miner and wearing a bandana over his face, stopped the stage and ordered the driver to unload the strongbox filled with gold. The driver followed the gunman's instructions. As soon as the strongbox was on the ground, the bandit ordered the stage to proceed on its way. The driver headed for O'Neals, where he reported the robbery.

A sheriff's posse rode to the spot where the holdup took place. Instead of clues, they found a fire burning out of control along the stage road and up Hildreth Mountain. Any tracks there might have been had been covered up by the fire. They found neither gold nor a holdup man.

A few months later, three men were walking from O'Neals to Hildreth. The first winter rain had come, leaving the air fresh and clear. The area that had been blackened by fire seemed cleaner, too. As they neared the spot where the robbery had taken place, something glittery in the bank along the road caught their eyes. As they looked closer they saw the bars of gold. They had been hidden in a hollow stump that burned in the fire. The rain had washed away the ashes that had covered them. The men stashed the gold in their packs and hurried on, wondering what to do. They couldn't sell the gold bars without being caught. Using an axe, they hacked several ounces from one of the bars. In Millerton they traded the gold for supplies and money.

When the gold arrived at the mint, officials became suspicious that the gold might be from the Abbey Mine. They tracked the men and arrested them. Eventually, they had to let them go because it was determined that they were not responsible for the robbery. The U.S. government got the rest of the gold, but the real robber was never caught.

Tucked away in the foothills of Madera County, then Fresno County, is a town that first owed its name to a wildcat. It seems that during the very wet winter of 1885-86, so many stagecoach travelers on their way to Yosemite stopped at Bowen's tent hotel for dinner that the owners ran out of meat. The travelers saw dead wildcats hanging outside the kitchen and were told that this is what they would be served. The town became known as Wildcat Station.

Year after year the winter rains were so heavy that the stage road leading from the valley to Wildcat Station would became almost impassable. It was certainly very dangerous for the horses that got bogged down in the mud. To solve this problem, the San Joaquin Valley and Yosemite Railroad was incorporated by the Southern Pacific Railroad early in 1886. The twenty-one-mile railroad branch line ran from Berenda into the hills with its terminus at Wildcat Station. A turntable was built at this point so the locomotive could be watered and turned around, ready for the trip back into the valley. Travelers wishing to continue on to Yosemite boarded a stagecoach and made their up through Grub Gulch and Ahwahnee to Yosemite Valley.

The first train arrived in March of 1886, a post office was established in July of that year, and the town received a new name. No longer Wildcat Station, the town was now to be called Raymond for Mr. T. Raymond of the Raymond-Whitcomb Travel Association of San Francisco. Businesses and churches were built for the growing population of the town.

Two trains came into Raymond daily during the tourist season. It became a common sight to see private railroad cars belonging to celebrities sitting on a side track while their owners visited Yosemite.

The rail line also was important in establishing Raymond as the main freight depot for the mountain area. Supplies for the Madera Sugar Pine Lumber Company and shipments for the Raymond Granite Quarry provided business for the railroad that continued to operate until 1956 when it was abandoned.

The town of Raymond, in the foothills of Madera County, was important for its railroad, but it also has another important resource.

In the early 1880s, Luke David homesteaded on land near Raymond. He chose the spot because a spring of water was located there. He certainly did not choose it because of all the rocks that were on the land. He thought they were worthless. Fresno sheep owner and brick maker Frank Dusy thought otherwise and purchased the land from David. When the railroad was being built through the area in 1886, one of the engineers noticed the many rocks on Dusy's land and thought they might have value. Locals, however, called the land "Dusy's rock pile." The land was purchased by F. E. Knowles, who organized the Raymond Granite Company. The quarry operation began in 1888.

The granite that comes from the Raymond quarry is considered by many to be the finest in the country. After the 1906 earthquake, Raymond granite was used to build all the buildings in the San Francisco Civic Center. Many of the buildings at the Berkeley campus of the University of California also were built of Raymond granite.

Producers in Hollywood found another use for the quarry. Two movies, *The Fountain Head* and *Spencer's Mountain*, were filmed there.

The quarry changed ownership several times. Today, it is owned and operated by Cold Spring Granite Company of Cold Spring, Minnesota, a business that is over a hundred years old. It is administered by the descendants of the founder, Henry Alexander, a Scots quarry worker.

Some of the more recent projects using Sierra White granite from the Raymond quarry are located in San Francisco—the Chevron and Yerba Buena buildings and the San Francisco Main Library.

For those who want to experience a little taste of the past, there are rich opportunities to do just that in the foothills of what was Fresno County before it became Madera County in 1893. Our traveler sets out on an autumn afternoon to journey up a winding road that follows a portion of the old stage road to Yosemite. Leaving Madera on Road 28½, he travels to Avenue 21, where he turns east. After a few miles the road curves and becomes Road 600, the road he will take all the way to Ahwahnee. The terrain changes as the road begins its ascent into the foothills. Soon he reaches the town of Raymond. Here, several historic buildings still stand. One building, today a tavern, dates from 1879, and was at one time the Shaw Brothers Store. Next to it is a boarding house that was built in 1896 after the railroad had been built to Raymond.

The third building really catches our traveler's eye. Built in 1914 by Nelson Luke, it has always been a general mercantile store. The exterior of the building is sheathed in squares of pressed tin. Inside, the pressed tin can be seen covering the ceiling. The original shelving still displays items for sale. All the purchases are rung up at the original counter, which is built of wood and contains bins filled with rice and beans. The store today is divided in half. A restaurant shares space with the general merchandise; a tavern awaits visitors in the other half of the downstairs.

Leaving Raymond, the road winds upward through an area rich in Gold Rush history. The mines are quiet now, and the towns are gone. At Grub Gulch, the traveler stops to read the historic plaque placed there by the Grub Gulch Chapter of E Clampus Vitus. Only an old corral is left in this area that was once inhabited by three thousand people.

Continuing on the twisting road and marveling at the vistas it provides, the traveler thinks how difficult it must have been to travel by stagecoach in those days. All too soon he reaches Ahwahnee and Highway 49, the road known as the Golden Chain. Our traveler turns right, heading to Oakhurst and then to Fresno and home.

A Racing Legend

On May 30, 1955, the citizens of Fresno were listening to their radios with rapt attention. One of their own, Billy Vukovich, was racing his car down the speedway in Indianapolis on his way to an unprecedented third consecutive victory. Torn between feelings of pride and apprehension, it was hard to think about anything else that warm spring day. As Vukie's car kept negotiating curve after curve, the announcer's voice kept pace. Then the unthinkable happened. Roger Ward's car was coming out of the southeast turn when it went into a spin and stopped beneath the foot bridge straddling the back stretch. A car driven by Al Keller spun across the track from the infield and hit Johnny Boyd's car, pushing it in front of Vukie's. Vukie hit Boyd's car, plunged over the guard rail, over and across a service road, and burst into flames. He couldn't escape from the wreckage. Shock and disbelief spread through Fresno, covering the city in a mantle of grief. It was incomprehensible that one of our own could meet such a tragic end with victory so near.

Billy Vukovich's family moved to Fresno when he was six months old. During his teenage years, his family lived on a ranch on Temperance Avenue, just south of North Avenue, in the Lone Star district. He had a stripped-down Chevrolet that he loved to race up and down the streets of this area. Soon he graduated to midget racing and won his first victory in 1941. In 1947 he won the Pacific Coast midget-racing championship. In 1950, he won a national title.

In 1951, Vukovich made his debut at the Indianapolis Speedway. He came in tenth. In 1952, he placed seventeenth. Then came 1953. It was hot in Indianapolis that day. The racetrack temperature soared to an unprecedented 103 degrees. For a Fresno boy used to hot summers, this was not a problem. Vukovich won handily. In 1954, he won again. Then 1955 came and, with it, tragedy.

Later that year a granite memorial was placed in front of the Memorial Auditorium to honor Fresno's racing hero. It was moved and today, it stands at the northwest corner of Selland Arena—a permanent reminder of a remarkable man who wrote his own unique chapter in the tales of our valley.

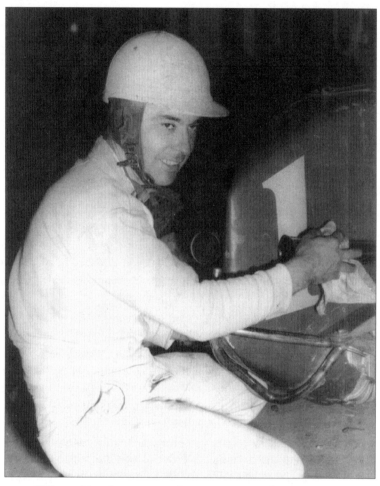

When this photo was taken in 1948, Billy Vukovich had won the Pacific Coast midget-racing championship and was well on his way to a national midget-racing crown. By 1954 he'd won the nation's premiere car racing event, the Indianapolis 500, two times.
Courtesy of The Fresno Bee Library.

Auto racing has long captured the hearts of Fresnans. In the second decade of this century, local drivers like Eddie Waterman, Tom McKelvy, and Earl Cooper, driving comparatively primitive racers, competed on the old dirt track at the fairground with nationally known drivers like Barney Oldfield and Eddie O'Donnell.

In the 1920s, the board speedway at the Fresno Fairground took center stage. During both the Raisin Day celebration and the fair, the speedway drew crowds who watched Jimmy Murphy, Joe Thomas, Tommy Milton, Gaston Chevrolet, Ralph DePalma, Earl Cooper, and Eddie O'Donnell race. In their two-seated race cars, with their mechanics huddled down beside them, they reached the then incredible speed of 116 miles per hour. The crowd thrilled as they watched the cars going lap after lap until the final moment of victory for one of the lucky drivers.

None of this, as it exciting as it was, compared to the years that one family in Fresno held center stage in the racing world. The name Vukovich became a household word all over the country. The patriarch, Billy Vukovich, Sr., started as a midget racer and went on to thrill the Fresno community by winning the Indy 500 in 1953 and 1954. Tragically, he was killed while headed to a seeming victory in 1955. Like his father, Billy, Jr. started out driving midget racers. In 1966, he won the Bay Cities Racing Association outdoor championship. In 1968, he made his debut at Indy, finishing seventh. During his twelve-year career at Indy, he had six top-ten finishes.

Then young Billy III made his appearance. In 1981, he made his debut in midget racing at the Madera speedway. A year later, he was named Valley Midget Racing Association rookie of the year. In 1988, Billy raced at the Indy 500, winning not only the Rookie of the Year award, but establishing his own place as the third generation of his family to race at the event. Then on November 25, 1990, tragedy struck the Vukovich family once again. While practice racing at the Mesa Marin Raceway in Bakersfield, young Billy's car slammed head-on into the third-turn retaining wall. He was going 130 miles per hour. He died from massive head injuries. The death of one so young and full of promise brought sadness to the Fresno community. Once again, as they had mourned the death of Billy, Sr. in 1955, Fresnans grieved for one of their own.

The name Vukovich is forever part of the history of the Indy 500. It also occupies pride of place as one of the great legends of our valley.

The newly completed Fresno Memorial Auditorium in 1936.
The Image Group from the Laval Historical Collection.

In 1933, the Fresno Chamber of Commerce spearheaded a bond election for a convention and community center that would become a focal point of pride for Fresno. The project would provide jobs for many who were out of work because of the Depression. In 1934, Fresnans voted favorably for the $375,000 bond issue. In 1935, a Public Works Administration grant for $190,000 was added. The firm of Allied Architects of Fresno was hired. The building was constructed.

On New Year's Eve, 1936, the Fresno Memorial Auditorium was dedicated. Following a parade, five thousand people filled the building for the official ceremonies. David E. Peckinpah was the general chairman. A 200-piece band played "Stars and Stripes Forever." M. E. Griffith delivered the address. Afterward, hundreds of people filled the dance floor, swinging and swaying to the music of Sherman Dix and his orchestra.

The auditorium has been the site of many major community activities. The 1956 California Democratic Convention, plays, circuses, fraternal conventions, automobile shows, opera, ballet, dances, graduations, and a host of other events have been held here. Eddie Cantor, Frank Sinatra, Ray Charles, and other famous stars have trod its stage. In 1970, the Fresno Community Theater began presenting plays in the 500-seat theater that was built within a portion of the main arena. In 1992, the name of the building was changed to the Veterans Memorial Auditorium. In 1996, a restoration project that included restoring the Anthony Heinsbergen art deco murals in the foyer was completed and the structure was listed in the National Register of Historic Places. Today, the building houses not only the Fresno Playhouse, Fresno Lyric Opera, Memorial Auditorium Restoration Society, and National Legion of Valor Museum, but approximately twenty other performing groups who also rent the theater each year. Sixty-three years after its dedication, the building continues to serve the Fresno community.

The Veterans Memorial Auditorium sits on an elevated site that encompasses an entire city block. It is bounded by Fresno, O, Merced, and N streets. The land slopes from Fresno Street down to Merced, creating a dramatic potential for landscaping.

With this in mind, a committee set to work during the year the building was constructed—1936. Headed by Zella A. Taylor as the chairman and sponsored by the Parlor Lecture Club, the committee began a visionary task. They decided to honor twelve of America's great women leaders during the past one hundred years by the planting of trees that would be dedicated to them. A number of local organizations were invited to participate. Each chose one of the twelve ladies to sponsor. The list is impressive and reads as follows: Jane Addams, sponsored by the Fig Garden Woman's Club; Susan B. Anthony, the Native Daughters of the Golden West; Clara Barton, the American Red Cross; Carrie Chapman Catt, Friday Club; Mary Baker Eddy, First Church of Christ Scientist, Fresno; Julia Ward Howe, Fresno Women's Post American Legion; Helen Keller, Progressive Home Club; Mary Lyon, Business and Professional Women; Amelia Earhart Putnam, Zonte Club; Harriet Beecher Stowe, American Legion Auxiliary; Francis Willard, Women's Christian Temperance Union; and Dr. Mary E. Wooley, American Association of University Women.

The next task was to choose varieties of trees that would create a beautiful landscape as they matured. Deodar Cedar, Atlas Cedar, Weeping Mulberry, Cork Oak, Date Palm, Magnolia, Holly Oak and Monterey Pine trees were selected and duly planted on the site.

Today, these trees still are part of our Fresno landscape. They provide shade and beauty in downtown Fresno. A plaque, located at the entrance to the auditorium, memorializes their special significance.

The African-American Legacy

At the corner of Fulton and Sacramento streets just south of Divisadero, a large modern building can be seen. At one time it housed a bank, but today it is the home of the African-American Historical and Cultural Museum of the San Joaquin Valley. The museum traces its beginnings to the centennial of the Fresno District Fair in 1984. Jack Kelley and Rutherford "Bud" Gaston were asked to sit on the fair's board of directors. They began compiling a list of black people who had made contributions to Fresno County during the last hundred years in such diverse fields as education, sports, religion, and government. They began to think about creating a museum that would be a repository for information and artifacts that would tell the history of African-Americans in the San Joaquin Valley.

The museum became a reality with the help of the city and county of Fresno, the state of California, and the support of Fresnans of many different backgrounds. As you walk through the main gallery, you view a large collection of photographs of leaders in Fresno's black community that represent the first, only, or outstanding person in their particular field. Each photo is a history lesson for the school children who visit. A stained glass window on the landing leading to the upstairs gallery, titled "Generations Never to End," was crafted by artist Tim Williams and dedicated to Jordan, Simeon and Issac Young, members of the first black family in Fresno County. It was donated by the families of Hiram, Jordan, Simeon, and Issac Young and portrays the major contributions to the economic, cultural, and political development of Fresno County by African-Americans.

The upstairs gallery houses artifacts and pioneer photos. A large patio outside is being built for outdoor cultural and family events. The museum is administered by founder Jack A. Kelley, Executive Director Ms. Rubi Pegues-White, and a twelve-member board of directors. Keith A. Kelley, Carolyn Golden, Ida M. Jones, Ann Gaston, Bessie Miller, Thomas Ellis, Alan Simpson, Lewis Jackson, Kehinde Solwazi, Ethel King, Ben Quillian, and Jean Kennedy-Douglas comprise the board.

The museum's mission is to promote an understanding, ap-

Simeon and Carl Young serving as American doughboys in France during World War I.
Courtesy of African American Historical & Cultural Museum.

Reverend Simeon Young was born into slavery in South Carolina in 1850. After gaining his freedom, he graduated from Biddle University in Charlotte, North Carolina. He received his theology degree in 1887. He came to Fowler in 1912. He farmed during the week and preached in church on Sundays. This photo was taken on his Fowler farm on July 4, 1928.
Courtesy of African American Historical & Cultural Museum.

preciation, and awareness of African-Americans historically and culturally, throughout the San Joaquin Valley. After touring this facility, the visitor comes away with a deeper appreciation of the role this very important cultural group has played and continues to play in the history of our valley.

One of the great leaders in the history of Fresno's African-American community was born in Tennessee. During the early years of his life, he lived in Indiana, Ohio, and Michigan. While attending Wayne University in Detroit, he was a playground director for that city's department of recreation. He graduated from the College of Liberal Arts at Howard University in Washington, D.C. He received letters in five different sports and was considered one of the all-time great athletes at Howard University. He moved to New York City and enrolled in a graduate program at Columbia University.

In 1944, he arrived in Fresno to become a United Service Organizations Club director. For nineteen years, he served as the director of the B Street Community Center. He had held the same post at the USO Center in San Luis Obispo before coming to Fresno. During his tenure as director, the Fresno center developed social and recreational programs that served fifty-three adult groups and forty-eight youth groups.

Not only in his professional life did he serve his community, but in his volunteer time as well. He was past president and a founding member of the West Fresno Optimist Club and served on the 1951 Fresno County Grand Jury. He was a member of the Fresno Joint Recreation Commission and a member of the executive committee of the Fresno Citizens Committee on Education and National Recognition for Social Welfare in the State of California. In 1976, the California State Senate passed a resolution honoring his community service.

In recognition of Cecil C. Hinton's outstanding service to his community, the B Street Community Center was renamed the Hinton Center in his honor. At the time of his death in 1987, there were many successful men in Fresno who had grown up attending the community center and considered him their mentor and inspiration. Perhaps, they are his greatest legacy to this community.

On the morning of April 8, 1972, William Arthur Bigby, Jr. stepped forward. His wide smile reflected pride and happiness for, on this day, he was taking part in the dedication of a new housing project that would bear his name. Bigby Villa, located on Lorena Avenue between Bardell Avenue and Clara Street, was a $3.58 million low income housing project. The 180 units were built by Catholic Charities Housing, Inc. in cooperation with the Redevelopment Agency of Fresno. The fact that the dedication was held on the fourth anniversary of the passage of the Fair Housing Law was appropriate. Bigby had served on the citizens' advisory committee that was the forerunner to the Fresno City and County Housing Authority.

William Bigby was born in Colusa, California. His family moved to Fresno when he was seven years old. He attended Fresno schools, and, in 1912, became the first black graduate of Fresno High School. He served his country during World War I, attaining the rank of first sergeant in the Army. Fourteen months of his duty was in Europe. He would later be a founder of American Legion Post 511 and would serve as its president. He became president of the Negro Citizen's Advancement League of West Fresno in 1927.

Mr. Bigby was a charter member of the Second Baptist Church and a member of the Prince Hall Order of the Free and Accepted Masons. He was a 33rd degree Mason. He was a retired clerk for the State Board of Equalization. Many agencies and charities in Fresno, including the Boys Club of Fresno, the United Givers, the March of Dimes, and the Red Cross, were recipients of Bigby's generous gift of volunteer time. He was one of the first directors of the Valley Children's Hospital and served for sixteen years on the Edison High School Advisory Board.

At the time of his death, at age eighty-eight, in 1981, Bigby had received many honors from his community. Indeed, he is remembered as one of the most, if not the most, outstanding citizen in the history of Fresno's black community.

Jack A. Kelley

Visitors to the African-American Historical and Cultural Museum of the San Joaquin Valley are often greeted by a charming gentleman. As he guides them through the photos and exhibits, his enthusiasm is contagious. The more he talks about black history in the Central Valley, the more they want to know. He reminisces about men like William Bigby and Cecil Hinton and their role as motivators for many young men in the black community. When he talks about the school children who tour the museum his voice softens. "I tell them to have good study habits—to learn to spell and read well," he says. "I tell them to have respect for all human beings." Jack Kelley tries to instill these messages in the children who visit this museum that he founded.

Jack Kelley was born in Edmonton, Alberta, Canada, in August of 1920. His family moved to Bakersfield, where he attended elementary school. In 1941, he graduated from Tulare Union High School. He excelled in football, basketball, and baseball and was named to the All City Team. His high school baseball coach was the legendary Pete Beiden. He was named All County & Valley in football. He entered Fresno State College and continued his participation in sports.

In 1945, at the end of his sophomore year in college, Kelley enlisted in the U.S. Army. After his tour of duty ended, he returned to Fresno State and completed his bachelor of science degree in physical education. He married Rosa Conley in 1946 and was hired as a counselor for the California Youth Authority the same year. Three years later, in 1949, he began his career in law enforcement and became the Fresno Police Department's first black sergeant and detective. He served his community in this capacity until 1971, when he left the force to train minority students in law enforcement.

In the late 1980s, Jack Kelley decided to follow his heart by establishing a museum that would be a repository for information and artifacts about the African-American community of the Central Valley. He wanted it to be a place where young people could learn about their heritage and where all the people of our Central Valley could learn about the unique contributions of the African-American community. His dream became a reality in 1989.

A Mountain Pass Called Pacheco

When the sea breezes of the Pacific Ocean beckon, many valley residents travel through the Coast Range Mountains' Pacheco Pass to the Monterey Peninsula or to Santa Cruz. How did this road get its name? Did you know that this route has borne travelers and witnessed happenings that are filled with the romance and legends of early California?

In the early 1850s, Andrew Firebaugh operated a ferry service on the San Joaquin River at a place that became known as Firebaugh's Ferry—the present-day city of Firebaugh. He also operated a trading post. To increase his business, he decided to build a toll road over the mountains to the coast. The only pass from the coast to the valley was a dusty trail that had been used by the Indians as a trade route. The valley Yokuts would meet the coastal Ohlone beside an artesian well and exchange acorns and animal pelts for salt, shells, shellfish, and sea fish. Casa de Fruta today stands at the site.

On June 21, 1805, the feast day of Saint San Luis Gonzaga, Spanish explorer Gabriel Moraga discovered the pass and named a creek nearby for the saint. The pass took its name from the creek—becoming the San Luis Gonzaga Pass. In 1846, John C. Fremont and his men rode through the pass on their way to Sacramento. The Gold Rush of 1849 saw increased use of the route to bring supplies from the coast to the gold fields of the Sierra foothills. Notorious bandits Joaquin Murrieta and Tiburcio Vasquez traversed the pass many times, sometimes committing crimes along the way. Later, the pass became part of the first overland mail route and the Butterfield Transcontinental Stage Line. Stage coach travel added its own piece of romantic lore.

On February 6, 1856, the Monterey Board of Supervisors granted Firebaugh permission to build his road and collect tolls. In the spring of 1857, the road was complete. Firebaugh named the road Pacheco Pass in honor of Francisco Pacheco, whose family owned the vast Rancho San Luis Gonzaga that extended over the entire pass.

Bell's Station

For the traveler who wends his way through the mountain pass of the Coast Range on his way to Monterey, the road rises from the valley floor past the San Luis Dam, sweeps between the hills, soars to the summit, and, finally, drops to the flat lands of the Hollister Valley. It is about a twelve-mile drive. It takes the traveler past diverse scenery and vistas—all in the space of a few minutes. Until the San Luis Dam was built, the highway followed the old stage road. Today, the highway on the valley side of the mountains follows a new route and then picks up the old route shortly before the summit is reached. However, one historic site along the way is still there—Bell's Station.

In the late 1850s, a stage would leave Firebaugh's Ferry and travel toward Pacheco Pass—a forty-mile drive that took four hours, if lucky, with time for rest stops at Temple's Ranch, Lone Willow Ranch, and the San Luis Rancho at the entrance to the pass. A stop was made at the toll booth, for the pass was a tollroad. The location of this is subject to debate; but, probably, it was near today's entrance to the San Luis Reservoir's Dinosaur Point. The next stop was at the Hollenbeck Stage Station owned by William Hollenbeck. In the 1860s, it was sold to Lafayette F. Bell, who changed the name to Bell's Station. It was not only a stage stop, but also a telegraph office. Since it was on the route of the Butterfield Overland Mail from Saint Louis to San Francisco, news from the East could be telegraphed ahead.

Across the road is a spectacular landmark—a mountain peak called "Lover's Leap." Local lore says that an Indian princess leapt to her death from this mountain because of a broken heart.

The original Bell's Station burned down in 1932, but has been rebuilt—restaurant and all. Although the sound of the bugle heralding the arrival of the stagecoach can no longer be heard, Bell's Station is, for many, still a stopping place on the trip through Pacheco Pass and still evokes the romantic history of California.

Francisco Pacheco

Wagon maker Francisco Perez Pacheco arrived in California in 1820. He was born in Guadalajara, New Spain, now called Mexico, in 1790. He married Feliciana Gonzales y Torres, who was descended from the Aztec chiefs of the Valley of Mexico. In 1820, they, along with their two children, boarded the frigate *Cleopatra* and arrived in Monterey in May of that year. During the decade of the 1820s, four more children were born to the couple, and one died.

An Indian uprising in 1824, at the Santa Inez and Purisima missions, caused the governor of California to send troops to quell the disturbance. Pacheco participated in the action, acquitting himself with distinction. He was awarded with a piece of property in the town of Monterey and the rank of ensign in the army. Within two years, Pacheco petitioned to acquire a tract of land. His request was denied, but his desire to become a cattle rancher would continue. Meanwhile, he began to be involved in politics and attained the position of commandante of the guard of the Customs House.

In 1833, Pacheco's desire for land was finally realized. He became the owner of a large part of the Rancho Ausaymus y San Felipe near present-day Hollister. He continued to add to his holdings and by 1840 he owned 42,299 acres of choice land. Three years later his son Juan became the owner of the huge Rancho San Luis Gonzaga adjacent to and east of his father's rancho.

When the Gold Rush of the late 1840s brought a tremendous influx of people into California, the demand for beef increased and so did the value of Pacheco's cattle. Francisco Pacheco supported statehood for California. However, statehood brought problems—especially the question of property rights of Mexican Californians. He spent years in litigation until the patents were finally granted for the ranchos owned by his family. In 1855, his son Juan died, and the large Rancho San Luis Gonzaga passed to Francisco. In 1860, Francisco Pacheco died. The legacy of this distinguished man is the mountain pass that bears his name—Pacheco Pass.

Andrew Davidson Firebaugh

One of Fresno County's earliest pioneers began his career in the westernmost part of our county and, toward the end of his life, settled in the foothills of the Sierra, where he made lasting contributions.

Andrew Davidson Firebaugh was born in Cedar Grove, Virginia, on September 29, 1823, the seventh of sixteen children. His birthplace was a two-story log house on his father's plantation. Like many other farm boys, he grew up working beside his father's slaves, doing such chores as hoeing.

By his early twenties his adventurous nature began to surface. He left for Texas where he signed up in the 1st Regiment of the Texas Mounted Riflemen Volunteers and served through the war with Mexico from 1845-48. A year later, he headed for California. He joined Major James Savage's Mariposa Battalion and was with Savage when his unit discovered Yosemite Valley in 1854.

By 1874, Firebaugh had crossed the San Joaquin Valley and was farming near the Coast Range Mountains and the San Joaquin River. The river was the second largest in California and hard to cross. He decided to operate a ferry and, on the west bank of the river, a trading post. It is not clear whether he started the ferry or purchased it from another, but he was the owner in 1854. Called Firebaugh's Ferry, the trading post is the site of the present-day city of Firebaugh. The Mexican workers who helped him build his store and ferry coined a special name for him—*colorrojo*—because of his fiery red hair. In 1856-57, he built a toll road over the mountains that became known as Pacheco Pass. A year later Firebaugh's Ferry became a stop on the Butterfield Overland Mail Route.

Firebaugh sold his holdings and went to Missouri with a friend, Jack Burgess. He met Burgess' sister Susan, whom he married in 1860. They returned to California, eventually settling in Watts Valley. In 1870, they moved to Dry Creek. Firebaugh became one of the five trustees who founded the Academy School. On June 26, 1875, Andrew Firebaugh died and was buried on the ranch he homesteaded. His hillside grave is on private land located ten miles above Academy. It may be truly said that his influence spanned the breadth of Fresno County.

The Chief of the Yosemite

The great Indian chief Tenaya was born on the eastern slope of the Sierra Nevada, the son of an Ahwahnechee chief and a Mono Indian woman. The Ahwahnechee were the first Indians to live in a great valley called Ahwahnee in the Sierra. Today this valley is called Yosemite. Most of the tribe died from disease. Many of the survivors fled because they thought the valley was cursed. When Tenaya was a young man, he visited the valley and decided to stay and begin a new tribe that would include the surviving Ahwahnechee as well as members of other tribes who had married into the Ahwahnechee. He proclaimed himself chief and gave the tribe the name Yosemite, which meant grizzly bear.

An elderly shaman told Tenaya that as long as he controlled the valley, his tribe would prosper. Then he cast a spell on the valley to keep it safe. He told Tenaya that if white men on horseback entered the valley they would bring evil, his tribe would be destroyed, and he would be the last chief.

White men had heard tales of this mysterious valley—that it was deep within the mountains of the Sierra and inaccessible to them. They knew it existed because Indians from the valley made raids into the surrounding areas, stealing the white men's horses and mules and plundering their homes.

During the Mariposa Indian War of 1851, the Indian Commission ordered Major James Savage and his Mariposa Battalion to subdue these Indians. Companies B and C left their camp fifteen miles below Mariposa on March 19, 1851, under Savage's command. Rain and snow in the higher mountains made travel difficult. On the third day, they captured a village of two hundred Nuchu Indians living on the south fork of the Merced River. They ordered several Indians to take a message to Chief Tenaya. They returned with word that Chief Tenaya would come to them. Chief Tenaya arrived alone and, with great dignity, asked them to leave his people alone. Savage urged him to go to the Indian Commission and make a treaty. Tenaya said he would bring his people to Savage's camp. Tenaya returned to the valley. It seemed to him the shaman's prophecy was coming true. In our next tale of the valley we will continue his story.

The first view of Yosemite Valley has never failed to enchant visitors. This is as true today as it was when Major James Savage and his troops first saw the valley on March 27, 1851. *The Image Group from the Laval Historical Collection.*

Major James Savage and his Mariposa Battalion, under orders from the Indian Commission in 1851, had sought out the chief of the Yosemite Indian tribe, Tenaya. His tribe inhabited a great valley that no white man had entered. A prophecy foretold of disaster for his people if the white men came. Members of the tribe had been stealing horses and plundering homes belonging to the white man. The commission wanted a treaty with the Yosemite, to move them out of their valley called Ahwahnee, and into the San Joaquin Valley.

Savage's men were encamped along the Merced River near an Indian village they had just captured. Chief Tenaya returned from his valley, came to their camp, and apologized for stealing from the white man. He promised that his people would come to their camp and make a treaty. Savage waited for twenty-four hours, but the Indians did not come. Savage and fifty-seven of his men, with Chief Tenaya leading the way, began the trip to the mysterious valley and Tenaya's village.

Halfway to the valley, seventy-two members of Tenaya's tribe met the troops. Savage asked Tenaya where the others were. Tenaya said they had fled—that these people were the only members of his tribe left. Savage called him a liar. He ordered all the Indians back to his camp with the exception of one who would be his guide. They continued their journey.

They soon came to the mysterious valley of the Yosemite Indians. It was March 27, 1851. They searched the valley and found only empty huts—all the Indians who had not surrendered had fled. The exception was one elderly woman who had been left behind because she was too old to climb the rocks. The soldiers provided her with food and then returned to their camp outside the valley. Gathering all their Indian prisoners together, they began the descent into the foothills. After several days, the Indians escaped. Many were coaxed back—only the Yosemite tribe refused to return for peace treaty talks. In the aftermath, Tenaya's favorite son was killed. The chief had lost not only his tribe, but, as he expressed it, the "child of my heart." After the Mariposa Indian War ended, Tenaya and his immediate family were allowed to return to the valley. A year later, in 1852, he was murdered, stoned to death by Mono Indians. The prophecy had been fulfilled. Tenaya was the last great chief of the Yosemites.

A Valley Discovered

During the Mariposa Indian War of 1851, Major James Savage, his soldiers and an Indian guide were traveling through the Sierra on horseback in search of the valley called Ahwahnee—the home of the Yosemite Indians. Many of the Yosemite were prisoners of the Americans; the remaining reportedly had fled from their village. The soldiers were going to verify their departure.

It was March 27 and the ground was covered in snow, making the journey difficult. The path they were following was steep and dangerous. All at once they came to the edge of a high cliff. There, three thousand feet below and stretching before them, was a valley of incredible beauty. Forming a backdrop to the lush landscape was a sheer rock cliff that rose from the valley with majestic dignity like a towering sentinel of ancient grandeur. A haze hung over the valley and clouds shrouded the higher mountains, lending a mystic quality to the scene. One of the soldiers, Dr. Lafayette Bunnell, wrote of his feelings as follows: "This obscurity of vision but increased the awe with which I beheld it, and as I looked, a peculiar exalted sensation seemed to fill my whole being, and I found my eyes in tears of emotion. I can (now) depart in peace, for I have here seen the power and glory of a Supreme being; the majesty of His handy-work is in the 'Testimony of the Rocks.' That mute appeal—pointing to (the sheer cliff) El Capitan—illustrates it, with more convincing eloquence than can the most powerful arguments of surpliced priests."

The soldiers continued on their journey, descending into the valley and camping that first night in a meadow near the falls today known as Bridal Veil. After dinner they began to talk about a name for the valley. After much discussion, it was decided to name it for the Indian tribe which they had just forced to leave the valley. It was thus that Yosemite Valley was named.

Downtown Fresno was once composed of not just commercial and government buildings, but of lovely neighborhoods as well. Large and small Victorian homes, tree-lined sidewalks and green lawns created an appropriate counterpoint to the buzz of activity in the business district. Today, only remnants of these neighborhoods remain. However, one area, just north of Community Hospital, still has a large number of its original housing stock. Although it has suffered from neglect, it has an active neighborhood association that is working to create a better environment.

One of the homes in this neighborhood dates to 1899. Deputy County Surveyor Scott McKay built it for the most romantic of reasons—as a home for him and his new bride, Helen Jewett McKay. The wood framed house has a wrap-around porch as befits its corner situation—a perfect place to sit on a summer evening and greet the neighbors who strolled by. One interesting feature of the home is the two-room basement that was used as a living room and kitchen during Fresno's hot summers.

Scott McKay was born in Indiana and received his education there. He graduated from the University of Indiana in 1891 with a degree in civil engineering. He was hired by the San Joaquin Light & Power Company as a construction engineer in charge of building reservoir pipe line ditches. In 1902, he was nominated for the office of county surveyor on the Republican ticket and won the election handily. He served for four consecutive terms of four years each—totaling sixteen continuous years of service to the people of Fresno County. Under his leadership, many of the finest scenic roads were built in the foothills of the Sierra. He contracted pneumonia on a business trip to Tollhouse and died on May 4, 1918. His home on North Clark Street still stands—a silent but tangible reminder of a fine man who served his community well.

The Harlow Home

The residents of the Tower District have become leaders in the movement to preserve the historic architecture of Fresno. By their efforts they have, in many ways, taught the rest of the city how to go about preserving not only buildings, but neighborhoods. The Tower District Plan paved the way. So, too, did the restoration of the Tower Theater. Now, live theater, antique shops, bookstores, coffee houses, fine restaurants, and charming homes are plentiful—with more to come in the future.

The Tower District has another notable resource. It contains probably the largest single concentration of craftsman architecture in California. Bungalows, large and small, abound. The craftsman style came out of the Arts and Crafts movement of the latter part of the nineteenth century. It reflected a departure from Victorian architecture with its dependence on ornate details and a return to beauty, unity, and simplicity.

One of the Tower District bungalows, listed on the City of Fresno's Register of Historic Resources, is a fine example of the craftsman style. Built in 1913 by C. W. Harlow, a carpenter and building contractor, the exterior features a large front gable and six-inch clapboard siding. A porch spans the front of the home. Like many craftsman homes, the interior showcases the use of local wood. The living room features crossed ceiling beams, three-inch picture and ceiling moldings, and eight-inch baseboards. The fireplace is flanked by built-in bookcases. A large built-in china hutch in the dining room has leaded glass doors. Tri-paneled doors can be found throughout the house.

The neighborhoods of the Tower District are filled with craftsman homes built around or just after the turn of the century. As we approach the turn of another century, their charm and simplicity are attracting a whole new generation of Fresnans, many of whom are buying and restoring them. Perhaps, these homes will live on to see another hundred years of gracing these special areas of our city.

A House Built with Whimsy

Every October when Halloween ghosts and goblins scamper through Fresno neighborhoods yelling "trick or treat," thoughts often turn to another kind of ghost—the kind that might haunt a house. As more of our historic homes bite the dust, the fewer possible haunts seem to be around. There is one historic home, however, that looks the part—indeed, it seems to be made just for things that go bump in the night.

Located on a parcel of land on South Chestnut Avenue is a home that was built by Andreas Jansen in 1924. Rather than build a simple two-story house, Mr. Jansen let his imagination soar. The result was one of the most interesting and delightful combinations of architectural styles in the city. Basically Queen Anne in design, it combines all sorts of decorative motifs. Although it is a two-story wood frame house, it appears from the outside to be multi-level. The front of the house has a two-story porch with large square columns. The porch on the second-story level sits under a large gable that is hipped under the eave. It is embellished with a fan motif ornament. There are several other gables at different roof levels which tease the viewer into thinking there are more than two stories in the house.

The *piece de resistance* is an octagonal tower structure that sits atop the roof supported by two-story octagonal columns which are adjacent to the two-story front porch. It is attached to the roof between two gables. It has windows on each of its eight sides that look out on the world from its three-story height—just the sort of structure that teases the imagination. Looking like a decorative element on a tiered cake, its only real purpose is to adorn, but it also suggests sinister goings on and, maybe, a hint of romance.

When so many of Fresno's Victorian and Queen Anne homes were torn down, part of the romance of our city was lost. It's nice to know that a little bit of that has been preserved on South Chestnut Avenue.

The neighborhood just north of the Community Hospital was, at the turn of the century, filled with many lovely small Victorian homes owned by middle class families. A few large homes existed. Most of them are gone, but one notable residence remains. Situated on the northwest corner of McKenzie Avenue and Clark Street, this two-story craftsman-style home was built around 1905.

The two-story wood framed structure has a hipped roof with deep, overhanging eaves. It is simple in design as are most craftsman-style homes. Its most noteworthy feature is the interesting brick detailing in the porch that wraps around the front and side of the house. It has been relatively unchanged since it was built.

The man who built this home was George Shipp, the son of one of Fresno County's earliest residents. His father, William Walter Shipp, came to Fresno County from Mississippi in 1868 and settled in the Dry Creek area. He engaged in sheep raising. George was educated in public schools in Mississippi and in a private school in Fresno. From the time George was eight years old he worked with his father on the ranch and became an expert sheepman. In 1887, William sold his holdings in Dry Creek and moved his sheep to a ranch on the San Joaquin River. The ranching operations were turned over to George, who was twenty-two years old. George purchased an interest in the business. In 1891, he married Abbie Webster of Vacaville. Later, George leased property near Kerman where he ranged sheep in the winter, taking them to the mountains in the summer. He also engaged in cattle ranching. He bought ranches near Reedley, a vineyard in the Scandinavian Colony, and a 160-acre ranch on Blackstone Avenue where he raised peaches and figs.

The home he built on Clark Street stands as a reminder of one of Fresno County's early pioneer families who played a major role in the development of agriculture in our county.

May of 1903 held a great deal of excitement for those who lived in the Central Valley. A very popular president, Theodore Roosevelt, was going to pay a visit. The first part of the presidential visit took place in Yosemite where, in the company of John Muir and others, Roosevelt enjoyed the grandeur of the scenery and discussed forest protection with Muir. He was on a private camping vacation, but on one afternoon greeted crowds of well-wishers. He was clad in khaki pants and a torn sweater—evidence of his informal visit. A sign reading "Hello Teddy" was held aloft by a young boy. Roosevelt stopped and gave him a lecture on showing proper respect to a president. The boy stammered, "Yes, Mr. President," and looked properly scared. The warm hospitality and hero-worship of the residents was very much in evidence that afternoon. One important outcome of this visit was the president's support of making Yosemite Valley and the Mariposa Grove of Big Trees part of Yosemite National Park. This was accomplished soon after the president's visit.

After leaving Yosemite, President Theodore Roosevelt took a stagecoach down the mountains to Raymond. He had received a request for a public appearance and speech from the people of that town. After he arrived in Raymond, he strode to the porch of Bowen's Store, where he gave a rousing speech to the large group assembled there.

The president then boarded the train for Berenda, where he was greeted by hundreds of people waving flags and cheering. They had come from as far away as Hanford, Fresno, and Madera to see their president, who was also the famous Rough Rider—the hero of the Spanish-American War. He exhorted the crowd on the virtues of the work ethic that, he believed, was the basis for all that was good in America. The crowds were still cheering as his train pulled out of the station. They returned to their homes and communities, but they never forgot the visit of President Theodore Roosevelt to the great Central Valley.

The Pleasanton Cafe

Homer Sterios stands with an unidentified woman in the interior of the Pleasanton Cafe in the late 1910s. Note the curtained booths on the right.
Courtesy of Evelyn Sterios Fiorani.

The most colorful street in the downtown business district at the turn of the century was I Street, today known as Broadway. One of the most memorable businesses on I Street was a restaurant called the Pleasanton Cafe. Its story begins in this way:

In the first years of the twentieth century, two brothers, Harry and Dee Sterios, recent emigrants from Greece, settled in San Francisco. In 1906, the city suffered a terrible earthquake. In the aftermath of the devastation, Harry was paid ten cents by the city for every rat he caught. The two boys washed dishes and worked in various restaurants. They saved their money and bought a small coffee shop on O'Farrell Street that consisted of one long counter. In 1913 or 1914 they sold it and came to Fresno, using their profits to buy the Pleasanton Cafe from their cousin Christopher, who had started the restaurant in 1900. World War I had begun. Both boys were drafted into the Army. Dee served his tour of duty in the United States. Harry went abroad as a French interpreter for the Army. When the war was over they returned to the cafe.

The owners and staff of the Pleasanton Cafe at 1017 Broadway in the 1930s. Left to right, Democratis (Dee) Sterios, Harry Sterios, Homer Sterios and Andy Sterios. John Sterios stands on the right.
Courtesy of Evelyn Sterios Fiorani.

When a patron entered the door of the Pleasanton Cafe, he was greeted warmly by Harry or Dee Sterios. He would see a long counter that extended part way across the back of the restaurant. Along a side wall, was a line of curtained booths, which offered privacy to diners. The center of the room was filled with tables. Once seated, the patron was served by Andy Sterios. Chef Homer Sterios ran the kitchen. They were brothers of Harry and Dee. The tables were set with white linen cloths and the waiter wore black pants and a starched white jacket.

The Sterios family operated the Pleasanton Cafe until the late 1950s, when redevelopment plans for downtown called for demolition of their building. Then, sadly, the restaurant had to close. The cafe, like the historic Fresno County Courthouse, fell to the wrecker's ball. It was the end of an era and a special way of life that was downtown Fresno.

A Young Lady's Lament

It is often not only illuminating, but sometimes amusing to peruse the newspapers of another era. The customs, concerns, and priorities of one hundred years ago are very clear when reading a newspaper of that time. An outmoded turn of phrase or usage of a word can often add a great deal of enjoyment to even a casual look at the periodicals of that time. But, usually it's just the glimpse one gets of society that is truly fascinating.

In the November 20, 1885, issue of the *Fresno Evening Democrat*, a letter to the editor appears on the Local News page. Written by a young Fresno woman, it expresses her concern and outrage about a matter dear to her heart. In her opinion, too many of the young men of Fresno preferred to find wives in other cities. Offended by this, she wonders if these young men think the young women of Fresno are not good enough for them. She says that many of the young ladies of her acquaintance are "intelligent, industrious and in every way worthy of the love and esteem of any young man." She goes on to humbly say that, "I do not claim to be such a person myself, but I speak for other young ladies of my acquaintance." She was truly puzzled that the young men of Fresno enjoyed socializing and often dancing with Fresno girls, but felt they had to go to San Francisco or to some other city to find a wife. Then she turned her pen to another matter—the miserliness of many of the young men of her acquaintance. She found it maddening that the young men of Fresno happily socialize with local young ladies as long as it doesn't cost them anything. If they have to hire a carriage or pay for dinner, they make themselves very scarce. She called on the young women of Fresno to refuse to dance with them and to refuse their company on all occasions until they can find it within themselves to be less selfish.

One can only wonder how this young woman would feel about the world today—a world in which women often offer to pay for dinner and travel far from home to meet their future husbands.

One of the most attractive buildings on Van Ness Avenue just south of the commercial district of downtown Fresno is the James Phelan Building. One of its distinctive design elements is its color—it is built of brick that is a unique golden hue. In 1914, when the building was constructed at a cost of $90,000, it was one of the first automobile showrooms in Fresno. Over the years it has housed the local dealerships for Maxwells, Pierce Arrows, Cadillacs, and Hudsons. One interesting feature in the building was a ramp that went from the first floor to the second floor garage. It is the only local building of its time that was built for its particular purpose that is still standing. In the mid-1970s, the building was remodeled for its present use as an office building.

James C. Phelan was born in Colorado on October 25, 1867. He received his education in Colorado and New Mexico. In New Mexico he became involved in the grocery and butcher business and had his own store at age nineteen. In 1893, he married Myrtie Dickinson. Their marriage was blessed with seven children. They came west to Fresno in 1905. When Mr. Phelan built his showroom at 700 Van Ness Avenue in 1914, he was the San Joaquin Valley agent for the Maxwell, Mitchell, and Marmon automobiles and the Kleiber and Maxwell trucks. He employed between forty and fifty men to work in the various departments of his dealership. He continued selling motor vehicles until he sold the business in August of 1919.

James Phelan was a member of the Woodmen of the World, the Knights of Pythias, and the Young Men's Christian Association. He was a loyal member of the Democratic Party and was very active in community endeavors. One of his particular interests was working as an advocate for better roads.

The Phelan Building on Van Ness Avenue stands as a reminder of a major transitional period in our history—the time when the automobile began to replace the horse and carriage as the most popular form of transportation.

Before redevelopment projects in the early 1960s caused most of it to disappear, the street called Broadway vibrated with an energy unlike any other downtown street. In the early days of our city it was called I Street. In 1919, a group of I Street merchants petitioned to have the name of the street changed to Broadway to eliminate confusion with J Street addresses. It seems that it was often hard for the postman to distinguish between the I and the J. The name was changed to Broadway. This was probably influenced by the popularity of the silent films and vaudeville shows that were held in the street's White theater. Giving the street the name of New York City's "Great White Way" must have seemed appropriate.

Before 1900, livery stables, feed yards, grocery stores, hardware stores, Kutner-Goldstein store, banks, the Grady-Fiske Opera House and Beer Hall, Radin and Kamp's Store, the City Bakery and Cafe, several small hotels and lodging houses, and the grand Hughes Hotel graced I Street.

In the years after 1900, the street began to undergo changes. W. Parker Lyon opened his used furniture store. The White Theater opened its doors. Fresno's first city hall, which would later became the headquarters of the police department and police court, was built at Broadway and Merced Street. With the advent of the car, the livery stables began to close. In their place two- and three-story buildings were built, each with the name of the owner and the date of construction emblazoned at the roof line. Many cafes and bars opened. Offices, clothing stores, furniture stores, and barber shops appeared. Some of the bars had rooms at the back that could be entered from the alley. This is where gambling took place. Above these stores and offices were hotels—some legitimate, others operating outside the law as "houses of pleasure." A well-dressed gentleman could be seen accompanied by a beautiful woman entering the curtained booths of some of the cafes—later to adjourn to the hotel upstairs. Broadway had a pulse of life unlike any other part of downtown.

In the early 1950s, Mayor Gordon G. Dunn, labeled "No Fun Dunn," led the effort to "clean up the town." The result was a

Broadway, the most colorful street in Fresno, in the early 1920s. This photograph of a parade was taken in front of the Pleasanton Cafe at 1017 Broadway. *Courtesy of Evelyn Sterios Fiorani.*

temporary closing of the brothels and gambling houses. After a little while, they reopened. It wasn't until the redevelopment projects of the 1960s tore down all the buildings, replacing them with parking lots and a ponding basin, that they were closed permanently. Colorful Broadway was gone, and the vice interests moved to other parts of the city.

Asa S. Edgerly

In 1887 a gentleman came to Fresno County from Nebraska. He purchased 280 acres of hogwallow land on what would become Blackstone Avenue. His name was Asa Edgerly. Born in New Hampshire in 1834, he had received his education in that state and had graduated from New Hampton College. He taught school for nineteen years. Then he moved to Vermont and served as state agent for the Continental Life Insurance Company. He moved to Nebraska, where he was engaged in farming, the hardware business, and building rental houses. After selling his Nebraska properties, he came west to Fresno.

Edgerly and his son, William, began improving the hogwallow property, located at what is today the southwest corner of Blackstone and McKinley avenues. They set out vines and planted fruit trees. William also owned a twenty-acre peach orchard nearby.

About the same time, Asa Edgerly joined with T. C. White and William Harvey in the real estate business. They purchased eighty acres of land that they named the Belmont Addition. Since several lawyers bought property along the main street of this tract, Edgerly suggested they name the street Blackstone for the famous English jurist, Sir William Blackstone.

In 1888, Asa Edgerly built a large building at the corner of Fulton and Tulare streets that was known as the Edgerly Building. For fifteen years, the post office was a tenant in this building. Later, that property was torn down and replaced by a large Radin and Kamp store—a building that later housed J. C. Penney Company and, unlike many early buildings, still stands. Edgerly also built three buildings at the corner of Tulare and O streets and purchased lots at the corner of Kern and M streets that would eventually be filled with structures built by other members of the family.

In June of 1918, Asa Edgerly died. Like many other pioneers, he spent many years of his life investing in his vision of Fresno's future.

The Women of Millerton

In our tales of the valley we have learned a lot about the town of Millerton, but there is yet another story to be told. What was life like for the few women who lived in this rough and wild gold mining camp?

Life in this frontier community was not easy for women. The majority of the men were rough in appearance and manner. Many of them had been working in lumber or mining camps away from the refining influence of women. Often their manner of speech was coarse. They worked hard. When there was an opportunity to play, their play was rough. They had few social skills and most did not have polished manners. The miners carried knives and pistols. Few men walked around unarmed. Gambling was an important amusement for men—a card game called "rounce" was a favorite. Saloons were everywhere, drinking was a problem, and delirium tremens was a common ailment.

For a woman at Millerton there was little to do outside keeping her home. There were no social clubs, no study clubs, no sewing circles, no church groups—in fact, there were no churches at all. It wasn't until after 1872, when people were beginning to move to Fresno Station that monthly church meetings were held and a Sunday School set up. Even then, there was no church building. An improvised altar for Catholic worship was set up at the Fort Miller residence building. When the Methodist circuit rider came to the area, the services were usually held at Big Dry Creek. The women at Millerton found their only source of entertainment was visiting with their neighbors and exchanging gossip.

Most Millerton couples had very large families. The Gillum Baleys had ten children, the Russell Flemings had nine, and the John A. Pattersons had eleven. With no permanent school in Millerton, the children were home all day. This surely gave the women of Millerton something to do—a full time job. Life on the frontier was not a lot of fun.

In the early years of Fresno, groups advocating abstinence from alcohol, such as the White Ribbon Reform League and the Women's Christian Temperance Union, were popular. They had many members and held public meetings, hoping to draw others to their cause.

One local gentleman by the name of Jack B., who definitely did not espouse their cause, had been in jail several times. In September of 1885 he was out of jail, but he had not forgotten his friends on the inside. Whether it was the heat of a late summer Fresno day that made Jack think of liquid beverages or the need to give a special gift to his friends, history does not say. Suffice it to say that Jack picked up a large bottle of whiskey and proceeded to walk through town on his way to Courthouse Park. After circling the courthouse several times to make sure that no one was watching, he headed for the back of the jail. Perhaps the heat may be blamed for what happened next; but, at this point, he threw caution to the wind. He broke a rear window.

When the jailer found him, Jack had placed a funnel in a hole in the iron shutter and was pouring whiskey into it. Needless to say, the jailer was not amused by this and called for help. Officers Barker and Smart came running and arrested Jack on the spot. Jack did not take very kindly to being arrested and put up a good fight. Quite a struggle ensued, but they finally got Jack into jail. They got as far as the jail cell when Officer Smart let go of Jack so he could open the cell door. To open the cell, Smart had to remove the heavy lock from the door. Jack, taking advantage of the momentary freedom, lashed out and kicked Officer Smart as hard as he could. This wasn't a very good idea, but Jack was desperate. Smart raised the hand holding the lock and brought it down to rest on Jack's head. Dr. Leach was summoned to dress the resulting wound. Jack had a headache for sometime thereafter, but at least it wasn't from drinking the whiskey.

The Reverend Jacob Legler was one of the founders of the Cross Church on March 15, 1892 and served as its pastor until 1899. *Courtesy of the American Historical Society of Germans from Russia.*

In southwest Fresno there is a small remnant of a neighborhood that sits beneath and adjacent to the interchanges of Highway 99, Golden State Boulevard, and Highway 41. It is not easy for the traveler to find his way into this area. It is almost totally cut off from the rest of the city. However, it is worth a visit. Historically, this neighborhood was called Germantown or "Rooshian Town." It was the center of culture for the many Volga Germans who began settling in Fresno in the late 1880s. These were German families who had settled in Russian during the reign of Catherine the Great. They later left Czarist Russia and sought freedom in America. Many engaged in farming. Those who did not settled in this small Fresno neighborhood bounded by Ventura Street, California Avenue, and the Southern Pacific Railroad tracks.

The centerpiece of this neighborhood was the Free Evangelical Lutheran Church. Although its congregation moved north, the building still stands. Its distinctive white and gold steeple is visible from both Highway 99 and Freeway 41.

Another structure in this neighborhood is notable also. Built in 1900, the home of Carl Legler sits on a corner lot on E Street at

Reverend Carl Legler served as pastor of the Cross Church from 1902 until 1913. In 1912, Rev. Legler baptized 163 children into the church, the largest number of infant baptisms in one year in the history of the church.
Courtesy of the American Historical Society of Germans from Russia.

Monterey. Of Eastlake Victorian style, this charming home was built by the Rev. Jacob Legler, who organized the Cross Church. He urged his nephew, Carl, a school teacher who taught in the German community living on the Volga River in Russia, to come to Fresno. Carl made the journey, bringing his large family with him. They moved into his uncle's home on E Street. The year was 1902.

Carl decided to change careers and became a minister. He served in this capacity for St. Paul's Lutheran Church for many years.

Today, the home of Carl Legler is an empty shell—the victim of a fire. Will someone come to its aid and restore this charming piece of Fresno's history or will it, too, like so many other buildings, disappear? Only time will tell.

The Marshal & the Smoking Gun

On October 31, 1885, just three days after the board of trustees of the brand-new City of Fresno met for the first time, a shooting incident occurred in a downtown saloon. It happened in this way.

About four o'clock in the afternoon pistol shots were heard in Rupert's Saloon. The sounds abruptly pierced the autumnal air with such a staccato sound that everyone started running in their direction. This may seem a little strange. One might think that it would be the better part of valor to run away from such a noise, but our hearty pioneer ancestors allowed their curiosity to overcome any thoughts of flight.

Among the throng was a reporter from the *Fresno Expositor*. As he rushed down the street, he began to steel himself for the tragic and, perhaps, bloody scene that he was about to witness. When he reached Rupert's Saloon, he cautiously opened the swinging door and looked in to see if it was safe to enter. After all, he didn't want to be hit by a stray bullet. To his amazement he saw County Assessor W. J. Hutchinson standing in the room holding a smoking revolver. Sitting in a chair in front of Hutchinson was City Marshal C. T. Swain. The reporter's first horrified thought was, "Is the marshal hurt? Is he dead?" A second glance told him that the marshal was very much alive. Another gentleman, whose rather improbable name was Noble Pickle, was standing next to the marshal. As the reporter watched, Assessor Hutchinson handed the gun to Mr. Pickle. He noticed that beads of perspiration were welling up on the assessor's forehead. He also noticed that the faces of the marshal and Mr. Pickle were ghostly white.

It seems that Marshal Swain had just purchased a new self-cocking revolver. Assessor Hutchinson was looking at it when it suddenly discharged. The bullet hit the floor, glanced up, hit the ceiling, and hit the floor again, leaving all three gentlemen rather shaken. The crowd dispersed. At the next meeting of the board of trustees, laws were passed regarding the use of firearms in the city. Ironically, now anyone wishing to discharge a weapon would have to obtain a permit from the marshal.

Life in early Fresno was rarely dull.

Our tales of the valley have recorded many family events—births, marriages, anniversaries, and deaths—but the story that is about to be told is remarkable in our history. It is the story of four generations of a Dos Palos family. They are average people who, like the majority of Americans, have quietly lived their lives in the best way they could, striving to raise their children to be good members of their community. However, they have managed to achieve something that few families have—four consecutive generations of this family have celebrated fifty years of marriage.

Our story begins in Nodaway County, Missouri, where on February 15, 1882, Joseph Edward Sniffin, better known as J. E., and Sarah Elvira Kuhn were united in holy matrimony. They moved to Sylvia, Kansas, where they resided for a number of years before coming west to Dos Palos in 1906. J. E. went into farming and became a well-known rancher in the Dos Palos area. He also served as a preacher for the Church of Christ. He died November 22, 1933. He and Sarah were married for fifty-one years.

On November 13, 1908, Thomas "Ted" Sniffin, the son of Joseph and Sarah, married Rillie Sims In Clarinda, Iowa. He was a trapper for Miller & Lux. Their marriage lasted fifty-two years, until Ted's death in Dos Palos on November 12, 1961—one day before their fifty-third anniversary.

The third generation of our story begins with the marriage of Thomas' daughter Aretta to Lawrence "Pony" George on February 24, 1929. Mr. George was the Signal Oil Co. distributor in Dos Palos for many years. After retirement, he went into farming. At the time of his death on August 8, 1985, they had been married for fifty-six years.

On February 7, 1949, in Dos Palos, Betty George married Marvin "Bud" Wooten. Betty taught school and Bud engaged in farming. On February 7, 1999, they became the fourth consecutive generation of the Sniffin family to celebrate their Golden Wedding anniversary—continuing the remarkable legacy handed down through their family.

Just three weeks before the citizens of Fresno were to vote on the incorporation of their city, an event happened which, perhaps, helped to persuade people that the services a real city could offer were sorely needed. A real fire department was certainly a necessity in a town that was full of wood frame buildings—many of which had been rebuilt due to fire.

At one o'clock in the morning of September 7, 1885, Fresnans were awakened by the sounds of gunshots accompanied by cries of, "Fire!" This traditional method of rounding up volunteer firemen was effective yet again as many sleepy-eyed men rushed out into the night to help fight the latest fire. What followed next was a comedy of errors.

The fire was confined to two buildings just south of the Grady Opera House. One housed the agricultural implement company of Hogue & St. John; the other the firm of J. H. Northcraft, dealer in wagons and buggies. The volunteers hitched horses to the one fire engine in town and raced to the fire. They pointed the hose toward the flames, turned it on, but no water came out. The suction on the engine had shrunk so much it would not raise any water. They rushed to the water works and hooked up the hose to their fire plug. But, since their hose was only 500 feet long it would not reach far enough to touch the fire. Next they ran to the Southern Pacific depot and borrowed Agent Smith's 100-foot hose. They attached it to their hose, but, alas, even with this additional footage, the hose only reached to the north end of the Opera House. By this time the two buildings were entirely consumed by the fire.

The Opera House and the other buildings nearby were saved from damage by a group of citizens who formed a bucket brigade and managed to get enough water to the site to keep them from harm. Perhaps, it was this event that was the last straw and gave the citizens of Fresno the motivation needed to finally vote to incorporate their city on September 29, 1885.

When the conversation turns to cattle raising in Fresno County, one name is sure to be mentioned—Blasingame. Since the early 1860s, the Blasingames have been engaged in stock raising in the Academy area.

Jesse August Blasingame was born in Talladega County, Alabama. After serving in the Mexican War, he heard about the discovery of gold and decided to take his chances in the gold fields of California in 1849. Bringing several men with him to help in the mines, he traveled through the Isthmus of Panama and on to California. Although he was successful as a miner, he decided to try his hand at something that would guarantee a better income. He moved to the foothills of Fresno County, to the Big Dry Creek area, and turned to raising cattle, sheep, hogs and horses. He became one of the largest land owners in that area—his land stretched from Academy almost to Friant, a distance of nine miles--and included 12,000 acres.

Blasingame married Mary Ogle, a native of Missouri, who had come west with her family in an ox team train. They had two sons. They returned to Alabama in 1870 to settle some family business. Then they went to Texas and spent a winter there. He purchased two thousand head of cattle that he and his sons intended to drive across the plains and mountains to California. When they reached Humbolt Wells, Nevada, they shipped the cattle to San Francisco, Sacramento, and Colfax. He made a good profit from the venture. The Blasingames returned to their home near Academy. Five more children were born to the couple.

Jesse and Mary Blasingame moved into Fresno in 1878. He made many contributions to the communities of both Fresno and Academy. He was one of the founders of the Academy School, the vice-president of the Fresno County Bank, and was active in church work. He built the Ogle House, one of Fresno's finest hotels. After his death in 1881, Mary built the Blasingame Block at H and Tulare streets. She died in 1908.

Jesse Blasingame's descendants still live at Academy and raise cattle on the same land as their ancestor did so many years ago, providing another chapter in the tales of our valley.

Childbirth Amid the Tumult

During the wee hours of the morning of July 4, 1898, Myrtle Rowell, the wife of Chester Harvey Rowell, gave birth to their first child, a son. They had been in Fresno only a few short months and were living with Chester's uncle, Dr. Rowell, at the corner of K (Van Ness) and Tulare streets. Chester had just begun to work for his uncle as editor of the *Fresno Morning Republican.*

Anyone who has been through the experience of childbirth knows only too well that it is usually a trying time for both the father and the mother. On this night in particular, the patience of Myrtle and Chester was tried to the breaking point. In fact, the events were so awful that it moved him to write a scathing editorial a few days later.

This is the story of what happened that night. Right across the street from Dr. Rowell's home was the Fresno Beer Hall. At the rear of this establishment was a garden with a high wooden fence. After dark, it became a gathering place for women of a certain type who were admitted into the garden through a door in the fence. The night in question was one of Fresno's fine balmy summer evenings. A breeze wafted through the trees in the back garden bringing a touch of coolness after the hot summer day. Gentlemen began to enter the garden. Soon, the merriment was in full sway. Voices and laughter grew louder and louder, probably because the consumption of beer was keeping pace with the rest of the evening's activities. Around 2:00 A.M. someone picked up a cornet and began to play rather discordant renditions of the "Marseilles," the "Star Spangled Banner," and other popular and patriotic songs. This continued off and on for what seemed like hours. The lovely breeze brought all these sounds right into the bedroom where Myrtle was trying to give birth to her son. Furious with the police for not enforcing the laws that were supposed to regulate the saloons, Rowell, through his editorials, led the fight for a new city charter that was voted into effect in 1900. It probably all stemmed from that horrible July night.

Fresnans, like the citizens of communities throughout the country, loved to celebrate the Fourth of July. Pageants, parades, fireworks, and events in Courthouse Park were part of the traditional Fresno Fourth. However, on July 4, 1898, the celebrations took on new meaning because the United States was at war with Spain.

On February 15, 1898, the battleship U.S.S. *Maine* was sunk in Havana Harbor. War with Spain was declared on April 21. On May 1, the Battle of Manila Bay began, and on July 3 and 4, the Spanish fleet was sunk. The United States was poised to invade the Philippines. Feelings of patriotism were heightened. It was a time to wave flags and celebrate democracy.

The events of these days moved Chester H. Rowell, the editor of the *Fresno Morning Republican* to write in his July 3 editorial: "Not in a generation [when news of Gettysburg and Vicksburg arrived] has there been such a national holiday celebrated with so much earnestness as tomorrow will be...There will be processions and fireworks, peanuts, red lemonade and bucolic gallantry, but, beneath this surface runs the current of patriotism, strong and deep as it only does when fed by the storms of war. There is a patriotism of peace, just as there is a baptism of common life, but it is war which brings out heroism hitherto unsuspected, and rouses the latent patriotism of the whole people to full self-consciousness. When devotion to country is being daily measured in lives, when the keenest interest of each individual is the objective and success of the nation, no one can be so far absorbed in himself as to forget that he is but the part of a whole to which he owes all that he is. The Fourth of July oration will {contain} more than empty phrases. It will be a day for earnest men and women, as well as small boys, and will end with a fresh-eyed patriotism, instead of relief from the reign of the firecracker."

So it was that on July 4, 1898, Fresnans celebrated their nation's birthday with patriotic fervor and thanksgiving for the blessings of freedom.

A Dog Named Babe

The story of the creation of three mountain lakes, Huntington, Shaver and Florence, is part of the larger story of the massive undertaking by the Southern California Edison Company to develop and implement its Big Creek-San Joaquin River hydroelectric project. This project, started in 1911 by Fresno's Pacific Light and Power Corporation that was absorbed by the Southern California Edison Company in 1917, took many years to complete. Its result was to create not only the three lakes, but to build six dams, eight tunnels, and five power houses and to provide hydroelectric power and water to Central and Southern California.

In December of 1920, Florence Lake was being developed. It was necessary to get food, mail, and medical supplies from Camp 60 at the upper end of Huntington Lake to Camp 61 beyond Kaiser Pass, high in the Sierra. The snow was deep, making the roads impassable. It was decided to recruit an Alaskan dog sled team and a driver. Jerry Dwyer arrived, along with Patsy, Dooley, Trim, Riley, Whiskey, Barney, and Babe, the lead dog.

Jerry treated the dogs like his children, feeding them fresh fish, especially their favorite salmon, whenever he could obtain it. Because the snow sometimes caused the dogs problems, Jerry had leather shoes made for their feet. Babe was Jerry's favorite. For two winters, the team performed its mission well—taking the necessary provisions to the workers at Camp 61. Then, in September of 1922, Babe died in Jerry's arms. He buried her on the crest of Kaiser Pass. Her grave and later Whiskey's and Trim's were marked by the U.S. Forest Service. The editor of the *Covina Citizen*, G. F. Rinehart, who had visited Jerry and Babe many times, wrote a tribute to Babe. The first and last stanza are as follows:

"On the topmost reach of Kaiser Crest
Where the clouds commune and weep,
In a granite tomb 'til the crack of doom,
Babe lies in her last long sleep,...
When the Tourist conquers the tortuous steeps
With the Kaiser Pass as his goal
He will pause and rest on the wind-swept Crest
Where lies this Dog with a soul."

The Lynching That Wasn't

In May of 1892, A. G. Haskins of Centerville was walking alone along the foot plank of a flume when he was beaten severely. He died several days later; but not before he accused Michael Blume, a man Haskins had asked to leave the site of a picnic a few days previously because Blume was bringing whiskey into the grounds. On June 16, Blume was arrested, charged with murder, held without bond, and, instead of being brought to the county jail in Fresno, he was placed in a rickety Sanger jail with no guards. He had asked not to be taken to Sanger because he feared for his life. Haskins had been a man of influence and held in high regard. Feelings were running strongly against Blume.

At 11:00 the next night, eight or ten masked men who had keys to the facility entered the Sanger jail. They bound Blume's hands, threw him into a wagon, and took him to the flume where Haskins had been murdered. They asked Blume if he recognized the spot. He said he did not. They asked if he had murdered Haskins. He said no. They placed a rope around his neck and threw the other end over one of the crossbeams of the flume. They drew the rope upward and hung Blume until he was unconscious. Then they lowered the rope, waited for him to regain consciousness and asked him to confess. He would not. They hung him again until he was unconscious and then lowered him a second time. Then they took him back to Sanger and threatened him that if he told anyone about this, they would hang him again.

The next morning Constable Hill arrived at the jail. Hill asked Blume if he was all right. Blume told him what had happened. Hill took Blume to Fresno and turned him over to the sheriff who had Dr. Maupin examine him. Aside from a dislocated windpipe and red rope burn around his neck, the doctor felt he would be OK. District Attorney W. D. Tupper decided he had better investigate the goings on. Community feeling was high. Everywhere people were talking about the failed lynching—one of the stranger and more frightening events in the tales of our valley.

Red Lights & a Senator

T he purveyors of the "world's oldest profession" have been the subject of a story or two in the tales of our valley. Often a colorful part of the history of a community, it is never a dull story.

In 1900 Madera, the red-light district was on a block bounded by Fourth, Fifth, F, and G streets. Here five bawdy houses did a flourishing business. Sheriff John Barnett tried to clean up the situation, but there was one problem. It was not against the law. That changed in 1918 when the "Red Light Abatement Act," authored by State Senator Edward E. Grant, was passed.

The senator, hearing of Madera's red light district, came to the community to do something about it. He arrived at Sheriff Barnett's office wearing tattered clothes with a three-day growth of beard, and a friend, Mr. Remegie. He informed the sheriff that he wanted the three of them to conduct an investigation. They headed for F Street where they entered one of the houses by the back door. They were taken into a reception room, where negotiations began. Remegie and another man left the room with two girls. Grant made notes. The following day, Grant insisted that the sheriff arrest the two girls and the madam. He did, but he found that local opinion was divided about the matter when everyone got to court. Joseph Barcroft, the attorney for the defense, accused the sheriff of exceeding his authority by arresting the women without a warrant. He then got into an argument with the district attorney and the sheriff regarding morality and Madera's image.

By afternoon, the crowd in the courtroom had doubled. A young man was called to the witness stand and testified that he had been at the house on the afternoon in question, had seen neither the senator nor the sheriff, and had spent his time playing cards while the girls sewed. Under questioning, Grant had to admit he did not know what was going on in the room next to the reception area. The charges were dropped. Everyone went home. The senator left for other cities where his crusade might find greater support.

The Man with Three Wives

To many historians Major James D. Savage has become a figure of almost mythic proportions. Certainly no one in the history of our Central Valley was able to communicate with the local Indians as well as he. In his diary, Robert Brownlee, who served under Savage in the Mariposa Battalion, recalled his first meeting with Savage and paints an interesting picture of an unforgettable man.

In 1850, before the outbreak of the Mariposa Indian War, Robert Brownlee was operating a tent store in Mariposa. The two men met for the first time when Savage came into Brownlee's camp one day. He was wearing neither shoes nor a hat, but only a cotton shirt that reached to his knees. Three of Savage's Indian wives were following him in single file, with the eldest in the lead. Their ages seemed to be about sixteen, fourteen and twelve. Savage's appearance was of one who would have rough manners and speech. Brownlee was amazed when Savage asked for food for the women in a way that showed he was a man of education. As Brownlee would later learn, Savage was fluent in English, French, German, and several Indian dialects. The visitors stayed for several hours. The women looked at all the merchandise in Brownlee's store. Savage let them pick out whatever they wanted. When they finished shopping, the bill came to seventy-five dollars, which Savage paid with gold dust. He then invited Brownlee to visit him at his store on the Fresno River.

Brownlee, being fascinated by the man, immediately closed his store and followed Savage and his wives as they made their way back to the Fresno River. When they arrived, he showed Brownlee his living quarters in the back of his store. Brownlee wondered what the accommodations would be for a man with three wives. He soon found out. Bed consisted of four logs laid in a square with blankets and a sheet. At night the four crawled under the blankets and asked Brownlee to join them. Hiding his eyes, he did so. Life along the Fresno River in 1850 was interesting, indeed.

Madera's Triumph over the Railroad

In 1872, the Southern Pacific Railroad laid its track through the Central Valley. The cities of Modesto, Merced, Berenda, Borden, and Fresno came into being—each given birth by the Southern Pacific and blessed with regular rail service. In 1876, a flume was built with its terminus in a new city, Madera. Created without the railroad's permission, it grew up alongside its rail line. The Southern Pacific bosses were furious. How dare anyone create a community such as this without asking! Who did these folks think they were? Feelings ran so high that when Madera petitioned the railroad for a depot, they were told to build their own.

By December of 1911, the residents of Madera had had enough. Not only had they been treated like second class citizens, but another situation arose that made them even madder. Every evening at 9:05, train Number 50, the express train from Fresno to San Francisco, roared through Madera at top speed. It was extremely dangerous since there were no crossing arms at the tracks to protect Maderans, and the fact that it did not stop in Madera was insulting to this fast-growing county seat. It stopped at Modesto and Merced.

Tempers were raging. A letter was sent by the Madera Chamber of Commerce to the vice-president of the railroad, who sent a representative to Madera to assure everyone that their complaints would be dealt with. Number 50 continued to roar through town every night. The city trustees threatened the Southern Pacific saying that unless their demands were met, they would pass an ordinance requiring the train to slow to five miles an hour while passing through Madera. The ordinance was drafted in the presence of the railroad's agent, Charles E. Fleming, who urged the trustees to delay a vote on the new law until he could talk to the Southern Pacific owners.

Meanwhile Number 50 continued its cannonball run every night. A new threat was placed on the table. The trustees told the agent their city was not far away from the Santa Fe tracks. They would do business with them! The railroad had one week to give an answer. The answer came immediately. Number 50 began stopping in Madera. Madera won—not only the dispute, but its rightful place as an equal with the other Central Valley cities.

There is a site on the San Joaquin River that has a rich history. To one driving through this place, its history is not readily apparent, but once one knows this history, the drive will never be the same again. Today, the little community of Friant marks this spot. Before it was Friant, it was Pollasky. Before that it was Hamptonville. And, even earlier, it was the place where J. R. Jones ran a ferry. It was called Jonesville or Jones Ferry. It was here that David Cowan Sample crossed the San Joaquin River with his herds of sheep on his way to Big Dry Creek. Our tales of the valley have talked about Jones and Pollasky, but for whom was Hamptonville named? We will find out.

William R. Hampton was born in Grand Rapids, Michigan. He came west to Stockton in 1849 and entered the general merchandising business. He married a young woman named Catherine on September 4, 1862. They moved to Fresno County in 1867. Hampton went to work for J. R. Jones.

Later, Hampton purchased a tract of land on the south side of the river and set up his own merchandising business. He also built a home there for his family. The community known as Jonesville became known as Hamptonville. A large reinforced concrete bridge, the first in Fresno County, was built across the river.

Marcus Pollasky was a promoter of many projects—the most ambitious of which was a railroad extending from Fresno north along present-day Clovis Avenue out to Hamptonville. Pollasky's plan was to extend the rail line into the mountains. When the railroad reached Hamptonville, Hampton sold his interests in the town and moved his family to Fresno. The town became known as Pollasky.

William and Catherine Hampton died on the same day, June 13, 1908, in the Fresno home of their daughter.

The Shelbyville Swindle

If one were to write the history of swindles and con artists, one would have to include one of the most successful examples that took place right in our own backyard. Have you ever heard of Shelbyville?

In the late 1880s, there was a land boom in Fresno County. Agriculture was developing rapidly. Crops from Fresno were making their way into markets outside California. The word farming was becoming synonymous with Fresno County.

A showman named Guy Weber was working the circuit in some of the central states including Indiana, Ohio, Nebraska, and Illinois. He came through Fresno, heard about the rich soil and the bounty it produced, and came up with a brilliant idea. He purchased 2,600 acres of land, named it Shelbyville, had the deed recorded, and wove Shelbyville into his act. It became the teaser. Lots were given away by lottery. Every person who came to his show was given a golden opportunity to become the owner of land in the beautiful city of Shelbyville in Fresno County—a land like the Biblical promised land, flowing with milk and honey. People flocked to his show hoping to get California land for nothing. Those who won lots paid Weber directly for the deed, notarization, and seal. He made almost as much money on that as the highest assessed valuation of a lot—four dollars. He certainly made more than he had actually paid for the property.

If any of those who had become owners in Shelbyville had actually visited their property, they would have found that this piece of Fresno County real estate had a few problems. At one time it was good grazing land, but when water was brought in for irrigation purposes, the alkali in the subsurface rose to the top. Nothing, but nothing, would grow in the soil. It was as barren as the country around the Dead Sea. It was said that even the coyote chose a different route so he would not have to cross the bleak waste. The lots were not worth the taxes assessed against them. The land eventually reverted to the state and the con artist, richer by far, went on to greener pastures.

Ten miles southeast of Fresno is a small town filled with quiet tree-lined streets, charming homes and churches, and a downtown that is still the shopping hub for the community. In many ways, it encapsulates what many long for—the small town of yesteryear where everyone knows each other and the pace of life is slower. The man who gave his name to this town never lived in it. Indeed, his life is the very antithesis of the image this town projects. For he lived his life on a grandiose scale—flamboyance was his style.

Thomas Fowler was born on St. Patrick's Day 1829, in County Down, Ireland. He left Ireland when he was still young, traveling to New York and then to New Orleans, Texas, and, finally, to California in 1853. He then headed to Mexico with Thomas Davis and a man named Fisher. There they bought cattle that they drove into our Central Valley. In 1868, Fowler and Davis bought land along the Kings River in the area of present-day Minkler and Sanger. Their "76" brand was registered in Visalia and became well known.

As Fowler's cattle interests grew, he became interested in politics. A die-hard Democrat, he was elected to the state senate in 1869. Three years later the railroad was built through the valley. In May of 1872, it reached a point ten miles south of Fresno Station that was a convenient spot for Fowler to ship his cattle to market. A switch bearing his name was established here. His first shipments of cattle from Fowler's Switch occurred soon afterward. Fowler was at the height of his wealth and power. He considered running for governor, but got caught up in silver instead. He purchased the Empire Silver Mine at Mineral King—eventually losing his vast fortune.

Thomas Fowler was a man of strong opinions that he voiced loudly. He has been described as boisterous, extremely popular, and a heavy drinker. Even though he never lived there, this colorful man will long be remembered in the tales of our valley for giving his name to the city of Fowler.

The man who would be remembered by historians as the first resident of Fowler Switch, in 1878, was something of an eccentric. John S. Gentry was a bachelor who lived in a run-down cabin with a dirt floor, a poor roof, and walls that were described as not comparing "favorably with the average chicken coop." By the middle of 1881, his cabin was still the only dwelling in Fowler.

The land on which it was located became a source of debate with the railroad. The owner said he was on a claim of government land; the railroad said they had "working title" to the land and forced him to move his cabin to what is today the corner of Main and Seventh streets. Gentry raised poultry, primarily turkeys, which some people said was appropriate because his cabin was suited to that.

By 1882, a few people had begun to farm land around Fowler, The railroad decided to build a depot. The men who were working on the project would take breaks and walk across the street to Gentry's cabin. They would disappear inside only to come out smacking their lips. One of them was heard to say that it is "blooming good stuff Gentry keeps in his cellar." It is assumed this was the first merchandise sold in Fowler. He also made money by selling bottled and canned goods to the transients who came to work in Senator Fowler's stockyard or in nearby sheep yards.

Gentry's turkeys caused quite a stir when trains arrived. The turkeys, who were allowed to run wild, took it upon themselves to personally greet anyone who met or got on the train. The turkeys would not leave until Gentry called two words to them that no one else ever understood, "Kaducha, Kaducha."

Gentry added a second story to his cabin, painted it, and called it Gentry's Hotel. He became the postmaster. In 1895, Gentry sold his property and headed for a mining claim near Coulterville. He had stayed in Fowler long enough to see the town grow into a real community and to become a legend in the history of that city.

Although John S. Gentry was the first man to live at Fowler Switch, there were others who had come before him and had been associated with the area around Fowler. In the 1860s, Frank Dusy grazed his fifteen thousand head of sheep on land between Fresno and the Kings River. He and William Coolidge built sheep-shearing pens at the switch. In 1874, a sea captain named C. H. Norris arrived in the Fowler area, started raising sheep, and built a large home north of Armstrong and Adams avenues, part of which still stands. After two years he returned to the sea. In 1884, he came back to Fowler and began planting vines and trees.

In 1881, the first real farm in the Fowler area was established by Amos Harris. Born in New York, Harris came west to Placer and Nevada counties in 1851 to mine for gold. His mining efforts proved to be very successful. He left the gold fields, taking a small fortune with him, and went to Michigan, where he worked in the mercantile business for three years. He met Antoinette Pelham, whom he married in 1859. In 1874, they came west to northern California and, in 1881, settled in the Fowler area. Antoinette, disappointed when she saw the barrenness of the land—with only a sheep-shearing camp and John Gentry's turkeys running about—pledged to make their portion of this desert bloom. She shared her vision with all who came to her door and lived to see her vision realized. Amos Harris planted their farm in raisin grapes, orchards, and alfalfa. Since their home was the only one between the railroad and Selma, it became a community gathering place. Both Amos and Antoinette played an active part in the development of Fowler. He served as school director. She was a charter member and president of the Fowler Improvement Association. She started the first Sunday school in Fowler.

By the end of 1881, the C. K. Kirby and the C. L. Walter families had settled in Fowler. In 1882, the Southern Pacific depot was built and a town site was laid out. The growth of Fowler had truly begun.

Fowler's
Merced Street
in 1912.

*The Image
Group from
the Laval
Historical
Collection.*

John Gentry's saloon was Fowler's first business. As in most valley towns, satisfying one's thirst, especially in the hot summer, was a number one priority. However, the next settlers who came to Fowler had different priorities. Most of them were churchgoing folks and did not approve of beverages that contained alcohol. The owners of the Grand Hotel were persuaded to close their bar in 1896 by the "dry" proponents in the town.

When the citizens of Fowler began discussing incorporating their town in 1908, the major issue was the "wet" and "dry" argument. Those supporting the saloon interests, called the Anti-Progressive Party, teamed up on one side; those advocating closing the saloons, the Progressive Party, on the other. The motto of the Progressive Party was, "Incorporate with No Saloons."

On March 25, 1908, the first meeting was held to discuss incorporation. Only those who wanted to close the saloons appeared at the meeting. A vote was taken, which was unanimous, to appoint Fred Nelson, Roy Palmer, and Amos Harris as a committee whose responsibility it would be to fix boundaries.

The saloon interests showed up at the next meeting held on April 4. Then a petition was circulated and presented to the board of supervisors on May 4. Enough signatures had been obtained, and the supervisors granted the community the right to hold an election for incorporation. At a meeting on May 18, the Progressive Party managed to nominate five trustees and close the nominations before the Anti-Progressives had an opportunity to nominate anyone from their side. Now the only recourse for the "antis" was to defeat incorporation. The campaign was heated. On election day, May 26, 1908, 97 percent of the voters in Fowler went to the polls. Incorporation passed. Two weeks later the new board of trustees outlawed the sale of liquor in Fowler. It was not until the election of June 20, 1933, that voters narrowly approved the sale of 3.2 percent beer.

Fowler's First Mayor

The first mayor of Fowler, Fred Nelson, was born August 8, 1866, in Utica, New York, the son of Danish immigrants. The family moved to Iowa and then to Minnesota, where he received his education. When he was nineteen, he came west to California following a brother who had settled in Oleander, just south of Fresno, the year before. Nelson worked on several ranches and then rented the 440-acre D. W. Parkhurst vineyard and orchard. He ran that operation for four years. In 1896, he married Mattie Donahoo and purchased ten acres of the Parkhurst holdings. Here, the young couple began their married life.

In addition to running the ranch, Nelson built a packing house where raisin, peaches, and pears were packed and shipped. As his success grew, he bought the Kutner warehouse in Fowler. Paul H. Hutchinson became his partner in the Fowler Fruit Company. Later, Nelson would become a stockholder in the California Associated Raisin Company and the California Peach Growers, Inc.

Nelson played a leading role in the incorporation movement in Fowler. He led the forces to keep the future city "dry," and won a place on the board of trustees. The city of Fowler was incorporated in 1908. Nelson was elected president of the board of trustees, making him the mayor of the new city. Laws were passed to ensure that no alcoholic beverages would be served inside the city limits. A humorous sidelight to this was recounted by a friend of Mr. Nelson's, Truman Runciman. After the huge, festive celebration of the vote to ratify Fowler's incorporation, Nelson and Runciman drove to Fresno. As soon as they arrived, Nelson asked Runciman if he'd like to go have a beer!

Mr. Nelson organized the Fowler National Bank in 1912 and, later, served as president of the First National Bank of Fowler. Mr. and Mrs. Nelson were active leaders in the Fowler community. They were instrumental in such projects as the construction of the United Presbyterian Church. After the Nelsons moved to Fresno in 1916, he continued to invest in farm properties not only near Fowler, but in other parts of Fresno County as well. Although his contributions to agriculture are numerous, it is for his role as Fowler's first mayor that Fred Nelson will be remembered.

A Brave Dog Named Dinkey

The naming of cities, rivers and mountains is a serious business. Often names are given to honor a person, but, in the case of one stream in the Sierra, the honoree was a dog. It came about in this manner.

Frank Dusy, one of our valley's earliest sheepmen and mountaineers, discovered Tehipite Valley in 1869. He always traveled through the mountains with his camera and took the earliest existing photos of the valley and the Sierra. One day, Dusy, accompanied by his little black-and-white dog, Dinkey, was returning from Tehipite Valley. He was walking along the bank of a stream and came face-to-face with a very large bear. Startled, he put his rifle to his shoulder and aimed it at the bear. He didn't aim as well as he should, however, and, instead of killing the bear, he only wounded him.

The bear became enraged and charged at Dusy. Dusy slipped and fell. The bear lunged over him, missing him, but only by inches.

In the excitement of the moment Dusy dropped his rifle. Now, frantic to find it, he searched for it, all the while thinking that the ferocious bear was probably going to kill him. The bear turned around and faced Dusy. He started to charge the man when Dinkey, seeing his master threatened, jumped into the fray. Dinkey, who had very sharp teeth, sunk them right into the bear's nose and held on for dear life. The bear was distracted by this long enough to give Dusy time to find his rife, pick it up, reload it, and fire one more time. This time Dusy took careful aim and killed the bear with one shot.

Our story does not end here. Sadly, before Dusy took that final shot, the bear lashed out at the dog. With one large paw, he pushed the dog away from him. His sharp claws tore the dog's side wide open. The poor animal crept over to Dusy and died in his weeping master's arms. Dusy named the mountain stream Dinkey Creek in honor of the brave dog who saved his life. Today, not only the creek, but a section of the Sierra called Dinkey Creek bear his name.

The Mason Building

During the era from 1913 to the mid-1920s, the downtown skyline of Fresno changed dramatically. A number of important tall office buildings were constructed. The skyline would remain relatively unchanged until the Del Webb Center was built more than thirty years later.

On March 1, 1918, an article appeared in the *Fresno Morning Republican* announcing the completion of the Mason Building on J (now Fulton) Street between Mariposa and Tulare streets. This modern office building was replacing the old Mason Block that had been built during the early years of the city. Designed by architect Eugene Mathewson, the new six-story structure was built of reinforced concrete faced with brick. Decorative terra cotta panels extended from the cornice to the fifth floor.

The interior of the building featured bitulithic floors and native oak. The most modern materials were used. Instead of marble, the wainscoting in the stairways and halls was composed of vitrolite, a material that was considered superior because it was not porous and, therefore, more sanitary. No moldings were used. All the woodwork was plain with doors that were flush to the wall and hung on invisible hinges. This was quite a departure from the ornate trims and moldings of turn-of-the-century architecture. Indirect lighting systems were used throughout the structure. Ice water poured from the drinking fountains on each floor. One very modern feature was the three-speed elevators. The Mason Building was only the third building in California to have them.

The owner of this modern addition to Fresno's main street was Mrs. F. E. Palmer of London, England. Her $200,000 investment seems reasonable by contemporary standards, but was a major expenditure in 1918. Unfortunately, she died only a few days after completion of the structure and, therefore, was never to see the building.

A Calaboose for Grub Gulch

In the early history of our valley, every community, big or small, had two essential buildings—a saloon and a jail. Indeed, it seemed the saloon made it necessary to have the jail. In many towns the jail had another, and perhaps, more romantic sounding name—the calaboose. Our story centers around the calaboose in Grub Gulch, one of the gold mining communities in the part of Fresno County that is today Madera County.

Grub Gulch had never had a calaboose. They had never needed one. If someone committed a serious crime they just hanged him. Those who committed lesser crimes were flogged or banished. These were simple solutions and quite effective. Lawbreakers stayed away from Grub Gulch. Texas Flat, a mining camp just over the hill, built a very fine calaboose. Its residents made fun of Grub Gulchers because they lacked one.

The Grub Gulchers decided they had better build a calaboose. They built the finest one they could. It was ten feet square and ten feet high. Ten-inch logs of hard oak comprised the walls—high in one of the walls was a window with iron bars an inch thick. The massive door had a big padlock on the outside. The Gulchers made sure that it was escape proof. They now had their calaboose—all they needed was a tenant.

Two days later Pete Timmons and Hank Brascomb were playing poker. An argument ensued. Pete shot Hank to death. They were about to hang Pete when they remember they had a calaboose. They confined Pete inside. Pete was not pleased and remembered that, even though they had taken his gun, he still had a knife. Standing on the one stool in the calaboose, he found he could reach the window. After four hours, he managed to pry two of the iron bars loose, but realized that the window was too small for him to crawl through. Exhausted, he leaned against the door. It flew open. In their eagerness to use their new facility, the Grub Gulchers had forgotten to lock the door.

When one leaves the town of Mariposa and travels south and west on Highway 49, the road known as the "Golden Chain," one will see beautiful country and will travel through places with colorful names like Mormon Bar, Usona, and Nipinnawasee. In the winters of 1849 and 1850, a group of Mormons camped at the place called Mormon Bar. It soon became a big mining camp. The name Usona is formed from the first letters of United States of North America. Nipinnawasee is an Indian word that means "Home of the Deer."

One settlement along the road has a name that so evokes the Gold Rush era that one would assume there is quite a tale behind it. And so there is.

Just west of Mormon Bar was another mining camp. Not long after gold was discovered there a fellow named Texas Pete Connors, who had left Texas just ahead of the law, arrived at the camp. He got into a poker game. He lost everything, including his horse. Everyone thought Pete was broke, but he still managed to have enough gold dust to buy food and whiskey at Tom Regen's saloon. Everyone was wondering where he got the gold. They soon found out. A miner found Pete in his tent stealing his gold.

With no horse, Pete had to head out on foot for the high mountains, running as fast as he could. His high-heeled boots were made for stirrups, not for walking. He was found only two miles from camp, sitting on a stump massaging his sore, blistered feet. He was brought back to camp, where he was tried and convicted. They took him to the nearest tree. His last wish was to die with his boots off. His feet were so swollen neither he nor anyone else could pull them off. The camp handyman came to the rescue with a contraption that consisted of a raised thick plank with a deep notch at one end. Pete put one boot into the notch, some of the men pulled, and the boot came off. The other one followed suit. After the rope was thrown over the tree limb and Pete was sent to his reward, someone asked what the contraption was. "A bootjack," said the handyman. The name stuck, and today Bootjack is still a settlement on the picturesque Golden Chain as it winds through Mariposa County.

The early history of our valley records the names of several women who made major contributions to the agricultural development of Fresno County. In 1878, four teachers, Lucy Hatch, Minnie F. Austin, Julia B. Short, and E. A. Cleveland, purchased a hundred acres that they developed into the Hedge Row Vineyards. They were true pioneers in the raisin industry. In the 1880s, Minna Eshelman, who was an authority on dairy cattle, pioneered in using scientific methods to raise the standards of cleanliness in the processing of dairy products on her Minnewawa Ranch. Her contemporary, Nellie Boyd, who was the first woman to manage her own West Coast theatrical touring company, settled in the Central California Colony and ran her own vineyard operation.

From those early years until the present time, hundreds of women have been involved in our valley's agriculture. Whether working side by side with their husbands or running their own ranching operation, they all played an important role in the number one industry in our valley. A common thread runs through the lives of all these women—love of family, of community, of the farm lifestyle, and of the soil of our valley that produces such an abundant variety of crops.

Every year five women who have roots in agriculture are honored for their important contributions to their communities. They are selected from the counties of our Central Valley. The awards are presented by the Common Threads Committee that works in partnership with the California Agricultural Educational Foundation-Templeton and California State University, Fresno, School of Agricultural Sciences and Technology, and the Ag One Foundation.

The 1999 awards honor Muriel Smittcamp of Clovis, Violet Jensen of Fresno, Jane Logolusa Bautista of Madera, Geneva Shannon of Visalia, and Micki Parker of Le Grand. The common thread they share with the pioneer women of our valley's agriculture is one of the important legacies of our valley.

Jacob Franklin Niswander

Jacob Franklin Niswander was born at Staunton, Virginia, in November 1871. His father, Issac, was a planter who fought in a Virginia regiment during the Civil War. Jacob was the fifth eldest in a family of nine children. When he was seventeen, Jacob came west to California, arriving in Fresno in 1889. To earn a living, he found work in the grain fields of the valley, driving the big teams of horses and mules. He saved his money and, after three years, returned to Virginia and enrolled in Bridgewater College. When he completed his studies, he returned to Fresno to a job with the Malaga Cooperative Packing Association. In six years time, he moved up the corporate ladder and purchased the company. The business was still small, but he worked to increase the volume of trade. He built it into a larger operation and bought another plant at Del Rey. In 1914, he sold them both to the California Associated Raisin Company.

During these years, he was engaged in farming, mostly orchards and vineyards. He continued to add to his acreage, eventually owning three ranches: one in Fresno, one in Madera County, and one in Clovis. Niswander firmly believed that the only way to successfully market vineyard and orchard products was through cooperation. He became a leader in the organization of the California Peach Growers, Inc., in 1915. He continued to serve the co-operative as vice-president and general manager. Twenty-six different plants were operated under the company—each one equipped for grading, processing, packing, and shipping. From these plants, dried peaches were shipped throughout the United States and to Canada, South America, and other foreign markets.

Jacob Niswander married Eula Shipp in 1901. They had four children. An active Rotarian and member of the Sequoia Club, Jacob Niswander will be remembered for the important role he played in the development of Fresno County's peach industry.

James Cash Penney Comes to Town

On March 17, 1952, an important figure in the world of American business was in Fresno to speak to the Rotary and Kiwanis clubs. The Rotary club met at the Hotel Californian, and the Kiwanis Club met at the Sequoia Hotel. His topics were, "Responsibility, The American Way," and "Looking Ahead." The club members were anxiously awaiting his talks because his story was the stuff of legend. The employees in his local store were also excited to meet him. It was the fiftieth anniversary of the founding of his very first store, and James Cash Penney was in Fresno as part of the celebration of this event.

In April 1902, J. C. Penney and his wife and baby arrived in the small town of Kemmerer, Wyoming. He had five hundred dollars in his pocket and a dream in his heart. He opened a little store and moved his family into the attic room above it. Here, with a table and boxes from the store for furniture, they made their home. He and his wife, with the baby at their side, worked long hours in the store. A second child was born who was put to sleep on the counter, wrapped in a blanket

The little store prospered, and soon they moved into a small house nearby. Not long afterward a second store was opened, then a third store, then a fourth, and a fifth, as one by one Penney opened stores across the country. In 1920, the first J.C. Penney store opened in Fresno at 959 Fulton Street.

Penney was not only a successful merchant, but a philosopher as well. He operated his business on the Christian principle of the Golden Rule. He was a dedicated Rotarian and believed in the Rotarian principle of service above self. He visited Rotary founder Paul Harris shortly before Harris died. The two men shared their experiences. That visit made a lasting impression on Penney.

By the time James Cash Penney visited Fresno in 1952, his empire included 1,617 stores nationwide. Penney, however, never forgot his humble beginnings. He spent two afternoons of his visit behind the counter of his Fresno store, waiting on customers just as he had in those days long ago in Kemmerer, Wyoming.

Billy Caruthers

The man for whom Caruthers was named was born on a farm in Vermont in 1840. As a young man William "Billy" Caruthers came west to California and settled in the area called Liberty near present-day Riverdale. He purchased three and one quarter sections of land from the state of California. Because it was considered desert land, he had to pay only a dollar and a quarter per acre. Until about 1888 he raised sheep on this land, then he switched to grain farming and cattle raising. He introduced Australian white wheat into the valley. He exhibited it at the Chicago Exposition in 1893 and took the gold medal. He married Ellen Wilson, a daughter of "Tobacco" Wilson, a pioneer cattleman in Wildflower, a community about ten miles away.

In 1888, the Southern Pacific Railroad began grading a line from Kerman to points south. Billy Caruthers realized the railroad would provide a shipping point for him and other grain farmers in the area. He offered the railroad a half-section of his land and suggested they locate a station and lay out a town site on the property. Town lots could be sold. In return, the railroad would give him half of the proceeds from the sale of the land and name the town Caruthers. The railroad owners accepted the deal and sent John Mills to be the first agent. News of the railroad's decision prompted two grain companies to locate their warehouses at the new town site. Valley Lumber Company of Fresno opened a branch store there also.

In the late 1880s a lawsuit was brought against Billy Caruthers that he lost. The court costs and attorney's fees forced him to mortgage his lands. He continued farming on his remaining property until the mid-1890s, when a depression forced him to sign his property over to O. J. Woodward of Fresno and to the San Francisco Savings Bank, who both held portions of the mortgage. Caruthers moved to Hanford, where he died in 1911 at age seventy-one.

A genial, good-looking man with strong Republican views, Billy Caruthers will long be remembered in the legends of our valley.

A street corner in Caruthers in 1918.
The Image Group from the Laval Historical Collection.

A Rich Lineage of Spanish California

As we Fresnans go about the hustle and bustle of everyday life, we don't often think about the California of two hundred years ago. The romance of Spanish California and the surnames that evoke that time—Pico, deAnza, Vallejo, Portola—all seem far away from our modern reality. For some Fresnans it is not removed from today's modern world at all—for them it is ever-present. For them it is all about their family.

The late Robert Vallejo Emparan was the Fresno County deputy agricultural commissioner for twenty-five years. He served his community well and was highly respected. What many did not know was that he had a lineage that, in itself, depicted the rich tapestry of Spanish California.

Of all the Spanish Californians in our history, no one stands taller than Don Mariano Guadalupe Vallejo, a general in the Mexican Army. He established a large rancho and hacienda in the Sonoma area and was active in governmental matters during the Mexican and American periods. He founded the town of Vallejo. His father was a member of the military guard that accompanied Father Serra into California. His great-great grandfather, Don Pedro Vallejo, was the viceroy of New Spain. Don Pedro's brother was the admiral of the ship that brought Columbus back to Spain in irons.

The first settlement on the shores of San Francisco Bay was founded by Juan Bautista deAnza in 1776. It had been a hard trip from Northern Mexico for the expedition, but it was made easier by the presence of a young widow named Dona Maria Feliciana Arballo y Gutierres who sang, danced, and told risqué stories each evening, lifting everyone's spirits. She became known as the "singing, dancing, laughing girl" of the de Anza expedition. At Mission San Gabriel she married Juan Lopez. Their granddaughter, Francisca, married General Mariano Vallejo. The Vallejos' daughter, Luisa, married Mexican Counsel Ricardo Emparan. They were the grandparents of Fresnan Robert Vallejo Emparan. And thus the rich tapestry was woven, linking the colorful era of Spanish California with twentieth-century Fresno.

A Visionary Project

High on a hill near Pincushion Mountain, in the foothills of the Sierra northeast of Fresno, a restoration miracle is taking place. Here, an important part of the tangible early history of our county—pieces that were thought gone forever—is being reassembled. It is a task undertaken by the Table Mountain Rancheria Band of Indians—the descendants of the Western Mono and Chukchansi Yokuts who have inhabited this area for thousands of years. It is their dream to create a Tribal Cultural Center in some of the historic buildings of Fort Miller where the story of the Native Americans of the area, the story of Fort Miller, and the story of the ranching period, when the Hart and McKenzie families lived in the buildings, can be told.

The Fort Miller Blockhouse was moved to Roeding Park in 1944 and was administered as a museum by the Fresno City and County Historical Society for many years until a lack of money to do needed restoration work forced the organization to close it. In the early to mid-1940s, when Friant Dam was being built, the McKenzie family, who had owned the Fort Miller property, dismantled the remaining buildings and stored them in a barn on high ground. There they stayed until 1990, when Mary McKenzie died. In the early 1990s, after a few items from the barn were removed, the remainder were offered at auction. The items that remained were vandalized.

In 1997, Bud Olsen, president of the Eastern Fresno County Historical Society, told Robert Pennell, cultural resources manager for Table Mountain Rancheria, the story about the barn and its contents. The Rancheria invited all those who had purchased items from the barn at auction to a meeting and asked them to return the items they had purchased so they could be part of the restoration project they envisioned. Miraculously, 65-70 percent of the materials were donated or sold back at cost. In our next tale of the valley, the story of the project, itself, will be told.

A Restoration Miracle in the Foothills

The project now underway by the Table Mountain Rancheria Band of Indians, the descendants of the Western Mono and Chukchansi Yokuts who have inhabited the foothill area for thousands of years, will create a Tribal Cultural Center in three restored historic buildings from Fort Miller.

The McKenzie family, who owned the site for many years, commissioned Pop Laval to take photographs of the buildings while they were still intact. Using these photos and dimensions of two of the buildings that the McKenzies had documented, the project began. The Rancheria's public works department and Robert Pennell, cultural resources manager for the Rancheria, did all the archaeology work. Up to 75 percent of the materials from the original buildings is being used. The rest of the needed material will be replicated. Two of the buildings were built of adobe. Some of the bricks had disintegrated. When possible, the material from these was mixed in with new material. The remaining adobe bricks were made the exact color and size the originals had been. Hans Sumpf Company of Madera did this part of the project. Scott Davison of local architectural firm LSBK Design is creating the reconstruction plans.

The blockhouse has been placed on a new stone foundation. The original logs still make up the walls of the building. The windows, doors, and roof are from the 1944 restoration. The officers' quarters is 75 percent complete with a replicated quartzite foundation and its original sashes, mantels, and door frames. The main house will be restored on a site adjacent to it. These two buildings will have temperature and humidity control and will be archivally sound—meeting the standards set by the Smithsonian Institute's Museum of Natural History. The commanding officers' quarters will be a stabilized ruin. To this will be added a visitor's center.

These buildings will make up the Tribal Cultural Center. They will contain exhibits which tell about the culture and history of the Native Americans of Table Mountain Rancheria, the history of Fort Miller, and the ranching period of the fort. A Tribal Cultural Park, landscaped with plants used in basketry, will be part of the center. An interesting historic irony may also be apparent in this project. The very buildings that were built to protect the first white settlers from the local Indians are now on tribal land. After this careful and thoughtful restoration, they will tell an important part of the history of our valley.

A Pre-Election Celebration

The year was 1884. It was September—just two months before the presidential election that would decide whether Republican candidate James G. Blaine or Democrat Grover Cleveland would be the next president of the United States. The town of Madera was founded when Republican Ulysses S. Grant was president. Since that time, Republicans continued to hold that office. It was almost more than staunch Madera Democrat, Captain Russel Mace, could tolerate. Mace decided that this election was going to be different. As a member of the county central committee, he was going to do what he could to see that Maderans supported Cleveland. "Let's have a pre-election victory party," he thought, "and invite not only the whole town, but Fresnans as well."

This news was heaven-sent to heavily Democratic Fresno. They could hardly wait to attend. However, having chartered only one car on the train to Madera, the one hundred and fifty attendees found themselves in extremely tight quarters—it was so crowded that some of their number found themselves riding in the caboose and in platform cars filled with wheat. This discomfort was forgotten when they reached Madera. Captain Mace was at the station to meet them. A brass band led the way to Mace's Yosemite Hotel, where they were joined by Madera Democrats. A turkey dinner, ample wine, and after-dinner cigars preceded the main speaker of the evening, Henry St. John Dixon, a Southerner who had been one of the settlers of the Alabama Colony and an ardent supporter of the Democratic cause. Bonfires and fireworks added to the festivities, delighting the crowds of Maderans who gathered outside the hotel.

Two months later, the election took place. Grover Cleveland won. A delighted Captain Mace could add another story to his repertoire and go down in history as one of the more successful prognosticators in the history of our valley.

The Foothill Town of O'Neals

For the traveler in search of a little tranquility—a peaceful break from the hectic pace of twentieth-century life—a driving trip into the foothills of Madera County can provide just such a respite. Leaving Fresno on Highway 41 and traveling north, the road crosses the San Joaquin River, curves, and then forms a straight-away that heads for the foothills of Madera County—passing Little Table Mountain to the east. When the ascent from the valley floor begins, marvelous vistas present themselves. Breathtaking views of the Sierra make the traveler forget all about the stresses of work. A right turn off Highway 41 onto Road 200 will take the traveler to North Fork and, ultimately, to Bass Lake. First, however, our traveler will enter Spring Valley and a small foothill community that is deeply rooted in the past—the town of O'Neals.

In 1866, Captain Russell Perry Mace married his second wife, Mrs. Jennie Cunningham Gilmore. They moved to Spring Valley which, during the Gold Rush, had been a real crossroads. Here they built a two-room home. Mace raised cattle, placer-mined, and ran a general merchandise store. In 1874, Mace and his wife left the area and moved to Borden.

Four years later, Charles O'Neal and his wife, Bettie, purchased Mace's holdings. They also operated a small hotel. When a post office was established on October 4, 1887, he was named postmaster. The village took his name—O'Neals. A school was built in 1889 to serve the fifty families in the area.

O'Neals became a hub for five stage lines that were owned and operated by Herman Bigelow. It was the main depot on the runs to Sugar Pine, Bass Lake, and North Fork from a number of valley locations. The stages hauled both freight and passengers. Relay stations were located along the runs to provide fresh horses when they were needed. O'Neals was an important center.

Today, O'Neals is primarily a cattle raising area, well off the tourist path. For the traveler passing through, it does provide a pretty vista or two—a nice escape from the frantic pace of city life.

In the early 1860s, a miner named Milton Brown built a cabin on the bank of the north fork of the San Joaquin River. Today, the area would be called the north fork of Willow Creek. His land was at the end of a wagon road traveled by shepherds and cowherds when they took their stock up the mountains into the summer pastures. They usually left their wagons and extra supplies with Brown and would return periodically to restock. They began to call the area Brown's Place. Other larger ranchers, including Miller and Lux, used the road by Brown's cabin because the snow in that area was usually gone a month earlier than the northern trail they had been using.

In the mid-1870s, a store and several saloons were built. There were enough people in the area by this time for an election precinct to be set up. The precincts in that area are still called Brown's today. In 1877, C. E. Stribbens extended the road deeper into the mountains to Alder Creek. He opened a store that sold "a few groceries, some cheap calico, and lots of whiskey." Because of the amount of whiskey sold, the Indians changed the name of Alder Creek to Whiskey Creek.

In 1880, C. M. Peckinpah and his six sons arrived in the area. They built a sawmill on the mountain that today still bears their name. Two years later, the North Fork Lumber Company built a sawmill that provided many jobs. On December 18, 1888, largely through the efforts of the lumber company, a post office was established in the company's store and the town became officially known as North Fork.

The United States Forest Service was formed in 1893, and, in 1905, established its local headquarters in North Fork. North Fork's historic role as a gateway to the mountains is as true for the tourists of today as it was for the shepherds of the 1860s.

A Stage Bound for Yosemite

The morning of May 4, 1879, dawned bright and beautiful. It was an exciting day for the residents of Fresno Flats (today Oakhurst). Everyone was busily setting homes and businesses in order and preparing for the celebration of a lifetime. Everyone was so excited that they could hardly believe this day had finally arrived.

A huge American flag was hung over the main road. By noon, all the citizens of the town had gathered near Hunt's Hotel to await the long anticipated moment when the very first stagecoach bringing travelers to Yosemite was due to arrive. The new Yosemite Road had been finished through their town one month earlier, and now the first tourists were arriving. The whole town had prepared a welcome fit for a king!

Everyone was waiting, but the stage did not come. Tensions began to build. Finally, at 2:30 in the afternoon, someone shouted, "Here it comes!" And come along it did—with the driver cracking his whip as the team of horses drove up the hill, under the American flag, and came to a stop in front of Hunt's Hotel. Henry Washburn, owner and manager of the Yosemite Stage and Turnpike Company, jumped down from the top of the stagecoach. The stage was late, he said, because the road was "heavy and not yet settled." Gunshots rang out as the eleven travelers descended from the stage. Now the celebration began in earnest. The crowd rushed forward, surrounding the stage and its passengers, who somehow managed to get inside the hotel for their dinner. Outside, the festivities went on with some drinking among the celebrants. A couple of brawls were played out by a few of the men in the community who decided to mix fisticuffs with their spirits.

The tourists came out to board the stage for the remainder of their trip. They were sent on their way like heroes and heroines. Over the years, thousands of tourists would wend their way through Oakhurst bound for Yosemite, but the memory of that May 4 would stand out above all others in the history of Fresno Flats.

Fred M. Roessler

The 1914 home of Fred M. Roessler. The Greek Revival style residence was built by contractor Hans Hansen who built many other homes in the area.
Author's photo.

One early resident of Fresno County, Fred M. Roessler, was born in St. Martin, Rheinish Bavaria, Germany, on August 24, 1857. His father was a viticulturist. He worked in his father's vineyard after school on Wednesday and Saturday afternoons. Under his father's direction, he learned the care of the vineyards and the method of pruning vines.

When he completed his education, he had a strong desire to see the world so he left home and boarded a ship bound for New York City. He arrived in 1873 and enlisted in the *St. Mary's*, a nautical school ship where he studied navigation. Having completed the course, he shipped out from Boston on the ship *Lathley Rich,* traveling around the Cape of Good Hope to ports of call throughout the Orient.

In 1874, he returned to the United States—first to San Francisco, then to Monterey, and eventually to Fresno County, where he settled in 1879. The lure of cheap land brought him to the Central Valley. He purchased forty acres of improved land for $1,600. He gradually purchased surrounding land until he owned 180 acres.

This formed the nucleus of a large vineyard of wine grapes. In 1892, he began making wine commercially and, in 1893, he built his first winery. Later, he built a larger winery with a capacity of half a million gallons. He built a large home with a park that was filled with ornamental and shade trees. It became a showplace of the area.

On May 3, 1890, Fred Roessler married Sina Johnson. Their marriage was blessed with three children: Elsie, Alfred, and George, who would, after his father's death, manage the family's business. They also had an adopted son, Ludvig.

During his lifetime, Fred Roessler invested in business property downtown and owned thirty acres at the corner of Cedar and Shields avenues. Today, his home still stands and is the administration building for the California Christian College. The Roessler Winery building is still part of the Discovery Center complex on Winery Avenue.

Paymaster Hanford Picks a Town's Location

There is a city about forty miles south and west of Fresno that came into existence in 1876. It is not on the direct line the Central and Southern Pacific Railroad Corporation took south through the valley, but is on a spur line that was laid in a westward pattern from Goshen. The line was intended to extend clear to the ocean, so that agricultural products could be shipped directly to the coast without having to go first to San Francisco or Los Angeles.

The United States government gave grants of land to the railroad on which they laid their rail beds. The railroad's paymaster handled the necessary details of buying, selling, and leasing these lands in addition to paying wages. The man who filled this position was originally from New York. In 1852, he moved west to California and became a friend of Leland Stanford, one of the railroad owners. He was offered the position of paymaster in 1869. He handled his job expertly, not misplacing so much as a penny during his years of service.

As a reward for his dedication and loyalty, his bosses gave him the honor of selecting a location for a town along the new spur rail line. He was told the new town would be named for him.

He chose the site carefully. It would be located just thirteen miles west of Goshen. So the town of Hanford was born—named for James Madison Hanford. He was proud of the town that bore his name and visited it often, but it was never his home. At the time of his death, in 1911, he was living in Oakland.

The drug store housed the business of J. T. Baker. Baker attended the town's first land auction and bought lots on Sixth Street. Here, he opened the first store.
Courtesy Hanford Carnegie Museum, Inc.

One of Hanford's most historical and interesting places to visit dates back to the 1880s. When the city was founded, in 1877, by the Central Pacific Railroad, many Chinese who had helped build the railroad decided to make their home in the new town. Other settlers from the region around Canton, China, arrived in Hanford. The area where many of them settled was called Chinatown. A part of that neighborhood still exists and is called China Alley.

The area was originally called Young Chow Alley because Young Chow owned a lot of the property on the alley. History does not record how or why the transaction took place, but the properties owned by Young Chow were transferred to Sue Chung Kee. The alley was then called Sue Chung Kee Alley. After his death it became known as China Alley.

Kee's son, whose name was Y. T. Sue, helped to establish the Chinese Center of Knowledge, a one-room school for children of all ages who went there five afternoons a week, after attending public school, and on Saturdays, to study Chinese language, customs, and culture.

A gentleman named Gong Ting Shu came to Hanford in 1883, settling one block from China Alley. He made and served noodles to residents of the area in the basement of his home. He later moved to a building on China Alley and opened a restaurant. Today, the same building and the adjoining ones house the five-star Imperial Dynasty Restaurant, still owned by his family—the Wing family.

China Alley was a city within a city. Among the businesses represented were a barber shop, grocery store, herbalist, tobacco shop, gambling house, the Sam Yup Association, and several restaurants. Today, the buildings on historic China Alley still stand. Many of them have been restored. A visit to this historic neighborhood transports the visitor to another and, perhaps, more colorful time in the history of the charming town of Hanford.

One of the most exotic and historic buildings in Hanford is the Taoist Temple. Located on China Alley, the building was constructed of bricks made here in 1893. It was built by early settlers who came from three regions near Canton, China. They formed the Sam Yup Association. The purpose of their new building was to provide housing for recently arrived immigrants from China on the first floor and to serve their spiritual needs in the temple on the second floor. Many years later, the first floor served as housing for senior citizens of the Chinese community.

Today, the first floor of the building is a museum. The first room you enter contains small exhibits and a gift shop. The other rooms have different themes. One features furniture from the herb store that used to exist on China Alley. Another has a kitchen theme. Here, donated items, including a snuff slicer, a small kerosene stove, and kitchen utensils, can be seen. The third room contains lottery items and mahjong sets from the gambling houses.

When you enter the temple on the second floor, you not only step into another world visually, but feel a sense of time suspended—the feeling of being in the presence of an ancient culture, yet one that transcends the modern world as well. Original lanterns hang from the ceiling. On one wall are the eight immortals, or patron saints, hand-carved out of cherry wood burl. Eight large ceremonial staves, tipped with pewter symbols of each immortal, line another wall. The main altar is dedicated to Kuan Kung, a hero who lived in the second century A.D., and who was later canonized.

In one corner is a small altar where joss sticks—sticks of incense—may be lighted. The petitioner lights the joss sticks and kowtows, or bows, before the altar and prays. Then he may make an offering. Thin papers representing clothing or money can be lighted and placed in an octagonal ceremonial incinerator—the smoke carries the offerings to heaven. Teak wood and marble chairs, original lanterns, moon-shaped fortune telling blocks, candelabras, and embroideries grace the room and tables.

When you leave, it is with a deeper appreciation for the culture the Chinese pioneers brought to our Valley.

The first Chinese settlers came to Hanford in the early 1880s. They worked in the rich farm lands of our valley, built homes and opened businesses. They first settled in a section of Hanford near the railroad, around Fifth and Sixth streets. Later they moved to the eastern end of Seventh Street. A portion of this area later became known as China Alley.

In the early 1900s, a school opened in the basement of the Sue Chung Kee building on China Alley. The teacher was herbalist Y. T. Sue. Later, the school was relocated to a room in the Taoist Temple building.

Members of the Chinese community decided that they wanted to build a school building. After eight years, they managed to raise ten thousand dollars. The building was built. It consisted of one large room that housed not only the classroom, but also a library, a small kitchen, and a place for the teacher to sleep. The cornerstone was laid during a special ceremony on April 26, 1922. The school continued to be supported by donations from the Chinese community.

The school, which was called the Chinese Center of Knowledge, was dedicated at a ceremony held on December 28, 1922. The event was enhanced by the presence of the Chinese San Francisco Consul General Dr. Kollang Yih and his wife. The school was richly decorated with Chinese and American flags, lanterns, crepe paper, and fresh flowers for the occasion.

In 1967, the building was donated to the City of Hanford by the Chinese community to be used by a theater group called the Kings Players. The building has been modified for its new use as a theater, but Chinese motifs have been used as well. Theater-goers pass through a moon door to enter the building and large Chinese characters adorn the proscenium arch. The theater is used throughout the year and provides entertainment as well as an important piece of history for the people of Hanford.

The Washington Irrigated Colony

In 1878, three men, Wendell Easton, J. P. Whitney, and Allen T. Covell organized the Washington Irrigated Colony on eleven sections (7,040 acres) of land south and southwest of the Central California Colony. They spent almost twenty-five thousand dollars advertising lots in their new venture. Easton traveled to Germany, Sweden, and Australia, trying to attract settlers to the area. Not one person bought land. Easton was not discouraged. He brought people from San Francisco by train. Again, no buyers. He chartered another train. This time his luck changed. Five of the eleven sections sold. This represented 385 farms. Soon more parcels sold. The colony was launched.

The organizers of the colony purchased water rights from the Fresno Irrigation and Canal Company. Each farm was guaranteed water. Homes were built. Vineyards and orchards were laid out. Teams of horses and stock animals were well fed—the colony produced rich fields of alfalfa. The colony soon had a surplus of milk. In 1880, Easton built a cheese factory on Cherry Avenue. It was a cooperative venture with settlers from both the Washington and the Central California colonies operating it. "Washington Colony Cheese" was sold to the public and became a source of pride to the colonists.

Allen T. Covell laid out the plan for a town. Blocks 360 feet square were intersected with streets. Two blocks were set aside for a school and a town hall. Two blocks were to be a public park—today, it is the Easton Park. Covell was the first resident of the new town that was named for him. Easton continued to develop and bring improvements to the colony lands surrounding the town. At some point, the settlers began calling the town Easton. Since the town was originally registered as Covell at the Fresno County Courthouse, it is still legally designated on maps and legal documents by that name. A drive down Elm Avenue today takes the traveler through the heart of Easton. The name Washington Colony can still be seen on the cemetery that serves the district—a reminder of the beginnings of this part of Fresno County.

Before the railroad came through the valley and created Fresno Station, the land was a desert—a wilderness of sorts—fit only for grazing animals. No one lived at the spot that would be the site for the new town. The nearest residents were twelve miles away. However, in 1865, William Helm brought his bride and his sheep and settled in this place on 2,560 acres of land he purchased from W. S. Chapman for one dollar an acre. They arrived in July, when the valley heat was uncomfortable by day, but the nights were glorious. The land was excellent pasturage for the sheep and proved to be an excellent investment.

William Helm was born in Durham, Ontario, Canada, on March 9, 1837, the son of Scottish parents. He made his way to California in 1856, at the age of nineteen. He tried his luck in the gold fields, but soon found that unprofitable. He spent the next three years as a butcher in Placer County. He saved his money and decided sheep raising would be a better way to earn a living. He was successful enough to afford a wife. He married Frances Sawyer Newman in 1865 and, with her by his side, ventured into a new life in the San Joaquin Valley.

Helm's initial holdings were just six miles from what is today the center of downtown Fresno. The winter camp for his sheep was on the site of today's Courthouse Park. He was the largest wool grower in Central California, but the nearest market was Stockton. It took three wagons drawn by ten mules twelve days to carry the wool to Stockton. When the railroad came through the valley in 1872, it was a great boon to Helm.

When Fresno Station was established, Helm built a residence in the new town. He continued his stock raising operations and improved and developed his land, building a ditch and bringing water from the Kings River for irrigation.

Over the years Helm added to his land holdings. He built the Helm Block at the corner of J (Fulton) and Fresno streets. He was an organizer and vice-president of the Bank of Central California. He witnessed every step in the development of the agricultural flowering of our valley. His commitment to the Fresno community was unwavering. It continues through his descendants who still call Fresno home.

El Camino Viejo

Modern travelers zipping along Interstate Highway 5 or Highway 33 on our valley's west side probably think they are traveling on rather new north-south routes through California. It might surprise our travelers to know that these are not new routes, but ones that have been in use for hundreds of years.

After the missions were established along California's coast, travelers found that the road linking the missions, called *El Camino Real* or the King's Highway, was a good way to travel because accommodations were provided at the missions and the pueblos that dotted the road. However, there were some travelers who chose an alternate route, an inland road that was faster and was far removed from the watchful eye of the Spanish authorities. The road was called *El Camino Viejo a Los Angeles* which means the Old Road to Los Angeles—a road that followed prehistoric Indian trails. There were no accommodations on this road. Travelers traveled from watering hole to watering hole and slept under the stars.

El Camino Viejo came over the mountains from Los Angeles, then turned west, skirting the base of the Coast Range foothills. When it reached just south of present-day Fresno County, it divided. The western branch kept on its course near the hills, passed near the present-day city of Avenal, and continued north. The eastern branch went east of the Kettleman Hills, then swung north, passing near present-day Riverdale, on to Las Juntas (near Mendota), then turned west and reunited with the western branch. The road continued over the Altamont Pass to what is today east Oakland.

El Camino Viejo was a quicker route than the coastal road, but slow by today's standards. The best time one could make by ox-cart was one mile an hour, traveling through tule swamps and over hot barren plains. The next time you zip along Interstate 5 think of the earlier travelers on that route and be grateful your journey can begin and end on the same day.

In our last tale of the valley, we followed the route of El Camino Viejo, the old road on our valley's west side. Now let us talk about some of the people who traveled its length.

The first travelers were the Indians, who used a series of trails through the area for hundreds of years. Before them, the wild animals of the valley—elk, antelope, bear, and small animals—wandered from water hole to water hole through the foothills and ravines. In the mid-1700s, the old Indian trails were forged into one trail by the early Spanish and Mexican refugees, who used the trail because they could travel between the two major settlements of Rancho San Antonio, the site of present-day east Oakland, and Rancho San Pedro, south of present-day Los Angeles, without attracting the notice of the Spanish authorities. The desperadoes of the period—horse thieves and cattle rustlers—could safely ply their trade along this road.

Legend has it that in 1822, an eloping couple, Ramon Solorzona and his beautiful Chilean bride, traversed the trail in a creaking, wooden-wheeled ox-cart, with the bride's father in hot pursuit. He chased the couple all the way to Fort Ross, but did not catch them.

The padres from the coastal missions and the Spanish military would come through the mountain passes and make raids on Indian villages along El Camino Viejo, taking Indian boys and girls between the ages of seven and fourteen to serve them as house servants or vaqueros.

Later, the Camino was used by sheepmen and cattlemen who drove their herds and took hides and tallow to markets on the coast. Bandits used the road, too. Tiburcio Vasquez and Joaquin Murrieta were familiar sights along the Camino. It was along the Camino at the Arroyo de Cantua that Murrieta allegedly was killed. And, it was along El Camino Viejo that the first settlers arrived in the west side of our valley. The names of these settlers—Kettleman, Kreyenhagen, and Domengine—still live on in the tales of our valley.

Two Wild Towns in the West

In the first half of the nineteenth century, a number of Spanish and Mexican people settled in the west side of present-day Fresno County. The Spanish-speaking people who were born in California called themselves *"Californianos,"* thus setting themselves apart from the immigrants from Mexico. They established a few settlements along the route called El Camino Viejo.

One of these communities was on the San Joaquin River just three miles northeast of present-day Mendota. It was founded around 1800, making it one of the oldest, if not the oldest, settlement in what is today Fresno County. Its name was Las Juntas which means the Junction or Rendezvous. Its beginnings are shrouded in some mystery. It is thought that on one of the valley raids made by padres and soldiers in search of Indians, some of the soldiers were quite taken with the local Indians. After their return to San Juan Bautista, these soldiers deserted and returned to the Indian village, intermarried, and settled down, starting the new community. Over the years the population would grow to around two hundred fifty residents. It also would develop the reputation as the wildest town in the San Joaquin Valley. Thieves, gamblers, cattle rustlers, and bandits like Murrieta and Vasquez would rendezvous there. Since justice was lax, or even non-existent, it was a refuge for desperadoes of all kinds.

Another settlement developed just to the east called Rancho de Los Californianos. Its reputation was even worse. If a desperado in Las Juntas felt the law might find him, he high-tailed it for the rancho, where he was certain to be safe.

There were also many law-abiding citizens in these early settlements, but the wild reputations of these communities overshadowed them. Even though these towns are gone, their stories live on, giving a certain piquancy to the legends of our valley.

The Wells of the Chane Indians

One of Fresno County's earliest communities was at a point where three creeks, the Jacalitos, Los Gatos and Warthan, flowed into each other six miles east of present-day Coalinga. This spot was the location of an ancient Indian village. It was called *Poso Chane* (Shaw-nay) which means wells, or pools, of the Chane Indians. The Chane Indians were affiliated with the Tache tribe who lived around Tulare Lake. Coastal Indians came to the Poso to trade with the Taches. Most of the Chane Indians were captured by the Spanish and taken to missions on the coast.

Because the area was swamp land, it was filled with tules, wildflowers, and animals. The surrounding land was fertile and perfect for agriculture. About a dozen Spanish and Mexican families settled here and farmed the land. They also ranged cattle and horses. Later, American families moved to the Poso, built homes, and opened stores.

In the early 1850s, an Irishman with curly hair was living at Poso Chane. Because of his hair the Americans gave a new name to the settlement—Curley's Springs. The name, however, was not widely used. Poso Chane is the name that endured.

In 1854, the family of Narcisso Higuera settled at the Poso. Higuera became the first important stockman in the area. His cattle roamed as far east as Tulare Lake. Higuera established a headquarters for their vaqueros at the lake in an old adobe dugout. This was about three miles northeast of present-day Kettleman City.

In 1862, a major flood wiped out the great pools of water at the Poso. The Higueras left, not only because of the change in the terrain, but because they were not holders of a Mexican land grant and had not filed for a homestead. California was now a state and they were subject to United States law.

Today, the Poso Chane is gone. Instead of a swamp, the area is a desert. The hoof beats of the cattle and the cries of the vaqueros are lost in the mists of time.

Nothing evokes the romance of Spanish California more than place names. The El Camino Viejo through the valley was studded with words that are descriptive of the terrain, the flora, the fauna, or the purpose of the site.

The southernmost name on the Camino as it begins its trek through the San Joaquin Valley is *Aguaje de Santa Maria* or the Spring of Saint Mary. An ancient spring marks the spot of an Indian campground which the Spaniards named for their favorite saint. Another site on the Camino was named when a group of Spanish explorers camped on the site in the early 1800s. A severe earthquake hit, cracking open the ground, enabling fresh, clean water to pour out for their use. They named the place *Aguaje de Los Temblores* or Earthquake Springs.

Another important place on the trail was *Aguaje de Mesteno* or Mustang Springs. Here, Chico Martinez, who was known as the King of the Mustang Runners, had his place of business. Martinez captured the mustang horses that ran wild on the plains. He put them in corrals and traded, loaned or sold them to travelers on the Camino.

Agua La Brea or Tar Springs was named because the water in the spring was covered with oil. This water hole was located near the present-day road from Hanford to Paso Robles (Pass of Oaks). In 1867, one of the first oil wells in the San Joaquin Valley was drilled here. *El Arroyo de Las Garzas* was named for herons that nested at this spot. The first American who settled there was Dave Kettleman.

The final place we will visit was called *Rancho Centinella* by the Spaniards. It was a vaquero camp. Don Francisco Pacheco built a one-room adobe called the *Centinela*, or the Sentinel, at this place, which he thought marked the eastern boundary of his *Rancho San Luis Gonzaga*. Today, the site is marked by the community of Santa Nella, a name that is a romanticized version of Sentinel, one that evokes the saints' names of the cities along the coast. Unfortunately, Saint Nella never existed.

The First Congregation Church of Fresno located at San Pablo and Divisadero. Photo taken on June 8, 1920.
The Image Group from the Laval Historical Collection.

On the southwest corner of Van Ness Boulevard and Yale Avenue, deep in the heart of the Fresno High School neighborhood, an imposing church building can be seen. Deep terra cotta in color, the long mission-style structure contains a chapel at the south end of the building and, at the north end, a two-story sanctuary capped by a colorful dome. According to the minister at the time the building was constructed, Dr. John H. Gregg, the colors symbolize the following: red for divinity; gold, purity; blue, faith; and green, new life. The building is home to the First Congregational Church of Fresno, a congregation that can trace its beginnings to the year 1882.

The first Congregational service in Fresno County was held on June 6, 1880, at the Grange Hall in the Central California Colony south of Fresno. About twelve people attended the service, which was conducted by Dr. J. J. Warren. A small church was organized with the assistance of the Reverend S. V. Blakeslee, a missionary connected with the Congregational Home Mission Society. On

January 8, 1882, he led a service in the Templars Hall. A series of services was held on alternating Sundays at the Metropolitan Hall located on the 1000 block of I (now Broadway) Street.

In May of 1882, an organizational meeting was held. The congregation consisted of three men and six women. Dr. Blakeslee was named the first pastor. After a fire destroyed Metropolitan Hall, the members met in the Hawthorne School building. In December of 1882, the Reverend Blakeslee moved to Selma. The Reverend George E. Freeman was called to serve the congregation. The membership began to grow. On September 3, 1883, their first church was completed and dedicated. It stood at the corner of K (Van Ness) and Inyo streets.

In 1912, the congregation moved to a new building at the corner of Divisadero Street and San Pablo Avenue. This structure, designed by Starbuck and Clark in the English parochial style, still stands. In December 1949, the congregation moved north to its present location where, having just undergone an extensive restoration project, it hopes to continue to serve the needs of its people for many years to come.

World War II Comes to Fresno

World War II had a direct impact on many Central Valley families. Husbands, sons, and fathers left home for far-away places to fight to preserve liberty. For those at home, the reality of ration stamps, the unavailability of certain goods, and the call for the purchase of war stamps and war bonds became part of daily life. Each family had its own story to tell. Our story today will focus on the memories of one little Fresno girl.

The day the letter from Uncle Sam arrived, she was only nine months old—too young for any memories of what that day meant or how it would affect her life. Her Daddy left—he didn't go too far away—only to the Presidio in Monterey. He would soon go farther away and, for the next five years and ten months, she and her mother would move eleven times—often back to her grand-parents' home in Fresno—in their attempts to live near his Army base.

In 1942, he was sent to a top secret Army Intelligence School in Chicago. He was gone for many, many months. Later, they learned that he had top secret orders to head for North Africa with his unit, which would parachute in before the troops landed and infiltrate the area. His orders were canceled as he prepared to leave, saving his life because none of his unit returned.

The last years of the war were spent at the Presidio in San Francisco. The little girl and her mother moved to Berkeley, living in several different rental houses during the next two years. She remembered one air raid. They were at her Aunt Elizabeth's house. The sirens went off. Everyone rushed around drawing the black-out curtains. Then they headed for the basement and waited several hours until the all-clear signal sounded.

The day the war ended, everyone poured out into the streets, dancing and hugging. Her Daddy took her up to the Top of the Mark Hopkins Hotel so she could watch them dismantling the antiaircraft guns on the top of all the tall buildings in San Francisco. The end of the war meant they could come home to Fresno. She was five, almost six years old. It was a joyous homecoming. They were one of the fortunate families because her father had survived.

The March against "Demon Rum"

At the turn of the century, the forces of Prohibition were on the march, in some instances, fiercely so. Beverages containing alcohol were said to contain a "demon" and were evil. The forces to prohibit the sale of these beverages were, therefore, on the side of righteousness.

The cause was not new. One of the first citizens of Fresno County, Moses J. Church, was a Seventh-day Adventist who believed strongly in practicing temperance. One of the provisions of buying land in his Temperance Colony, in 1877, was to abstain from making and selling beverages containing alcohol. Two years earlier, the Good Templars Lodge, a group advocating abstinence from alcohol, was formed. Other groups throughout the county during the late 1870s and the 1880s also advanced the cause. The Temperance Alliance, the Women's Christian Temperance Union, the White Ribbon Reform League, the Prohibition Club, and the Anti-Saloon League had chapters in valley towns.

Selma, however, was the first Fresno County community to meet the issue on the government level. Sentiment for prohibition had been growing. The first public incidents were initiated by seven women of the Selma Women's Christian Temperance Union. They entered several saloons and asked to pray and sing. They were asked to leave. This turned into a public debate. Anti-saloon petitions were brought to the city trustees, who rejected them. The 1904 election campaign for Selma's board of trustees featured temperance candidates. Suddenly, Selma received statewide attention. Well-known Christian temperance speakers arrived in Selma, armed with their Bibles and their message of living the pure life. The election of 1904 turned into a challenge for residents of Selma—the moral character of their city was on the line. The outcome? The largest voter turnout in the history of Selma voted the three temperance candidates into office. Selma would soon go "dry." It would be followed four years later by Fowler. Coalinga was the last Fresno County town to do so. The forces of "good" were on the march throughout the country, resulting in the passage in 1920 of Constitutional Amendment XVIII, outlawing alcoholic beverages. It was repealed in 1933.

Federal law enforcement officers are seen pouring hundreds of gallons of alcoholic beverages into Dry Creek Canal in 1919. *The Image Group from the Laval Historical Collection.*

The Year 1945 in Fresno

The year 1945 was a roller coaster ride of emotions for Fresnans. World War II had been going on for a long time, but, by the end of 1944, events were looking very good for the United States and its allies. Hitler's forces were being attacked all along the western front, Russia was attacking him from the east, and the war in the Pacific was going well. The theater of war was moving away from the United States Pacific Coast and nearer Japan.

Early in the year, Japanese evacuees were released from internment camps and were returning to their homes in Fresno County. On March 7, an announcement was released by the Department of the Navy that a new 6,000-ton antiaircraft cruiser was being built. It was to be christened the USS *Fresno*.

On April 12, there was a shocking news bulletin. President Franklin D. Roosevelt was dead—the victim of a stroke. A stunned citizenry reacted by calling the local radio stations and the *Fresno Bee*. The *Bee* had already gone to press. The editor ordered the presses stopped so the paper could be reworked to feature the story in the afternoon edition. Full coverage was given on all the radio stations. Flags were lowered to half-mast, and a public service was planned for April 14, with Dean James M. Malloch of St. James' Episcopal Cathedral giving the address. Rabbi David L. Greenberg of Temple Beth Israel and Monsignor James G. Dowling of the Shrine of Saint Therese assisted in the service, which was held in the Memorial Auditorium.

On May 7, the war ended in Europe. On May 8, the citizens of Fresno gathered in Courthouse Park for a service of thanksgiving presided over by Mayor Zeke Leymel. It was a restrained celebration because the war was still raging in the Pacific.

On August 14, Japan surrendered. World War II was over. People poured out of their homes and businesses for unrestrained rejoicing. A thanksgiving service for people of all faiths was held in the First Christian Church. At last, the boys could come home. However, out of the 18,000 Fresno County boys who served their country, 550 did not come home—their sacrifice and that of their families was painfully recorded in the tales of our valley.

Hanford's Carnegie Museum

One of the most unusual buildings in Hanford's downtown can be found on East Eighth Street. Designed by architect George McDougall, it is set apart from other buildings by its interesting style. Called Richardsonian Romanesque after Henry Hobson Richardson, an influential architect of the late nineteenth century, the building features a tower, rounded arches, and a stonelike foundation. According to one architectural historian, this building is second only to the buildings at Stanford University as fine examples of this style in California. It was constructed with $12,500 given by Andrew Carnegie and housed the Hanford Public Library from 1905 to 1968, when a new library was built. It was slated for demolition, but, due to a group of caring citizens, the building was saved. In 1971, the city leased the structure to a non-profit corporation formed to administer a historical museum within its walls. In 1975, the building opened to the public once again. Since then it has been home to the Hanford Carnegie Museum.

When one enters the building, one immediately feels a sense of history. The two main rooms are filled with exhibits that tell the story of the Hanford-Kings County area and give the visitor an idea about how people in this area lived, worked, and played. The majority of the items in the exhibits were donated by local people. Docents stand nearby to answer questions or to guide the visitor. A museum store tempts visitors with interesting books on the area, educational games, and gift items. A courtyard garden in the back of the museum invites visitors to linger. A poem engraved in granite can be found in one corner of the garden. Written by California Poet Laureate Charles Garrigus, the poem is dedicated to the museum.

The Hanford Carnegie Museum is also a resource center for researchers interested in the area's history. Housed in its architecturally distinctive building, the museum is an important part of Hanford's downtown and well worth a visit.

The Chautauqua Comes to Fowler

In 1874, two men in Chautauqua, New York, devised a plan to educate lay Sunday school teachers that would go beyond normal religious instruction. It would include classes, lectures, and entertainments that would expand their horizons. Their primary purpose was learning, not just appealing to the emotions. The plan they set in action sparked a movement that spread across the country. It brought national figures, entertainers, and lecturers together for a week-long series of open forums where the issues of the time were discussed. Dramatic presentations and musical entertainments were provided each night.

The Chautauqua, the brainchild of Dr. John Vincent and Lewis Miller, found its way into communities large and small. For a world without the modern communications we enjoy today—radio, television, and movies—the Chautauqua brought education and entertainment into every corner of America, especially rural America.

In the decade of the 1910s, the Chautauqua came to many of the communities of our Central Valley. In 1918, it came to Fowler. It did not arrive, however, without notice. For weeks, the events were heavily promoted. By the time the big day arrived, banners decorated the streets and shop windows, and the townsfolk were filled with enthusiasm and excitement.

The featured speaker was William Jennings Bryan, a onetime pacifist who, once the nation entered World War I, supported his country's involvement in the war. Other speakers were journalist Dr. Lincoln Wirt, Bureau of Information representative Dr. C. Bushnell, and Jacques de Beaufort, a Belgian Army captain, who described his war experiences. These talks helped to inform the citizens of Fowler about the war. A drama about the war, a string quintet, an operatic singing group, and a gentlemen who could imitate over three hundred bird songs provided part of the entertainment. While the adults enjoyed these presentations, the children had their own entertainment with storytellers and pageants.

So enthusiastic were the citizens of Fowler about the Chautauqua that they arranged for it to return each year until 1923, when interest began to wane. Radio and movies were now bringing the world to their door. The era of the Chautauqua had ended.

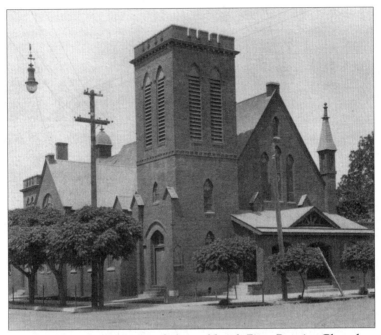

June 8, 1920 photo of the red brick First Baptist Church
building at the corner of Merced and N street.
The Image Group from the Laval Historical Collection.

The early history of the First Baptist Church of Fresno is
replete with peaks and valleys—successes and tragedies.
In early 1882, just nine years after the founding of Fresno, a small
group of enthusiastic Baptists met in the home of Mrs. William
Donahoo and organized a Sunday school. On March 18 of 1882,
the same group met in the Templars Hall for a formal organizational meeting. There were seven charter members of the newly
formed First Baptist Church. On November 7, they called the Reverend T. T. Potter as their first pastor. On December 27, three people
were baptized in the baptismal chamber Moses Church had built
between the banks of his mill ditch that ran down the middle of
Fresno Street.

The church continued to grow. On June 28, 1885, the congregation dedicated its first church building at Merced and J (Fulton)

streets. A year later, the church burned to the ground. The First Presbyterian Church let the congregation use its building for services. Two weeks later, it burned down.

In 1897, the Baptists bought lots at Merced and N streets and built a new church. It was dedicated in 1898. On July 4, 1899, the church burned down. This time the members made an important decision—the new church would be built of bricks. On March 18, 1900, the Baptists dedicated the new red brick church that would serve their congregation for the next fifty-two years.

In the mid-1950s, the members decided to move north to the church's present site on Saginaw Way. Eleven days before the dedication of the sanctuary, a fire caused $100,000 damage to the new church. The next night, Mahalia Jackson sang at the Memorial Auditorium. At the end of her concert, she asked people to donate money to the church. On May 3, 1959, a new sanctuary was dedicated and continues today to serve the congregation.

From its founding of a mission in Chinatown in the mid-1880s that became the First Chinese Baptist Church to its decision to keep its church in the heart of its city neighborhood, the First Baptist Church of Fresno has made and continues to make important contributions to the Fresno community.

From Collis to Kerman

Early in the 1890s, the Southern Pacific Railroad Company built a rail line from Tracy to Fresno. About twelve miles due west of downtown Fresno, a watering tank and pump were located on that rail line. A caretaker was put in charge, keeping the tank filled so there would always be plenty of water for the train engines, but his job was so lonely that after a few months he quit. In 1894, a post office was established at the site. It was named Collis for Collis P. Huntington, the president of the railroad. The Bank of California purchased a large tract of land as a speculative venture. The promoter of the project died, the bank became insolvent, and the property was liquidated. Two capitalists from Los Angeles, William G. Kerckhoff and Jacob Mansar, bought the land, which included the town site. The newly built Enterprise Canal nearby offered excellent opportunities for a colony development, and many people were attracted to the new town. In 1906, the town was renamed Kerman—a name that used the first three letters of the surnames of the two developers.

The new town began to grow. By 1910, Kerman's telephone service had forty-three subscribers. It had a volunteer fire department, a branch library, and the large Kerman Creamery Company. By the 1920s, Kerman was an agricultural paradise, popularly known as "The Home of the Thompson Seedless Grape." Ranches in the area also produced alfalfa, peaches, figs, nuts, berries, vegetables, and honey. At the end of World War II, Kerman's population had reach one thousand. On July 2, 1946, the town of Kerman was incorporated.

Today, Kerman boasts a population of 7,400 people. Three of the major employers are the Kerman Unified School District, the Kerman Telephone Company, and the Kerman Municipal Government. It also has several major businesses: Pacific Coast Packaging, Sun-Empire Foods, Schaad Family Almonds, Bianchi Winery, Mariani Raisin Company, KBC Trading and Processing Company, and Helena Chemical Company. It is still an agricultural center for grapes, cotton, almonds, and alfalfa. From its beginning as the tiny railroad stop of Collis, the city of Kerman has grown to play an important role in the economy of our Central Valley.

Main street and park in downtown Kerman in 1914.
The Image Group from the Laval Historical Collection.

Gustav Kreyenhagen was born October 14, 1821, in Hanover, Germany. His father was a scholar and editor; his mother, a gifted pianist. Gustav graduated from the University of Berlin with a degree in mathematics and languages. In 1848, he married Julia Hering, the daughter of a Lutheran minister. That year, they left Germany and settled in New Orleans, where he taught in a private academy. They then moved to Saint Louis. Gustav became a professor of Greek, Latin, mathematics and music at Washington College. It was here their two children died of cholera infantum, a disease common to the Mississippi Valley at that time. A third child, Emil, was born on December 1, 1853.

They decided to move to a better climate and headed west, going through the Isthmus of Panama on horseback and then by ship to San Francisco, where Gustav's two brothers, Edward and Julius, lived. Julia lost her hat in the strong winds on board ship and arrived in San Francisco bareheaded—a social impropriety at that time.

San Francisco was a city of wooden buildings and tents—a wild town with law enforcement in the hands of vigilantes. Gustav went into business with his brother Julius; they operated a general merchandise store. He continued in this business even though he and Julia moved across San Francisco Bay to Oak's Openings, a community that would later become Oakland. In 1860, they moved to Gilroy. Then, about 1867, they entered the San Joaquin Valley. For the next eleven years, Gustav operated a general store and a stage station and raised sheep at a place that became known as "Kreyenhagen's Corners" near Los Banos, a major center for freighters who hauled supplies by teams of mules and horses through the valley. By this time, four more children had been born to the couple.

In 1875, Gustav moved his family south. Traveling along El Camino Viejo, they settled at Poso Chane, east of present-day Coalinga. Gustav operated a store and a hotel and engaged in cattle and sheep raising on a large scale. Gustav Kreyenhagen died in February of 1890, leaving a widow and five children to mourn his passing. His descendants still own some of his lands. Their story will follow in another tale of our valley.

The Kreyenhagen Brothers

Emil, the oldest surviving son of Gustav and Julia Kreyenhagen, was born in Saint Louis on December 1, 1853. A year later, the family moved west. He received his education in the public schools of Gilroy and at St. Joseph's Academy in Oakland. In 1867, the family followed the El Camino Viejo over the Altamont Pass and into the San Joaquin Valley. They traveled south, settling near Los Banos, where they had a stage station.

Emil drove teams of horses and mules that hauled freight over the Pacheco Pass from San Jose to Los Banos. The trip took four days. In these days before the railroad, this was the only way large quantities of supplies could be shipped. When Los Banos began to grow, Emil and his brother, Hugo, became business partners with their father. They operated a hotel and store in the developing community.

In 1874, Gustav sent Emil farther south to a place called Poso Chane. Acting on his father's orders, he built a hotel, livery stable, store, and sheep corrals. In 1875, Gustav sold his holdings near Los Banos and brought the rest of his family, including his four other children Hugo, Adolph, Bertha, and Charles, to Poso Chane. He bought land between Garzas and Zapato Chino creeks and began a large stock-raising business. About 1887, the four brothers took over the business. They were running about ten thousand head of sheep and six hundred head of cattle. Later, they disposed of their sheep and devoted their energies entirely to cattle raising. They were the largest individual cattle growers on the west side and they were the first to raise grain on the west side of the valley. On July 14, 1916, they formed a legal corporation called Kreyenhagen's Incorporated.

Today, some of the lands are still owned by the Kreyenhagen family. The hills west of their ranching operation bears the family name—a name that will forever be remembered in the legends of our valley.

A Home for Latino Arts

In 1925, the palatial mansion of Mrs. Nellie Short was left to the City of Fresno to be used as a home for the cultural arts and a memorial to her late husband, Frank. Mrs. Short's dream did not materialize, and the home and property were sold. Among the companies who purchased the property were I. Magnin & Co. and Bank of America. The structure was enlarged and remodeled—it no longer looked like the original home.

Then in 1995, Arte Americas received a $250,000 Community Development Block grant that, along with funds it had raised through a capital campaign, enabled it to purchase the building.

Arte Americas was founded in 1987 by a group of educators, artists, and their friends who wanted to support Latino arts in the Central Valley. They wanted to provide a climate where local Hispanic artists, writers, and musicians would be appreciated and where future artists would be inspired to create. The local arts community and the public were supportive of their early efforts to develop their programs. Their first home was in the Warnor's Theatre building.

In the ensuing years, Arte Americas has grown and expanded its programs. The museum at 1630 Van Ness Avenue offers not only exhibits of visual and folk arts, but also offers education through exhibits, a resource library, and the development of curriculum and materials for schools. It also sponsors musical and dance performances and live theater.

With funding and support from the California Arts Council and from corporations, foundations, and individuals like Wells Fargo Foundation, California State Automobile Association, and writer Gary Soto, Arte Americas is continuing to work toward creating a premier Latino cultural center in Fresno that can be enjoyed and appreciated by the entire Central Valley community. It seems that the home that hosted the art and music of its day once again has a place for the arts within its walls.

One of the best known of the early day west side sheep ranchers is Adolph Domengine. Born in San Francisco in 1856, he was the son of a Frenchman, John Domengine, who was a successful miner in the gold fields of California. John Domengine was in the laundry business in San Francisco, but eventually turned to raising sheep on the San Luis Ranch on Pacheco Pass. When young Adolph was three, his Uncle Matthew took him and his two siblings to their father's hometown of Saint Abbiet in the Pyrennes Mountains.

In 1868, Adolph came back to California. He went to Los Angeles with his father to purchase a band of sheep—then he helped his father drive them to land near San Francisco. For the next twenty-two months he attended school in San Francisco. Then in May of 1872, he began herding sheep for his father on the San Luis Ranch. A year later his father sold the ranch to Simon Camy. Adolph continued working with Simon. In 1874, they moved the sheep to an area between Fresno and the San Joaquin River. Adolph worked for Miller & Lux for the next nine years. In 1883, he started purchasing land on the west side. By 1919, his holdings covered over a distance of twelve miles. He bought 3,200 head of sheep. Later, he would turn to Durham cattle. The distinctive brand was a D with a quarter circle above and an A.

The Domengine Ranch was located on Domengine Creek in an area that abounds in streams. It extended from the plains of the valley into the foothills of the Coast Range mountains. The ranch was first settled by George Hoffman in 1862. Lumber had to be hauled from Stockton to built the first cabin on the property. The land was sold to Bertram Yribarren, then to Peter Etchegoin, and then to Domengine.

In 1887, Adolph Domengine married Mary Pfitzer of Fresno. Their three children assisted their parents in the cattle business. After the deaths of the parents and the three children, the ranch was left to four Catholic charities. Soon after, it became part of Harris Ranch and remains so today—an important legacy in the tales of our valley.

Arthur G. Wahlberg

The Fresno State Normal School faculty poses for a photograph in the fall of 1919. Arthur G. Wahlberg is the third from the left in the back row. President C. L. McLane also stands in the back row, fifth from the left.
The Image Group from the Laval Historical Collection.

E ven though the frontier town of Fresno was more than a little rough around the edges, the people of this community longed for culture in their lives. When the Barton Opera House was built in 1884, it provided a beautiful setting for concerts and plays. Study clubs and choral groups attracted participants. The Central California Conservatory of Music offered lessons in instrumental music, voice, and elocution. It was into this environment that an eastern gentleman arrived.

Born on June 6, 1874, into a musical family, he had received instruction from some of the finest teachers. At the age of thirteen, he developed an excellent bass voice. By the age of fifteen, he was a soloist in his church choir. Two years later he became the choir's director. Later, he held the position of soloist and choirmaster of the St. James' Episcopal Church in Boston.

In 1897, he married Gertrude Blanche Graham, a lyric soprano. They had four children. In 1903, they moved to Fresno, where he went to work as a bookkeeper first at the First National Bank and then at the Bank of Central California.

He enjoyed the relaxed manners of his new city and began to get involved in cultural pursuits. His talents were immediately recognized. With Dr. Chester Rowell and Louis Einstein as sponsors, he organized and trained a male quartet for the Unitarian Church. In 1904, the First Presbyterian Church asked him to be its musical director, a position he held for many years. In 1906, he was named supervisor of music for the Fresno City Schools. When the Fresno Normal School was founded in 1911, C. L. McLane, the school's first president, asked him to be its director of music. He held this position for thirty-two years. As chairman of the finance committee of the faculty and students of the Fresno Normal School, his bookkeeping skills were used to assist the college. In 1912, he organized the Fresno Male Chorus.

The talents of Arthur G. Wahlberg were true gifts to the Fresno community—inspiring others and bringing beautiful music within the reach of all. In 1985, the recital hall of the California State University, Fresno, Music Building was renamed in his honor.

On June 25, 1825, in the town of Blankenhelm, Prussia, was born a man who would, in some sixty years time, be called upon to lead the brand-new city of Fresno. When he was nineteen, his family sailed for America on the ship *Agnes* and settled in Wisconsin.

In the spring of 1850, the west beckoned. On May 1, he set out for California with a team of two hundred wagons under the command of one Captain Taylor. The journey was fraught with numerous problems. Discontent and insubordination ran rampant, and wagons left daily as people decided to travel on their own. The young man and his partner also left the wagon train and headed out with their four mules and ample provisions. A rifle given him by his father was helpful in obtaining sage hens and wild ducks when their provisions began to get low. They made good time and arrived in Sacramento on July 20. They headed for the mines, staying at several locations before settling in for the winter at Blue Tent, a place on the Calaveras River. They made a great deal of money. When spring came, they headed south to see if the stories they had heard of the rich placer mining on the Fresno and San Joaquin rivers were true.

They arrived in Coarse Gold Gulch in May 1851, but the placers were soon exhausted. Our young man stayed and involved himself in mining and other pursuits. In November of 1862, Fresno County Clerk J. C. Johnson died. Our gentleman, William Faymonville, was appointed to fill the vacancy. In the next election, he was re-elected to the office. When his term ended, he went into real estate and, after Fresno Station was founded, moved to the new community.

In the election of 1885, in which the vote to incorporate Fresno was successfully passed, Faymonville was elected to the board of trustees, the governing body of the new city. At the first meeting of the board, he was elected president, which made him, in effect, the first mayor of Fresno. He served his city well. He died on February 2, 1889. A tall monument marking his grave can be seen in the Mountain View Cemetery.

The front facade of Hanford High School taken about 1970.
When it was torn down in the mid-1970s, it became the catalyst for an active preservation movement that resulted in the
creation of a downtown historic district.
Courtesy Hanford Carnegie Museum, Inc.

A visit to Hanford is a very special experience. The visitor
to this Central Valley city will see a Courthouse Square
with its restored historic courthouse and other public buildings
intact, a vital downtown business district, and historic homes,
buildings, and landscape looking much as they did many years
ago. According to architectural historian John Powell, "Hanford is
the valley's best-kept architectural secret." In an era when so many
valley towns have lost key pieces of their historic building stock,
how did Hanford manage to keep its intact?

In the mid-1970s, Hanford High School was scheduled for
demolition because it was said it did not meet earthquake safety
standards. It was a controversial issue, but the school was torn
down. The people of Hanford realized they had lost something
irreplaceable.

About the same time, it was announced that Kings County

government offices would be moved out of the historic courthouse and into a new government center. The City of Hanford made arrangements to lease the historic county buildings for one dollar a year for ninety-nine years. The move was made in the first part of 1978. In July of that year, the City of Hanford took possession of the county buildings. There were some who wanted to tear down the historic courthouse. A large number of the citizens of Hanford didn't want to lose this important symbol of their community. A citizen's committee was formed. They went to Santa Cruz to see a restored courthouse, to Los Gatos to see a restored school and to Sacramento to see the restoration work on the State Capitol. They met with officials at the State Office of Historic Preservation. They did their homework.

They came home and formed a Historic District in the downtown core. They made an assessment of the buildings within that area and, following the secretary of interior's guidelines, determined whether buildings were contributing or noncontributing. They set strict architectural controls for the exteriors of the buildings within the district and adopted a Historic Preservation Ordinance.

Today, Hanford's downtown is going through some natural evolution. A mall on the outskirts of the city is making an impact. The Hanford Heritage Trust, a private nonprofit preservation group, has been formed. A Historic Preservation Commission for the City of Hanford is in place and is working hard to preserve Hanford's historic building stock.

Hanford is a living legacy. Its special ambiance welcomes visitors and makes them want to return again and again.

Exterior of the Kings County Courthouse as it appeared about four years after its 1896 completion (above) and in 1942 (left). The building continues to grace the central plaza in downtown Hanford.
Courtesy Hanford Carnegie Museum, Inc.

The centerpiece of Hanford's Historic District is its Court house Square and adjacent Civic Center Park. The historic landscape of trees and shrubs nestles lovely and fascinating buildings, some of which date to just a few years after the city was incorporated in 1891. The park was once the seat of county government. It is no more, but, thanks to smart planning and community caring, the park and the buildings within it remain, creating a feeling of nostalgia for the small-town-America of one hundred years ago.

The Kings County Courthouse building, now restored for commercial use, was built in 1896. This three-story, neo-classical revival structure with Italianate influences housed county government offices until 1978. It is listed in the National Register of Historic Places.

Just behind it is a two-story brick and masonry building with Romanesque features. Designed by the McDougal brothers, it features a large arch over the entry and a tall, octagonal tower which gives the structure a castle-like appearance. Built in 1897 as the sheriff's office and county jail, it was designed to accommodate sixty prisoners. One of them, a lady named Mary, is said to haunt the building. Today called the Bastille, it houses a restaurant. Its outdoor patio is the setting for jazz concerts in the summer.

Across the park from the Bastille sits Hanford's Civic Auditorium. Designed by architects Coats and Traver in 1924, the classical revival building features a front porch with eight plain, ionic columns. The stepped parapet with its large clock gives the building a stately appearance. Many famous people have performed within its walls. John Philip Sousa, Benny Goodman, the Dorseys, Harry James and their bands brought the best music of their times to the citizens of Hanford.

In 1985, Hanford won the Helen Putnam Award for excellence in preservation of its downtown from the League of California Cities. The city has been honored several times as a Tree City, USA by the National Arbor Day Foundation. In 1998, Hanford was selected the regional winner in the "Prettiest Painted Places in America" contest.

KINGS COUNTY JAIL   HANFORD, CAL.

This 1942 photo shows the Kings County Jail. Built in 1897,
the building now houses a restaurant and is called the Bastille.
Courtesy Hanford Carnegie Museum, Inc.

From Cranes to Bass

Nestled in the higher foothills of Madera County is a lake that has been so much a part of the lives of many Central Valley residents that its name alone is synonymous with recreation. Bass Lake, for many, brings back memories of summer vacations, camping, boating—just plain old-fashioned fun and relaxation. What some may not know is that there was a time when Bass Lake did not exist—a time when the area covered by the lake was a peaceful valley.

From time immemorial, a broad, grassy meadow filled a deep valley due east of present-day Oakhurst. Teepees made of cedar bark, homes of the Eagle Clan of the Mono Indians, dotted the valley. Flocks of sandhill cranes nested there giving the valley its name—Crane Valley. The Indians lived on the wild ducks, geese, and deer that came into the valley. Acorns, elderberries, strawberries, gooseberries, wild grains, wild barley, and manzanita berries rounded out their diet. The north fork of the San Joaquin River, called Willow Creek, flowed through Crane Valley.

The first white men who came into Crane Valley married local Indian women. They farmed grains and vegetables. Later, cattle and hogs were raised here. The river was mined for gold, but there were no fish in its waters. In 1885, George Teaford brought buckets of trout from nearby Whiskey Creek and stocked the river.

In 1895, the San Joaquin Electric Company built a hydroelectric plant on Willow Creek. Five years later, a succeeding company built a dam across the creek. By 1910, the dam had been enlarged two more times, creating a lake 4.1 miles long and 1,880 feet wide. The Forest Service stocked the lake with bass, thus giving it its name of Bass Lake.

Ever since its creation, Bass Lake has been a popular recreation spot. Many of the resorts have fallen victim to floods or fires, including Ducey's Bass Lake Lodge, a local landmark. Now rebuilt on a new site near the Pines Resort, it once again welcomes visitors to this scenic spot.

A Visit to a Mountain Hideaway

Our travels through the mountains south of the Kings River in eastern Fresno County have taken us on a couple of occasions to a place called Clingan's Junction, named for William Clingan. There are still Clingans in the area—Bill's son Forest and his wife, Helen.

Their home is not visible from any road, but once the visitor negotiates the winding road and comes to the crest of the hill, he turns down the hill into a drive that brings him to a rambling stone cottage that is such a part of its landscape it blends into the hillside. A welcoming committee of guinea hens run quickly up and down the drive—their thick feathered skirts bouncing. Their long spindly legs end in high-arched feet that look for all the world like high-topped boots. They look like flustered Victorian ladies bustling about.

The traveler enters through a building that is filled with artifacts from the Old West. The saddle that Grat Dalton, the notorious bandit, used in his escape from Dalton Mountain has pride of place. Going through a door, one steps into a cozy, comfortable, charming room. A large stone fireplace in the middle of the room divides the living, kitchen, and eating areas. Windows look out on the mountains and the small valley between. Everywhere can be seen Indian baskets and artifacts of every kind. It is easy to tell that the residents love local history and craftsmanship. A large kettle on the hearth made the journey west with the Donner party.

The home was built by Bill Clingan out of native rock. It has been added to over the years as more room was needed. Later, a second structure was built for Helen and Forest. It is now Helen's studio where she paints portraits of the local Indians and the birds and animals that are native to the area. She and Forest have gathered local tales and Indian traditions into a book entitled *Oak to Pine to Timberline* and were two of the authors of *Fresno County in the 20th Century*. Their research has contributed greatly to the knowledge of the rich history of the mountain area.

Legends of our valley in the truest sense, Helen and Forest Clingan have created a rich legacy for us all.

For the traveler bound for Grant Grove in the Kings Canyon National Park, the most direct route is to travel east on Highway 180. After the ascent into the mountains begins, the traveler will go through the small community of Squaw Valley. He will soon come to a juncture in the road where a turnoff can be made to the town of Dunlap. This spot is called Clingan's Junction. The traveler might wonder how it got its name. This is the story.

In 1911, William Clingan arrived in this mountain area for the first time. He came here in a pack train and headed for Sampson Flat, where he camped with thirty other forest service officers. One of the highlights of his visit was seeing a log cabin with bullet holes in the logs—acquired during a shoot-out between a sheriff's posse and Sontag and Evans, the notorious train robbers. After a week's stay, he left on a six-horse wagon.

Bill Clingan returned three years later to take the post of district ranger. Two years later, he married Lorena Brewer, the teacher at Millwood School. In 1919, he went to work for Santa Barbara millionaire George Owen Knapp building and supervising summer camps at Bubb's Creek and later on the floor of King's Canyon. The camps were reachable only by pack train. Supplies were brought in in early spring. After the camps were set up, Clingan would bring in Mr. Knapp and his guests, packing them in from the Nevada side of the Sierra, which was a shorter trip. Bill's son, Forest, was old enough to help his dad on these pack trips.

In 1927, Clingan bought the Dunlap general store and moved his family to that town. In the late 1930s, surveys were being done for a new Highway 180 that would extend from Grant Grove to the valley floor. Some of the surveyors were staying with the Clingans, and Bill found out that the road would go through an area not far from Dunlap. The first flat area on that road was owned by Charlie Wilcher. Bill bought a 120-acre parcel from him. In 1940, Clingan built a store on the land that would be adjacent to the new road. About this time, the road was completed from Grant Grove to Clingan's store. At that juncture, the road to the valley split off between the old road and the new. Hence, the four corners at the juncture became known as Clingan's Junction.

In the fall of 1940, the store building was used as a rest stop for people on their way to the nation's Christmas Tree services, but, because of World War II, it did not open for business. After the war ended, the Clingan family opened the store and officially moved to Clingan's Junction. Today, Forest Clingan and his wife, Helen, still live in the area—a beautiful place with a colorful history in the mountains of Fresno County.

Smoke Signals in the Valley

We live in an era of instant communication. As soon as events happen they are transmitted all over the world instantaneously via radio and TV. It may surprise some of us to learn that our local Yokuts Indians had their own method of communication between valley tribes that, although it was not quite instantaneous, was rather quick and very effective.

On April 6, 1844, John C. Fremont was traveling through the San Joaquin Valley. He noted in his diary, "After having traveled 15 miles along the river, we made an early halt, under the shade of sycamore trees. Here we found the San Joaquin coming down from the Sierra with a westerly course. We had expected to raft the river but found a good ford, [probably Gravely Ford, below present Herndon] and encamped on the opposite bank, where...wild horses were raising clouds of dust on the prairie. Columns of smoke were visible in the direction of the Tule Lakes to the Southward—probably kindled in the Tulares by the Indians, as signals that there were strangers in the valley."

On another occasion, a party of Spaniards entered the southern end of the valley looking for Indians to capture to take to the coastal missions. Within four hours, there were columns of smoke rising from one lookout station to another along the Sierra and Coast Range foothills from the Cosumnes River in Sacramento County to the south end of Kern Lake.

The Indians dug a hole about two feet across and two feet deep. They built a small fire with dried weeds they stored for that purpose that they partially smothered to create a dense smoke. They used a wet blanket, wet tule mat, or wet skin—to interrupt the smoke and divide it into puffs. The smoke signals described the size of the invading party, whether or not it was hostile, the kind of people in the party, the direction it was traveling, and its actions. The alarm signal was a long series of short puffs. The all-clear signal was a series of widely separated puffs.

Because of their close allegiance and interdependence on one another, this ancient manner of communication by the many tribes of Yokuts was very effective. It got the message where it needed to go in the speediest manner possible. Even in our modern age, isn't that still what communication is all about?

Catherine Morison Rehart

261

Two views of the Coalinga Oil Field in 1921.
The Image Group from the Laval Historical Collection.

The man who is the subject of our story today was born on July 18, 1872, at Chester, Virginia. He was the son of a Civil War veteran who marched with Sherman's army to Atlanta. At the age of two, his family moved west to Shasta County, California, where he received his early education in a one-room schoolhouse. He completed his studies with a three-month course at a business college in Stockton. At age twenty-one, he was restless and wanted to leave home to seek his fortune. Two opportunities beckoned him—the gold boom in Alaska and oil strikes in Los Angeles. He stuck a stick in the ground—it fell north, so Alaska was the choice.

He headed first for Redding, where he worked in a stone quarry for two dollars a day. After two weeks, he hadn't made enough to buy a ticket for Alaska, but he could afford a ticket for Los Angeles so he headed south where he got a job hauling oil. He worked his way up from tool dresser to cable tool driller. After forming a partnership with Irving Carl, they drilled twenty oil wells. He drilled a well of his own and made five thousand dollars. He paid his bills, went home to Shasta County, and married Minnie Zumwalt.

In 1899, they moved to Coalinga for his health. He continued to drill wells and manage oil company properties and became known as one of the best oil drillers in the West. He found it was often hard to get the casing down a hole that had just been drilled, so he invented an offset bit that allowed him to drill the hole so that it was larger than the casing. He patented his invention. The Baker casing shoe was his next invention four years later. He began to build Baker Oil Tool Incorporated, a specialty oil tool business. During his long career, he would hold 124 U.S. and twelve foreign patents. Ideas for inventions came to him at night just before he went to sleep. He would run the ideas in his head for several days and then sketch them out. Among his numerous inventions was the elevator brake and the collapsible cup.

Reuben Carlton Baker not only ran a successful business but served the community of Coalinga in numerous ways, including holding the office of mayor, organizing the Coalinga Gas and Power Company, and establishing the First National Bank of Coalinga in 1908. In 1958, when Baker was eighty-seven, his company was returning two million dollars a month. He established the R. C. Baker Foundation which had a million dollars in assets. He directed that the earnings be used for education and research. Today, the R. C. Baker Memorial Museum of Coalinga is housed in the original building of the Baker Casing Shoe Company, which was deeded to the museum. It has been said of him that no one has had the opportunity to do more for Coalinga than R. C. Baker, and no one has been more faithful to duty and privilege than he.

Baker's Shoe Casing Company

In March of 1913, Reuben Carlton Baker organized a company for the purpose of taking over and promoting the patent he held on an invention called a casing shoe. This device was used in drilling oil wells. "It is a steel shoe put onto the bottom of the casing during the boring of a well" that makes the job easier. It was used in oil fields the world over. The company was called Baker Casing Shoe Company. Royalties on the patent were $1,000 to $1,500 a month. Five years later, in March of 1918, Baker purchased the S. R. Bowen Machine Shop in Coalinga. This shop had the necessary machines to manufacture the casing shoe and other pieces of equipment that Baker had invented and for which he had obtained patents. At the time, there were four employees, including Baker. The company's sales varied from $2,000 to $7,000 per month. In 1928, the company name was changed to Baker Oil Tools, Inc.

Over the years Baker added plants in Los Angeles and Houston, an office in New York, and sixty branch warehouses in the main oil fields throughout the United States. Venezuela and Canada were served through Baker Transworld, Inc., a subsidiary of the parent company. In 1958, when Baker died, the company's monthly sales were $2 million.

How did a man like Baker, who started with nothing, create such an impressive and successful business? Talent, which Baker had in great abundance, certainly helped. But Baker had another secret for success—a philosophy of business practice that he followed faithfully. His 10-step formula was as follows: "Spend less than your income; invest all surplus funds in good, safe securities; always finish the job you start and then start another; invest all surplus funds for income—not for speculation; always live within your income—PAY AS YOU GO; never borrow money, unless you are sure of a profit; always be honest with yourself (and all others); consider all people honest (but remember some are not); always seek good advice for your investments; and always re-invest the income from your investments." That his formula worked was evidenced by his success. Today, the company has been sold, but is still in business under the name Baker Hughes International.

A Trip to the Big Blue Hills

A journey across the west side of our great Central Valley to the town of Coalinga takes our traveler through varied farmlands and towns. Leaving Fresno and traveling south on Highway 41, an interesting route begins with a turn west on Manning Avenue. Heading west, the traveler will pass Raisin City. Originally named Ormus, which meant rattlesnake, the name was changed to Raisin when the first post office was opened in 1890. It soon became known as Raisin City. At the Highway 145 junction, the traveler turns south and passes through the small community of Helm. The vast, expansive space and the flatness of the valley floor impress him. Fields of green low growing plants seem to stretch forever—truck farming seems to predominate in this area.

At Five Points, the road angles toward the hills. The fields are filled with cattle. As the traveler speeds by the stockyards, the smells of Harris cattle permeate the air. After driving over Interstate 5, the road becomes Highway 33, the old El Camino Viejo. A sense of history overtakes the traveler as he thinks of the Indians who walked this way for hundreds of years and of the Spanish who chose this inland route to travel through Alta California. Now, rocking horse oil pumping units dot the hillsides—their steady rhythm bringing in another kind of harvest for Fresno County. A graceful ascent into the Big Blue Hills reminds the traveler to look to the north to catch a glimpse of Joaquin Rocks, where legend says the bandit Joaquin Murrieta met his death one grim July day in 1853. The road drops into Pleasant Valley. Soon, the traveler is in the heart of the city of Coalinga, ready to stop, rest, and do some exploring.

For the return trip, the traveler chooses to head east on Highway 198. He passes the luxurious and inviting Harris Ranch and then travels through miles of young vineyards. Soon, he goes by the Lemoore Naval Air Station, crosses the Kings River, and turns north on Highway 41, headed for Fresno. He arrives home tired but amazed at all he has seen, exploring a corner of Fresno County that often goes unnoticed.

In the 1880s, coal was being mined in the hills of southwestern Fresno County. In 1888, the Southern Pacific Railroad extended its line from Goshen to Alcalde, south and west of present-day Coalinga. A spur line was built from the mine to the railroad. Coaling Stations B and C were on the spur line. At the point where it joined the rail, Coaling Station A was established. The name was shortened to Coaling A and, eventually, to Coalinga. On July 22, 1889, a post office was opened at the station and given the name Coalinga.

Coalinga didn't really begin to develop until after oil was discovered and the first oil well was brought in in 1896. Then Frederick Tibbits opened a saloon, and Louis O'Neill built a store. A year later, the Blue Goose well was drilled and the oil began to flow—five hundred to a thousand barrels a day. The oil boom began. Soon other businesses appeared and, by 1900, Coalinga could boast about two dozen frame buildings. Tents and shanties also dotted the town site. The town became known as a free-wheeling boom town. Front Street, better known as Whiskey Row, had thirteen saloons that all did a rousing business. Many of them were also elaborate gambling dens and the sites of fist fights, brawls, and shoot-outs—all the stuff of legendary frontier lore. Water was a scarce commodity. It was brought by rail from Tulare on a train with the nickname "Old Sixbits." Then it was hauled into town by horse-drawn wagon.

Other businesses included hotels, blacksmith shops, livery stables, the Webb and May store, and Frank Cleary's insurance office. The first church was organized in 1900. In spite of the wild frontier flavor of the populace, the town had a literary society whose members met and discussed pressing issues of the day. Coalinga was incorporated on April 6, 1906. The oil boom continued well into the 1920s, bringing many people to the area.

Today, Whiskey Row is gone, but the City of Coalinga remains—an attractive community situated between the hills in verdant Pleasant Valley. It is home to the annual California Horned Toad Derby and the R. C. Baker Museum—two good reasons to visit this corner of Fresno County.

Coalinga's fabled Whiskey Row, located on Front (Main) Street between 4th and 5th streets. Before fire destroyed the row in 1912, the businesses provided lusty entertainment for both locals and oil field workers. This view is on an old postcard.
Courtesy of Dr. David Paul Davenport.

A trip to Coalinga should include a visit to the city's R. C. Baker Memorial Museum, dedicated in November of 1961. It is situated at 297 West Elm Avenue in a building that "was the original machine shop and office of Baker Casing Shoe...Mr. Baker purchased the building from S. R. Bowen in 1918 for $10,000. When the Baker headquarters was transferred to Los Angeles in the 1930s, the building was still used as a machine shop. It was donated by Baker Oil Tools to the City of Coalinga in 1959 to be used as a museum..." The museum, the oldest commercial building in Coalinga, is run by "a non-profit organization established for the purpose of preserving the geological and historical lore of the area."

As one tours the museum, it is evident that the group upholds its purpose very well. One entire wall of the museum contains glass cases that hold dozens of fossils of all kinds, petrified wood, shells from the prehistoric ocean floor, mastodon teeth—items that were discovered in the oil fields nearby and were donated to the museum. A mastodon skeleton, found in the Coalinga-Kettleman Hills area, is especially worth noting. Many photos accompany these artifacts and tell the fascinating history and prehistory of the land in and around Coalinga.

Other glass cases hold old photos of Coalinga and the families who pioneered here. Also exhibited are drafting tools, early cameras, watch fobs, antique telephones, and a telegrapher's key. A large assortment of Indian baskets, grinding stones, beads, and arrowheads remind the visitor of the first residents of the area. A large photo of Chief Ke-howt-za, the last chief of the Tachi Yokuts tribe, is prominently displayed. Other fascinating items include antique guns, Civil War sabers, musical instruments, china, silver, furniture, clothing, typewriters—even a wringer washing machine.

The R. C. Baker Memorial Museum was funded by Baker's heirs and the community. It is worth a stop on your next visit to Coalinga.

In the mid-1870s, more farms were being developed in the southwest area of Fresno County. Hoping to establish itself ahead of that development, the Southern Pacific Railroad decided to build a rail line west from Goshen. It would eventually extend to Tres Pinos in San Benito County. In 1877, the line was completed to a point just nine miles north of the county line and a station was established. A turntable was built so trains could turn around and head back to Goshen. On June 18, 1877, a post office opened. It was called Huron. Because of the sheep ranching in the area, Huron became a shipping center for wool and sheep. This continued to be true well after the turn of the century. During the years 1913-1915, more wool was shipped from Huron than from any other wool producing center in the country. As more people moved into the area and planted barley and other grains, Huron became a shipping point for those products, too.

The town began to grow and, by 1890, had a population of two hundred fifty. It boasted among other businesses a Kutner-Goldstein store, two livery stables, a blacksmith shop, two hotels, and Barnes and Meades Palace Saloon. Two years later, a fire destroyed some of the leading businesses in town. This tragedy would be repeated on February 9, 1919, when a fire swept through the town.

In 1916, the first deep well was dug for irrigation purposes just six miles east of Huron. Other wells were dug north and northwest of Huron at the Frank Diener ranch and the Jack O'Neill ranch.

The late 1920s brought a new period of growth. The first oil well in the Kettleman oil fields just south of Huron came in. Soon oil well suppliers and truckers established their headquarters in Huron to be near the railroad.

After World War II, more acreage was planted and crop yields increased. Packing houses and an ice plant were built. The population of the community increased, which led to Huron's incorporation on April 30, 1951.

Today, the fields around Huron are filled with row crops including broccoli, asparagus, and tomatoes. Lettuce is the main crop—all kinds of lettuce. Dole's Lettuce California and Fresh Express are the largest companies in the area. The lettuce that appears in the supermarket washed, bagged, and ready to eat is grown in Huron.

On December 31, 1998, Huron was given the designation of an Enterprise Community—one of only twenty cities in the country to be granted this distinction.

A Settlement Named Alcalde

In 1888, the Southern Pacific Railroad extended its rail line from Huron to a point just five miles southwest of Coalinga in Pleasant Valley. Coal was being mined nearby. Newly discovered deposits of oil, limestone, and gypsum made the line a profitable business for shipping these resources. At the terminus of the line a two-story depot was constructed. In October of 1888, a post office opened. The settlement was given the name *Alcalde*. Where did this name come from?

When Alta California was under Mexican rule, each city was presided over by the alcalde. He was, in essence, the mayor, but his powers were more far reaching than a person with that title under our system of government. The alcalde had both judicial and executive powers. His powers were unlimited.

One of the earliest residents of this new settlement was Tolton Turner Barnes. He was not only the local doctor, but the attorney, constable, and justice of the peace as well. Since he was a man who wore many hats, so to speak, and seemed to preside over all the needs of the people in the area, the local residents, many of whom were Mexican, gave him the nickname, "Alcalde." Soon, everyone was calling the settlement Alcalde. The name stuck.

As the natural resources of the area developed, business increased. Soon hotels, businesses, and homes were being built. Soon the twice-a-week train service became daily service. When the train arrived each day, two stagecoaches were there to greet it. The stages took travelers to the Coalinga Mineral Springs or over the Coast Range mountains to Priest Valley and Kings City in Monterey County.

Coalinga continued to develop, but Alcalde did not. At some point, it just seemed to fade away. Today, the settlement is gone. All that remains is a lone ranch house and a short road that bears the name Alcalde. The rest is consigned to history in the southwestern hills of Fresno County.

Edna Domengine's Kidnapping

On the night of June 29, 1908, Adolph Domengine, his wife, and sixteen-year-old daughter, Edna, were asleep in their home on their west side ranch north of Coalinga. Hearing gunshots, they were awakened and ran outside. They saw that their barn was on fire. Just then two masked gunmen stepped out from behind an outbuilding, told the family to put their hands in the air, and tied up Domengine's two sons and three ranch hands who, hearing the commotion, had come running out. One of the gunmen hitched two horses to Domengine's buggy and ordered Domengine and Edna to get in. The two gunmen jumped in and drove down the main road of the ranch. When they reached the gate, they ordered Domengine out and told him to meet them the next day at Jack's Springs in the hills west of Coalinga with five thousand dollars in gold as ransom. The gunmen drove off into the night with Edna. One of the men, Grover Cleveland Rogers, known as Cleve, took Edna to Jack's Springs. He hid her in a small ramshackle cabin. The other man, Tony Loveall, went to Coalinga.

By the time Adolph Domengine walked the two and a half miles back to his ranch his fear had turned to anger. He untied his sons and sent them to other ranches nearby to tell them of the kidnapping. Then he headed for town to inform Constable Ed Arnold. The news spread like wild fire. Posses were formed—each one heading out to Jack's Springs. The men had little trouble locating them because they found traces of a lunch Cleve Rogers shared with Edna on their journey. They spotted the cabin. The men hid behind large rocks outside. About that time, Ben Porter, who had gone for reinforcements, drove up in his car. Rogers, hearing the motor, rushed to the door of the cabin. A shot was fired at him, hitting the door jam. Rogers grabbed his shotgun, and using Edna as a shield, moved forward. He balanced his gun on Edna's shoulder and fired several times, nearly deafening her. The members of the posse came out from behind the rocks and began to close in on him. Rogers threw down his gun and surrendered. Edna Domengine was safe, but the story doesn't end here. In the next tale of our valley, we will continue the saga.

Chasing a Kidnapper

In our last story, we followed the 1908 kidnapping of Edna Domengine, whose father was one of the leading ranchers on the West Side. Our story ended happily with the capture of Cleve Rogers and the release of Edna. But, that is not the end of the tale—far from it. A second man had been involved, but where was he?

When Adolph Domengine rode into Coalinga to tell the constable about his daughter's plight, posses were formed to hunt the kidnapper. One of the men who joined up was a local named Tony Loveall, who told folks he was just "getting off of a four-day drunk." He rode with one of the posses, giving the appearance of a man eager to find the culprit. When his group headed up the canyon toward Jack's Springs, where the kidnapped was presumed to be, someone called out, "We've got him. It's Cleve Rogers." Loveall, hearing this, turned his horse and rode away from the group as fast as he could.

Sheriff Robert Chittenden arrived from Fresno in his car and took charge. He and several prominent Coalingans escorted Rogers to the Coalinga jail. Huge crowds had gathered yelling, "Lynch him!" Sensing real trouble, the sheriff went outside the jail and addressed the crowd, telling them they needed Rogers alive to find out who his accomplice was. The crowd calmed down. Going back inside, he interrogated Rogers who finally wrote the initials T. L. on a piece of paper. Chittenden knew of Loveall and rumors that he had once killed a man. He decided Loveall must be the other kidnapper and had joined the posse so he could kill Rogers if he was captured, thus protecting himself.

The sheriff and five of his men got in a car and headed out, looking for Loveall. For two days he led them on a crazy chase through the foothills and gullies of the Coast Range Mountains. Finally, he was captured and both he and Rogers were taken to Fresno where they were put on trial and convicted for the kidnapping of Edna Domengine—thus ending another colorful saga in the legends of our valley.

Arthur P. May

One of the first residents of Coalinga was born in England. He arrived in California in November of 1884. He first settled in Los Angeles, then moved to Tulare and Hanford, finally arriving in Pleasant Valley in 1888. He took up a homestead and timber claim which, at the time of his death in 1940, he still owned. Soon after he came, the railroad was extended from Huron to Alcalde. Two oil companies, Producers Oil and Home Oil, started business in the area in 1894. A little settlement was beginning to take shape along the railroad at Coaling Station A, where a poor grade of coal mined nearby was loaded on rail cars.

He opened a general mercantile store and became the settlement's first businessman. His store housed the first post office and had the only telephone. The phone was used by the oil companies and everyone else who needed to make long distance calls. He was the agent for Wells Fargo Company for twelve years. In 1897, he married Stella Kerr, daughter of an early settler and judge in the area. Their union was blessed by a son and a daughter.

By 1901, the population of the area was increasing, and our gentleman decided that since his business was growing he needed fire insurance to protect his large supply of goods. Since the building was built of wood and the town did not have a fire department, he could not get insurance. This problem was solved when he built a brick building. In fact, he put up a row of brick stores. People thought he was crazy—that there would never be enough business in Coalinga to fill them.

But he, Arthur P. May, had faith in the community. A couple of years later, he organized the town's first fire department. In 1906, Coalinga was incorporated. Arthur P. May was elected chairman of the new city's board of trustees—making him the first mayor of Coalinga. A man of many firsts, Arthur P. May also started Coalinga's first bank—right in his store. At the time of his death in 1940, May was living in Oakland, but returned often to the city that he helped pioneer—a city whose people, in turn, never forgot the man who had done so much for his community.

Arthur P. May's brick building at the corner of Front (Main) and 5th streets in Coalinga about 1904. Note the horse drawn wagon tied to the hitching post in front of the store.
Courtesy of Dr. David Paul Davenport.

Muir's Look at the Valley

On March 28, 1868, a Scots gentleman stepped off a boat and set foot in San Francisco. Three days later, he set out on foot for a trip that would bring him to the place where he would find his inspiration—the place of his heart. Before he reached that place a long trek had to be made. From Oakland he traveled south and then west, walking over the Pacheco Pass. Perhaps it's best to let him tell his own story. Here are the words of this man, John Muir:

"It was (April) the bloom-time of the year over all the lowlands and ranges of the coast; the landscape was fairly drenched with sunshine, the larks were singing, and the hills were so covered with flowers that they seemed to be painted...I wandered enchanted...aware...that Yosemite lay to the eastward, and that, some time, I should find it. One shining morning, at the head of the Pacheco Pass, a landscape was displayed that after all my wanderings still appears as the most divinely beautiful and sublime I have ever beheld. There at my feet lay the great central plain of California, level as a lake, thirty or forty miles wide, four hundred long, one rich furred bed of golden Compositae...along the eastern shore of this lake of gold rose the mighty Sierra, miles in height, in massive tranquil grandeur, so gloriously colored and so radiant that it seemed not clothed with light, but wholly composed of it, like the wall of some celestial city. Along the top, and extending a good way down, was a rich pearl-gray belt of snow; then a belt of blue and dark purple, marking the extension of the forests; and stretching along the base of the range a broad belt of rose-purple, where lay the miners' gold and the open foothill gardens—all the colors smoothly blending, making a wall of light clear as crystal and ineffably fine...it seemed to me the Sierra should be called, not the Nevada or Snowy Range, but the Range of Light."

This was John Muir's first look at our great Central Valley. It was an image that would remain with him throughout his life. He continued on his journey to the mountains of the Sierra where he would wander and work and leave an incredible legacy for all who came after him.

John Muir, seated on the ladder, with Murphy's Brass Band.

The Image Group from the Laval Historical Collection.

George Pope in the doorway of his tire business at 1340 Van Ness showing off his JD Harley Davidson motorcycle with sidecar. He purchased the motorcycle in 1928 for $585 from Wilson motorcycles.
Courtesy of Bud and Grace Pope.

George William Henry Pope was born January 12, 1899, in Newark, New Jersey. The family moved west to Pasadena after losing all their money in the panic of 1906. He assembled his first bicycle from pieces of metal, using garden hoses for tires.

In 1918, Pope and his brother-in-law, Dave Pinkham, left Pasadena on a motorcycle, pulling their trailer behind, and headed north because they heard there were more business opportunities in the growing town of Fresno. Pope did not have a chance to complete high school, but he had a natural genius for making anything mechanical work. For a few years he often visited his family in Southern California. Finally, he moved them to Fresno.

In February of 1919, he opened a tire business at 1209 Van Ness Avenue with a starting capital of $500. He worked hard—eating and sometimes sleeping at the shop. Honesty and good service became his hallmark—the backbone of his business. In offer-

The interior of Pope Tire Company showing the molds for recapping tires. The kettle that was used in the recapping process can be seen just to the right of the center of the photograph. *Courtesy of Bud and Grace Pope.*

ing service, he built up a loyal clientele. The store was so small that he did his recapping in a small corner of the building and service repairing on the sidewalk and in the street.

Riding motorcycles and flying airplanes had been George's passion since he was a young man. His flying skills enabled him to make quick deliveries to farmers who needed tires in a hurry. He would fly over the farm and, quite literally, drop them off.

He married Ireta Rudy. Their union was blessed with a son and a daughter. He moved his store to 1340 Van Ness Avenue and then, in the mid-1930s, to 1347 Van Ness. In 1939, he bought a lot at 1709 Broadway and built his shop there in 1941. The business remained at that location until it closed in 1998. When his son, George William, better known as Bud, was nine, he started working in the business dusting tires. They jointly ran the business until his father died in 1986. Bud continued the business until it closed on October 30, 1998.

One of Pope's specialties was customized recapping for race cars. They created custom molds so that each racer could have individualized tread on his tires—a sort of signature. Pope created a turned block design that Billy Vukovich, Edgar Eller, Johnny Boyd, and others used. They did the tires for the midget and hard top racers and for antique cars.

In 1989, Pope Tire Company was recognized as the oldest family owned and operated tire dealer in California. On October 30, 1998, George "Bud" Pope retired and closed the business. For those who love cars and auto racing, the name Pope will long be remembered in the history of our valley.

Pope Tire Company was located at 1347 Van Ness Avenue, their third location in Fresno. In 1941, the business moved to 1709 Broadway where it remained until Bud Pope retired in 1998 and closed the business.
Courtesy of Bud and Grace Pope.

Ice Cream with Your Coffee

There is a building at 1420 H Street, that has, since its construction, been associated with two of mankind's favorite pleasures—coffee and ice cream. Built in 1912-13 by the R. F. Felchlin Company, the building was designed as an ice cream plant for owners J. Arthur Benham and L. W. Wilson. Their ice cream business grew rapidly. They expanded the building in 1923. By the mid-1920s, the business had become the largest manufacturer of ice cream products in the valley. Other plants were opened in Bakersfield, Hanford, Porterville, Merced, and Visalia. Benham, who had come to Fresno in 1897 to work for Fulton G. Berry, decided to retire and sold his holdings in the company to Standard Creameries of Oakland in 1927.

Ten years later, in 1937, the building was purchased by Dale Brothers Coffee, who moved its operation to the new site. Joseph Dale and his twin brothers, Court and Wade, had been in the grocery business together in Tonopah, Nevada. After a fire destroyed their business in 1915, they moved to Fresno and began their coffee roasting business in a store on Van Ness Avenue. Over the years the business grew. At one time, Dale Brothers Coffee handled 80 percent of the commercial coffee accounts in the San Joaquin Valley. Joe Dale was one of the original underwriters of the West Coast Relays and was a great supporter of Fresno State College athletics. For his contributions, he was named to the Fresno Athletic Hall of Fame on November 3, 1965.

An outstanding feature of this building is the huge coffee can that sits atop its roof. Faced with the Dale Brothers hooded friar logo in rich orange, black, and white, the coffee can is a unique part of the Fresno skyline.

Although the building today houses a commercial photography studio, the coffee can still can be seen on the rooftop, a reminder of the years when the aroma of roasting coffee beans filled the air in this section of downtown Fresno.

Barrels of Benham's ice cream is delivered to Bowman Drug Co. at 2001 Mariposa St. *The Image Group from the Laval Historical Collection.*

The Ella Hoxie Home

There is a home on North Blackstone Avenue that holds a special connection to two families who pioneered in the town of Millerton. Unlike many of the homes built in Fresno before 1900, this one has suffered neither neglect nor demolition. Rather, this home has survived with its architectural integrity intact. Its design is a mix of Queen Anne and colonial revival box influences. Painted a light grey-blue with pristine white trim, the house fairly shines—pride of ownership seems to radiate from its walls.

In 1896, George Lafayette Hoxie built the home for his wife, Ella. George Hoxie was a son of Clark Hoxie, a member of the first board of supervisors at Millerton. In 1892, George Hoxie was elected county surveyor, a post he held until 1902. He served as city engineer from 1905 until 1909.

When Ella Hoxie died in 1899, the home was sold to Truman Hart, the son of Mary McKenzie Hart and Charles Hart, the first judge of Fresno County. Truman Hart served as mayor of Fresno from 1921 to 1925. He also served as county clerk from 1895 until 1899. He was active in the beginning of the oil mining industry in the Central Valley and helped to organize several companies. He served as the president of both the Oil City Petroleum Company and the Twenty-eight Oil Company. He was very successful in these ventures.

After Truman Hart died, his widow, Augusta, took Mr. Hart's sister, Mary McKenzie Hoxie, into her home and cared for her until she died in the home on November 15, 1935. Mary Hoxie was the first school teacher in the city of Fresno.

Today, the home at 251 North Blackstone houses K. Randolph Moore law firm—a rather fitting circumstance given the judicial and political involvements of the families who occupied it. It also provides a touchstone to our county's beginnings in the foothill town of Millerton.

The Pickford Family of Fresno

The story of one Fresno family begins in England at the height of the Industrial Revolution. On March 27, 1830, Oliver Pickford was born at Newton Moor, Cheshire County, England. He became a stationary engineer, a skilled job which required him to operate the boiler in such a way that production could be kept going at maximun speed without the boiler blowing up. He left England and immigrated to the United States in 1853. That same year, he married Mary Ann Hooley in Fall River, Massachusetts. They settled up river at Taunton, a small factory town. They had two children, Charlotte (Lottie) and James, who died in infancy. They moved west—first to Iowa and then to Trempeleau County, Wisconsin, where they lived for seventeen years. Eight more children were born to the couple. Oliver continued working as a boiler operator and a lumberman. He then tried his hand at farming and proved to be very successful. In 1876, the family moved to California, first to Oakland, then Cambria and, in 1881, they settled in Fresno. Their new home was a rough and tumble wild west town on the brink of becoming a city.

Oliver Pickford's oldest daughter, Lottie, married George Kohler, who had come to Fresno in the 1870s and was the owner of a successful butcher shop. The couple rented a boarding house at the corner of Inyo Street and Broadway, which Lottie operated. It was so successful that Lottie purchased the northwest corner of Van Ness Avenue and Merced Street from her father, who had bought it for $500 in gold coin, and built a three-story boarding house called the Kohler Hotel. She built a laundry behind the hotel and another laundry behind the boarding house on Inyo, which became the Kohler Laundry.

Lottie was one of the first female entrepreneurs in Fresno. A large woman who commanded such respect that even the members of her family called her Mrs. Kohler, she also had a kind heart. She adopted three children who were born to boarders who could not care for them and raised them as her own. Lottie died in 1919 while visiting her sister in San Francisco. Oliver Pickford died on July 25, 1913. We will share more about this family who made significant contributions to Fresno in later tales of our valley.

This photo of the Oliver Pickford family was taken in 1876. Top row: John, Thomas, and Lottie. Middle row: Mary, Olive, George, Harriet (Hattie), Oliver. Bottom row: Ernest and Christian Job (Joe).
Courtesy of Joel Pickford.

George Pickford, a son of Oliver and Mary Pickford, was born in 1861 in Trempeleau County, Wisconsin. He came to California with his family in 1876. During his teenage years, he worked at all kinds of hard labor and, for a time, was a cow puncher in Cambria.

After his family moved to Fresno in 1881, he worked in a butcher shop learning the meat business. Later, he opened his own meat market on the Merced Street side of the corner parcel his family owned at Van Ness Avenue and Merced.

In 1886, he married Ida Suder, who had walked across the Isthmus of Panama at age seven while journeying to California with her family. Her father was a Swiss-born tailor. In 1890, George began a series of ventures that showed his skill as a businessman. He bought the first of several businesses that were losing money, first the Pleasant View boarding house, then another one. When he sold them a couple of years later, they were on sound financial footing. His next purchase was the Armory Stables on J (Fulton) Street. When he sold it four years later, it, too, was financially sound.

In 1895, George Pickford bought the City Bakery and Cafe on I (Broadway) Street. The cafe became a popular place to eat for Fresno residents. The menu featured several kinds of sea food as well as standard fare. The bakery became very successful—baking and delivering up to eleven thousand loaves of bread every day. His brother-in-law, George Kohler, was a partner. Later, Kohler would leave the business and Pickford's son Rollin would become his partner. In 1908, they closed the business.

In 1908, Pickford mounted a successful campaign for a seat on the city's board of trustees. This was the year Dr. Rowell was elected mayor. During his three terms in office, Pickford established Fresno's Free Market at K and Fresno streets and a city-owned experimental sewer farm, and helped to draft the city's first general plan in 1915. He was Fresno's first market master. After leaving office, he became the bookkeeper for the Kohler Laundry company that his sons, Rollin and William, purchased from their uncle George Kohler.

George Pickford died on his eightieth birthday in 1941.

The Pickford owned Liberty Laundry as it looked in May 1937. The sons of George Pickford ran the business with George serving as bookkeeper. Rollin Pickford, Sr. is second from the right in the front of the photo. Will Pickford stands in the doorway.
Courtesy of Joel Pickford.

Rollin Pickford

We have told the story of the family of Oliver Pickford through three generations of self-made businessmen who, in spite of not having the advantage of a fine education, achieved a good measure of success. Now we turn to the fourth generation—to a man who was taught the principle of hard work, but who also inherited an artistic gift from his mother and grandmother that flourished in their sensitive care.

Rollin Alphonso Pickford, Jr. was born on May 23, 1912, in a small home at Calaveras and Divisadero streets. In a few weeks, Ruth and Rollin, Sr., moved with their son to George and Ida Pickford's (Rollin's parents) home at 645 P Street. The two families would always be close, either sharing a home or building homes next door to each other. Rollin, and later his brother and sister, would be raised as much by his grandparents as his parents.

From the time he was a small boy, Rollin Pickford loved to draw. By the time he was eight, he knew that he wanted to be an artist. He was a gifted child, skipping grades as soon as he started school. It was not until he was in the eighth grade that he took an art class. He painted his first watercolor and found his passion. He wanted to study art at Fresno High School, but his parents insisted he study pre-law. During the summers, he worked in the family laundry business—a hard, hot job.

He entered Fresno State College in 1929 and, despite his parents' wishes, majored in art. His first watercolor class from Professor Alexandra Bradshaw opened a new world of excitement for him. He transferred to Stanford University his junior year and obtained his degree two years later. The Depression was at its height, and jobs were scarce. For the next few years, he found seasonal work in the mountains of the Sierra. Living close to nature brought an appreciation that would become an underlying force in his work.

In 1936, he went to work as an illustrator for Fresno Photoengraving. Four years later, he formed Display Advertising, a free-lance partnership. During this period, two important people came into his life, Lanson Crawford, a watercolorist who reawakened Rollin's interest in the subject, and artist Tom Valiant. In Rollin's words,

Rollin Pickford, Sr.
holds his son, Rollin, Jr., in
this photo taken around
1916.
Courtesy of Joel Pickford.

"Lanson Crawford taught me how to see, and Tom Valiant taught me what to do with what I saw." He began to paint seriously. Over the years his style matured as he experimented with impressionism, cubism, abstract expressionism, primitivism, pointillism and minimalism. The seasons of the valley and the agrarian landscape inspired him, too. He worked not only in watercolors, but in oils and acrylics.

In the 1970s, he retired from advertising to paint full time. Now he divides his time between Pacific Grove and Fresno—finding beauty and subject matter in both landscapes. One thing has remained constant—his approach to painting. In order to paint an orchard, one must walk its length and breadth. He says, "To paint a nectarine tree...you have to have pruned one. To capture the noonday sun filtering through a canopy of grape leaves, you have to kneel in the dust."

Over the years, Rollin Pickford, through his work, has chronicled much of the valley's landscape and architecture that has been lost to development and growth. Besides this contribution to his community, he has given us all a far greater gift—an incredible body of artistic work that captures the subtle beauty of our valley in its many moods and seasons. A precious legacy, indeed.

The Home of Ingvart Teilman

When most residents of Fresno think of Teilman Avenue, they think of a street in the north part of our city. Although Teilman Avenue does go as far north as the San Joaquin River, it also runs through sections of south Fresno. Indeed, its origin is in that part of our city.

Directly south of Chandler Field there is a home that is set so far back from Kearney Boulevard that it almost goes unnoticed. The home was designed and built in 1915 by architects Bowen & Davis, who had offices in Visalia and Fresno. Driving up to the home, one is struck by its spareness of design and its perfect balance and proportion. It is immediately apparent that it is a craftsman home designed in the prairie style—an ideal design for the hot Fresno climate. Wide, tall windows that can be opened to catch the evening breeze are everywhere to be seen. The wrap-around porch and wide entry steps greet the visitor, inviting him to enter.

The inside is breathtaking. As you stand in the entry hall, your eye is first drawn to the glorious use of valley oak. From the staircase and wainscoting of the hall and living room, to the built-in window seats flanking the living room fireplace, the coffered ceilings of the living and dining rooms, and the built-in buffet that covers one wall of the dining room, the lush patina and richness of the wood are evident everywhere. Built-in bookcases, plate rails, leaded glass doors in the buffet, window details, and moldings—every detail of expert craftsman design is here. It is clear that the person who built this home for his family had an understanding of design and a commitment to creating beauty and function in his everyday living environment.

Walking through the home, one wonders about the first owner. Who was he? His name was Ingvart Teilman, and he was one of the signers of the articles of incorporation for the city of Fresno in 1885. In 1887, he became the city engineer. The street next to his home that intersects with Kearney Boulevard was named for him—Teilman Avenue.

Emmanuel Lutheran Church

Where once there were many, today there are only a handful of churches left to serve the downtown Fresno community. One of these is located in an area that is a proposed historic district. At one time it was surrounded by large, gracious homes. Today, few of these are left, and the church building sits quietly on a corner lot unnoticed by most Fresnans.

This is unfortunate because the building is one of the loveliest in the downtown area. Located on the northwest corner of Mariposa and U streets, it was designed by a master architect, Charles Butner, and constructed by master builders Thomas C. Irwin and William Hopkins. It is built of red and Indian red brick in the Collegiate Gothic style with a high pitched gabled roof. The outside entrance to the sanctuary features, according to architectural historian John Edward Powell, "an elaborate terra cotta...quoined surround, Gothic window tracery and planked doors with flat-iron straps."

The attached classroom building to the west of the church creates the outward appearance of an L-shaped building. Rising from the roof of this building is a three-story bell tower. A large deodar cedar tree is the outstanding feature of the landscaping.

The church was built in 1929 for the congregation of the Emmanuel Lutheran Church. Established in Fresno on March 9, 1890, the congregation initially met at St. Paul's Methodist Church. For thirty-three years, the members met in a building that once belonged to the Christian Church that they moved to Ventura and L streets. Then they moved into their new church on Mariposa and U streets. In 1965, the congregation moved north to a new building at East Floradora Avenue and North Angus Street.

In 1968, the Emmanuel Lutheran Church building was sold to the Carter Memorial African Methodist Episcopal Church, which still occupies the facility today. This lovely historic building continues to grace a historic neighborhood and bring beauty to downtown Fresno.

L. C. Wesley Super Garage

At the southeast corner of Van Ness Avenue and Kern Street in downtown Fresno sits a building that has a noteworthy background. Built in 1931 for L. C. Wesley, it was called the L. C. Wesley Super Garage. For car and truck owners, it was a very convenient place. You could leave your car here before work and pick it up at the end of the day. It offered one-stop service. You could have your car washed, polished, and greased. If your car radio wasn't working properly or the car's battery needed replacing, these problems could be fixed. If a tire was flat, it could be repaired. If the tire tread was too worn, new tires could be purchased. All this was available, plus another fine feature—covered parking. This was appreciated by customers not only when the temperature was over one hundred degrees, but also when the rain and fog of winter were at their dreary peak.

One might ask why, when there were other similar businesses downtown in 1931, is this business in this particular building worth noting?

Across Van Ness Avenue from the garage is the Californian Hotel. The hotel was designed by premier architect H. Rafael Lake in 1923 and constructed by the firm of Trewhitt-Shields. Lake joined the firm as the staff architect. The firm's projects included the Hollywood Roosevelt Hotel and Fresno's Wilson Theatre. Later, at the height of the Depression, Lake joined Allied Architects and designed the Hall of Records in Courthouse Park. In 1931, H. Rafael Lake designed the Wesley Super Garage building. The firm of Shields, Fisher & Lake handled the construction.

According to architectural historian John Edward Powell, "The property is important architecturally because it represents the earliest major use of art deco imagery in the community." Built of reinforced concrete in a Perpendicular style with art deco detailing and zig zag motifs, this structure is a unique example of this style of architecture. It now faces an uncertain future which may include demolition. If it is torn down, Fresno will have lost another piece of its architectural heritage.

Margaret Hudson

Tucked away in northwest Fresno is a series of enchanted gardens which flow from one to another through archways, paths and openings in the shrubbery and trees. Everywhere can be seen the sculptures for which the gardens' owner is noted—figures of animals, children and intriguing shapes, poking up from the ivy, on walls, on arches, delighting the visitor at every turn—a magical place. Small studios dot the gardens. When she was six months old, her parents, David and Sadie Metzler, brought her to the home on this property. It is here that artist Margaret Hudson lives and works.

Art was always her passion. She studied art at Fresno High School winning a scholarship to the California College of Arts and Crafts in Oakland. She took classes in watercolor and drawing, but left after a year to attend theological schools in the eastern United States. She spent four years in Japan, returned home and married Gil Hudson, a Ph.D. graduate from the University of California at Berkeley. They moved to Korea where he taught physics at the National University. Margaret taught English conversation.

Their four sons were born. Ten years later, they returned to the United States and spent a year in Green Belt, Maryland. While there, Margaret was told that she should work with clay. In that area of Maryland, the earth is clay so her backyard provided the material she needed.

Her first sculpture was an image of a grieving woman with her head buried in her arms—it reflected the poverty and suffering she had seen in Korea. Her second sculpture was a self image—a mature woman joyfully thrusting her arms heavenward. In her words, "I had to put pain into the clay before I could find joy. I knew now I had found a voice for my soul."

Gil was hired to teach at West Hills College so they moved to Coalinga. Both Margaret and Gil caught valley fever. Barely recovered, Margaret returned home to Fresno in 1970 with her four sons and very ill husband to care for her aging parents. She began to work with clay again.

With so much difficulty and struggle around her, she felt an intense desire to work with the earth—that by molding it in her hands, she could create beauty and transcend the pain of her daily life. She began to mold animals and birds—creatures that represented the beauty of nature, the continuity of life—her life on the acre as a child.

A friend suggested that she take her sculptures to a craft show at the College Religious Center. Other craft shows followed. A business began to grow. In 1977, she opened Earth Arts studio on Swift Avenue—still a busy place today.

The late Fresnan and artist Varaz Samuelian told her that unlike European sculptors who make an armature and build outwards, she works like a pre-Columbian sculptor who makes pots and turns them into sculptures. As she works on a seated figure of a woman, she builds the face gradually—picking the clay up in her hands, working it, rubbing it back and forth. She places it on the figure. As she works, the features start to emerge. She wraps the figure in a wet towel to set before the next stage.

Her parents' deaths, a divorce, the death of her son, and a recent illness, have all impacted her work. At each stage of her life, she has had to face pain; but, in each instance, it has brought new insight and artistic growth.

After the big freeze in 1990 demolished a series of wet clay sculptures, Margaret decided to find another medium for awhile. She began painting tulips and roses, finding in the imperfect flowers—the ones with petals missing or with torn leaves—a beauty of form that parallels the soul that has experienced great sadness and has gained substance through suffering. Her paintings vibrate with color and movement—they are filled with life.

Margaret Hudson's vision for the future is to continue welcoming the over 2,000 schoolchildren who flock to her gardens every year and to continue to create a place in her gardens where people can come and feel at home with the earth. She is creating a garden of plants that are native to our area so that children can experience the beauty that once was our valley. Artist, earth mother, gardener, legend—Margaret Hudson is one of Fresno's treasures.

Fresno Betsuin Buddhist Temple

Main entrance to the Betsuin Buddhist Temple. The statue of St. Shinran can be seen in the left foreground.
Author's photo

Just west of downtown Fresno, in historic Chinatown, there is a tall and imposing building that has been a fixture of the neighborhood for many years. Located on Kern Street between E Street and Highway 99, this building is home to the congregation of the Fresno Betsuin Buddhist Temple.

The first Buddhist service in the San Joaquin Valley was conducted in Fresno in November 1899 by Rev. Kakuryo Nishijima of San Francisco. He came at the request of local followers of the Buddhist faith. After the service, they asked the Rev. Nishijima if their group could become a branch of the San Francisco Young Men's Buddhist Association. On January 28, 1900, a local branch was formed. It met in a building at 825 F Street. A year later, the congregation received its first minister, drew up articles of incorporation, and became an independent congregation, no longer a branch of the San Francisco group.

On October 7, 1901, the congregation purchased the present site for $1,050 in gold coin. A three-story wooden building was constructed which was similar in design to the present building. This structure served the congregation until 10:15 p.m., May 30, 1919, when a fire broke out, destroying the building.

A fund drive was begun immediately for a new building. Architects T. Kurahashi and William C. Hayes were hired to design the new concrete building that was dedicated in a two-day ceremony on November 27 and 28, 1920. Many of the members of the congregation lived in farming areas where there were no schools. Their children stayed in the church dormitory and attended not only public school, but also the Japanese Language School on the grounds of the church.

During the 1920s and '30s, Buddhist Sunday schools were started in Del Rey, Bowles, Madera, Selma, Fowler, Dinuba, north Fresno, west Fresno, Sanger, Kingsburg, and Parlier. On November 4, 1936, the Fresno Buddhist church was granted the status of Betsuin. This designation was given because of the large size of the church and its congregation. The head minister of the Betsuin is called *Rinban*.

The temple closed during World War II. Many of the leading members of the Japanese community, as well as the priests of the temple, were interned in relocation centers. Throughout the war, Buddhist services were held in these centers. After the war, the congregation continued to grow and became one of the largest Buddhist congregations in the United States.

Today, the Fresno Betsuin Buddhist Temple is looking toward the future. Members of the congregation wish to look beyond their ethnic boundaries and become a part of the mainstream life of the Fresno-Clovis community. As it has for nearly a hundred years, this respected congregation continues to add to the rich texture of life in our great Central Valley.

In the Temple Garden

As one walks through the front garden of the Fresno Betsuin Buddhist Temple a statue can be seen. It has a most interesting story.

A man named Shinran Shonin, who lived in Japan from 1173-1262 A.D., held a position of authority at Mount Hiei, a monastery temple community. For twenty years he had struggled unsuccessfully to find enlightenment and peace of mind. He decided they could not be achieved. He resigned his position and left Mount Hiei. As he began his journey he met a Buddhist master named Honen, who taught him the way to religious fulfillment. The path that he followed led to the development of a branch of Buddhism called Jodo Shinshu. The Fresno Temple looks to Shinran Shonin as its founder. The statue in the temple garden depicts the revered man in his travel attire. The rocks at the base of the statue were brought from the Sierra.

The statue was donated by Seiichi Hirose of Takarazuka, Japan. Mr. Hirose's lifelong dream was "to create and present 100 statues of Shinran Shonin to different parts of the world." Since the first presentation of one of these statues to a temple in Japan in 1936, he has fulfilled his dream by seeing these statues go to temples all over the world. The Fresno statue was unveiled at a ceremony on March 21, 1965.

In another part of the garden stands a large bell tower. Hanging underneath it is a 3,000-pound temple bell. The bell is three and a half feet in diameter and is five feet nine inches tall. Donated to the temple by Yehan Numata, the brother of a former minister of the Betsuin, the bell is rung on special ceremonial occasions. The bell came from Japan, arriving at the Port of San Francisco. It was transported to the valley by Matsubara Trucking and was stored at the Matsubara ranch until the unveiling ceremony on October 29, 1980.

A walk through the garden of the Fresno Betsuin Buddhist Temple offers an opportunity for quiet reflection in this very special corner of downtown Fresno.

Two Architects Named Swartz

From the years 1890 to 1965, two gentlemen named Swartz, father and son, had distinguished architectural careers in Fresno. Alexander C. Swartz, the father, graduated from the University of Illinois College of Engineering in 1873. He was an engineer and surveyor. When a planned route for the Santa Fe Railroad through Colorado, New Mexico, and Kansas was being surveyed, he was the engineer in charge of the survey party. He came to Fresno in 1890 to make a survey for a railroad that was planned over the Pacheco Pass to the coast. The railroad was never built, but he stayed in Fresno and practiced architecture and engineering until he died in 1919.

Fred L. Swartz, Alexander's son, was born in Girard, Kansas, on June 9, 1885. He was a graduate of Fresno High School, class of 1903, and was a star player on the school's football team. He studied architecture at the University of Pennsylvania. After completing the two-year course, he returned to Fresno and became a junior partner in his father's architectural firm. After his father's death in 1919, he welcomed C. J. Ryland into the firm as his partner and changed the firm's name to Swartz & Ryland. The partnership lasted until Ryland moved to Monterey in 1932.

Throughout his career, Fred Swartz designed many notable private and public buildings. The Fresno State College Library, now part of the Fresno City College campus and included on the Historic Resource Inventory List for the City of Fresno; the T. L. Heaton School, which was torn down in 1971; the Alexander Hamilton Junior High School; the Scottish Rite Temple; and the city halls in Coalinga, Lindsay, and Porterville were all designed by Swartz.

In the mid-1930s Swartz became associated with Allied Architects. Two projects he worked on were the Fresno County Hall of Records and the Memorial Auditorium.

At the time of his death on October 13, 1968, Fred Swartz was regarded as the dean of Fresno architects.

Hobart Park

Driving east on Divisadero Street, then turning south on R Street, you may be conscious of a small area of lawn, a couple of picnic tables, and large trees to your right. You may have driven this route hundreds of times and never noticed it, or you may have noticed the green area and wondered, "What is it?" It is a good question because the smallish wedge of land looks a little like a park, but there is no sign or plaque to give it a name.

The answer to the question is: It is a park. And, it has a name—Hobart Park. It is old—ninety years old to be exact. This is its story.

In 1903, a well-known landscape architect named Johannes Reimers was hired by the City of Fresno to design the layout and supervise the planting of forty-acre Roeding Park. He was called the "official gardener" of Fresno. Three years later, in 1906, many of the eucalyptus trees on Kearney Boulevard were cut down. Reimers was very upset by this. He said, "You people here do not know what you have done. The pride of the state has been destroyed in a week, and it will take a generation to grow it again."

In the same year, 1906, Reimers was asked by the city to design and plant a park on a small parcel of land bounded by Q, Divisadero, R and Merced streets. Although the Santa Fe Railroad cut through one corner of the park, Reimers planned a central fountain, walkways, shrubbery, lawn, and trees. Unfortunately, the budget would not stretch far enough to include all these amenities; there was only enough money for the lawn and trees. Reimers planted a number of interesting trees including bottle trees, California fan palm, date palm, broad-leafed eucalyptus, guadelupe palm, Mexican blue palm, Mexican fan palm, silk oak, and southern magnolia trees. Situated in the center of the park is a magnificent *bunya bunya* or monkey pod tree.

Today, Hobart Park is filled with mature trees that lend a graceful softness to the downtown landscape. One wonders what will happen to the park when the Community Health System regional medical center is completed. Will it survive? Will it become a backdrop to the complex, providing a place for health care workers to relax during lunch breaks? Or, will it, like so many historic buildings, be considered expendable and paved over? Only time will tell.

A Woman Named Marjaree

On November 13, 1978, a horrifying incident occurred. A young woman of great promise, who was involved in important organizations in her community, and who was completing her degree in business administration at California State University at Fresno, was raped and murdered. It was another case of domestic violence, but this time there was a difference. The young woman's name was Marjaree Mason, and her death sparked a movement within the Fresno community.

The response was immediate. The Fresno community said, "No more," and turned to the YWCA for help. The YWCA already had a shelter for homeless women. Now they set aside a few rooms for victims of domestic violence. A group of volunteers started a twenty-four-hour hot line. Their grass roots effort let women know they had a place to go—a safe haven. In 1979, just a year after Marjaree Mason's death, the shelter that had been established at the YWCA was named the Marjaree Mason Center.

Out of this early effort, counseling programs began to grow. Over time the program evolved to include support groups, outreach services, community education presentations, children's services, treatment programs for batterers, and classes in legal options for battered women, anger management, survival skills for battered women, and parenting. In 1998, the YWCA of Fresno voted to leave the national organization and to rename the local organization the Marjaree Mason Center, Inc.

In 1999, the organization is marking its twentieth year of service to the Fresno community. According to Executive Director Tim F. Reese, its vision for the future includes increased outreach to other parts of Fresno and Madera counties, particularly the rural and foothill areas. Since the closest shelters are in Merced and Visalia, the need is great.

The history of our valley is filled with tales of triumph over tragedy. The tragedy of Marjaree Mason has brought a legacy of hope to thousands of women in our great Central Valley.

Judge Ernest Klette

The history of our valley is filled with tales of people who overcame incredible odds to achieve their goals. One such man is the subject of our story.

Ernest Klette was born in Montreal, Canada, on July 17, 1874. His father was a furrier. The family came west to California in 1876 and settled in a sparsely populated community near Bellview, just five miles from Millerton. The family lived under a large oak tree on their property while they built a small dwelling. They engaged in ranching and sheep raising. The children attended the local school, learning the rudiments of reading and writing. As Ernest grew older, he became an avid reader. He learned English grammar by reading books by Victor Hugo, Charles Dickens, and Mark Twain. His summers were spent in the mountains, taking the sheep to pastures in the high country. While tending the sheep, he read.

In 1893, Judge M. K. Harris of Fresno came to their home to officiate at the wedding of Klette's sister. Klette, not quite nineteen years old, was very impressed by Harris. Judge Harris became his role model. Klette began reading law books. He decided to run for justice of the peace, hoping it would aid his studies. He was elected. He resigned the post in 1902 to enter Stanford University. He paid for his schooling by taking summer jobs chopping wood and working in a grocery store in Friant. Two years later, he was admitted to the California Bar. He moved to Selma and opened his law practice there. A year and a half later, he moved to Fresno. He served on the board of trustees and, later, as the city attorney. In 1936, Ernest Klette was appointed to the Superior Court Bench.

In addition to the practice of law, Judge Klette was an author of some note. He penned several books including one about Joaquin Murrieta entitled *The Crimson Trail*.

Ernest Klette died in Fresno on November 17, 1950. He was a kind man who, in his law practice, served clients from all walks of life, regardless of their ability to pay. As a judge, he served his community with distinction for many years. From his humble childhood in the foothills of Fresno County to his years of judicial success, his story is an inspirational addition to the tales of our valley.

Notes

A PROUD TRADITION
Frank J. Sanders, biographical notes and history.
"Frank J. Sanders: Duke of Tulare Street is back," *Fresno Business Journal*, March 21, 1994.
The Fresno Bee, "Prior, Shelton Sell Auto Agency to Frank J. Sanders," no date.

FRESNO CITY ON THE SLOUGH
The Fresno Bee, May 2, 1952.
The Fresno Bee, May 5, 1952.

A HORSE & BUGGY DOCTOR
The Fresno Bee, January 25, 1955.

MEXICAN LAND GRANTS
Charles E. Dixon, *Rancho Laguna De Tache*, April 9, 1961.
Robert M. Wash, *The Rancho Laguna De Tache Mexican Land Grant and the "Witness Tree."*

THE WITNESS TREE
Fresno County Abstract Company, *Abstract of the Title to Rancho Laguna De Tache*, Freven.
Charles E. Dixon, *Rancho Laguna De Tache*, April 9, 1961.
Ernest Nielsen, *Boundary Tree—Laguna De Tache Spanish Land Grant,* February 11, 1961.
Robert M. Wash, *The Rancho Laguna De Tache Mexican Land Grant and the "Witness Tree."*

THE TRAGEDY AT MUSSEL SLOUGH
John Walton Caughey, *California,* Prentice-Hall, Inc., Englewood, Cliffs, NJ, 1953. pp. 382, 449, 450.
Wallace Smith, *Garden of the Sun,* Lymanhouse, Los Angeles. 1939, pp. 259-290.
Wallace Smith, *Prodigal Sons,* Christopher Publishing House, Boston, 1951, pp. 55-62.

A SMALL "WAR" IN A WHEAT FIELD
Wallace Smith, *Garden of the Sun,* Lymanhouse, Los Angeles. 1939, pp. 259-290.
Wallace Smith, *Prodigal Sons,* Christopher Publishing House, Boston, 1951, pp. 55-62.

AUNT LIL & THE GOLD NUGGET
The Fresno Bee, August 21, 1951.

FRESNO'S FAMOUS LANDSCAPE ARTIST
Paul O.Bingham and Beverly Bubar Denenberg, "Maynard Dixon as Muralist: Sketches for the Mark Hopkins Hotel Mural," *California History*, California Historical Society, Vol. LXIX, No. 1, Spring 1990, pp. 52-59.
Dixon, Maynard, *Rim-Rock and Sage*, The California Historical Society, San Francisco, 1977, pp. ix-xxix.
Donald J. Hagerty, *Desert Dreams*, Peregrine Smith Books, Layton, Utah, 1993, pp. xvii-xxvii.
Edwin Streit, "The Old Neighborhood," *Fresno Past & Present*, quarterly journal, Fresno City and County Historical Society, Vol. 28, No. 3, Fall, 1986, p. 7.
Robert M. Wash, interview and assistance in preparation of manuscript.

AN ASSASSIN IN OUR MIDST¿
Theodore Roscoe, *The Web of Conspiracy*, Prentice-Hall, Englewood Cliffs, New Jersey, 1959, pp. 516-523.
Robert M. Wash, "After the assassination of Lincoln did John Wilkes Booth escape and use Fresno as a hide-out¿¿!" *The Fresno County Sun*, May 19, 1995, p. 10.
The Fresno Bee, "Booth To Stay Buried," May 27, 1995.

A GANG OF BROTHERS
Frank F. Latta, *Dalton Gang Days,* Bear State Books, Santa Cruz, California, 1976, pp. 1, 2, 57-74.
Robert M. Wash, *The Dalton Gang*, unpublished paper presented to the Fowler Friday Evening Club.

ANOTHER DALTON
Frank F. Latta, *Dalton Gang Days,* Bear State Books, Santa Cruz, California, 1976, pp. 1, 2, 57-74.
Robert M. Wash, *The Dalton Gang*, unpublished paper presented to the Fowler Friday Evening Club.
Robert M. Wash, interview and assistance in preparation of manuscript.

AN EARTHLY PARADISE
Erwin G. Gudde, *California Place Names,* University of California Press, Berkeley and Los Angeles, 1949, pp. 50, 51.
Hubert Howe Bancroft, *History of California,* printed in facsimile from the first American edition, Santa Barbara, California, 1963, pp. 64-68.

Notes

Robert M. Wash, interview and assistance in preparation of manuscript.
THE MOTHER OF COUNTIES
  Owen C. Coy, Ph.D.,*California County Boundaries*, California Historical Survey Commission, Berkeley, 1923, Revised edition, Valley Publishers, Fresno, 1973, pp. 101, 178, 282.
  Scott Pinkerton, *Mariposa County Courthouse,* Mariposa Heritage Press, Mariposa, California, 1989, pp. 9, 15.
  Raymond F. Wood, *The Early History of Mariposa County,* Academy Library Guild, Fresno, California, 1954, pp. 28-31.
  "Donations to Mariposa County Courthouse - 1957", collections of Scott Pinkerton.
MARIPOSA'S JUDGE
  Leroy Radanovich, *Mariposa Gazette,* May 25, 1995.
  Robert M. Wash, interview, November 6, 1997.
THE BUTTERFLY
  Charles W. Clough and William B. Secrest, Jr., *Fresno County—The Pioneer Years,* p. 25.
  Robert M. Wash, interview, November 6, 1997.
  Trip to Mariposa, November 6, 1997.
A COURTHOUSE FOR THE AGES
  Owen C.Coy, Ph.D.,*California County Boundaries*, California Historical Survey Commission, Berkeley, 1923, revised edition, Valley Publishers, Fresno, 1973, p. 282.
  Scott Pinkerton, *Mariposa County Courthouse,* Mariposa Heritage Press, Mariposa, California, 1989, pp. 16-33, 67-69.
  Scott Pinkerton, *History and Description of Mariposa County Courthouse 1854,* Mariposa County Chamber of Commerce, Brochure.
  Scott Pinkerton, interview, November 7, 1997.
A MUSEUM IN THE MOUNTAINS
  Tour of Mariposa Museum and History Center, November 6, 1997.
  Muriel Powers, interview, November 6, 1997.
ONLY A PAPER WEDDING
  Fresno Morning Republican, December 23, 1899.
THE KEARNEY PYLONS
  John Edward Powell, "Charles Franklin," unpublished biographical sketch.
  John Edward Powell, interview, November 8, 1997.
  The Fresno Bee, June 2, 1933, p. 7-B. Files of John Edward Powell.
OLEANDER
  The Fresno Bee, date not available.
  Washington Union High School Centennial 1892-1992, Easton Historical Society, Fresno, 1992. pp. 79-82.
  Philip E. Tavlian, interview, April 20, 1998.
A MASTER ARCHITECT
  Matthew M. McGrath and John Edward Powell, "The Architect," promotional brochure provided by Manning Properties, 1997.
  John Edward Powell, interview, December 27, 1997.
A COLLEGE FOR FRESNO
  Dr. Harold Haak, "CSUF's Past, Present and Future," annual address to the Academic Assembly of California State University, Fresno, August, 1986.
ELK HORNS & STAGECOACHES
  William Harland Boyd and Glendon J. Rodgers, *San Joaquin Vignettes, The Reminiscences of Captain John Barker,* Kern County Historical Society, Merchants Printing and Lithographing Co., Inc. Bakersfield, 1955, pp. vii, 99-105.
  Raymond Ellena, "Burell," *Fresno County Centennial Almanac,* Fresno County Centennial Committee, Fresno, 1956, p. 86.
  Charles W. Clough and William B. Secrest, Jr., *Fresno County—The Pioneer Years,* pp. 105, 106.
  Robert M. Wash, interview and assistance in preparation of manuscript.
A FARM SHOW IN TULARE
  Bill Rawls, Assistant Manager, International Agri-Center, Inc., interview, January 12, 1998.
  Clyde Stagner, interview, January 12, 1998.
  Maria Rising, International Agri-Center, Inc., web pages for The California Farm Equipment Show and International Exposition.

Notes

THE TULARE COMMUNITY STEPS UP
  Bill Rawls, Assistant Manager, International Agri-Center, Inc., interview, January 15, 1998.
  Richard Rogers, interview, January 16, 1998.
THE LEGENDARY MAN OF BADGER PASS
  Nic Fiore, Ski School Director, Badger Pass, interview, January 22, 1998.
  The Fresno Bee, November 10, 1957.
  The Fresno Bee, November 5, 1967.
  The Fresno Bee, December 30, 1973.
  The Fresno Bee, February 7, 1982.
A MARDI GRAS IN THE TOWER DISTRICT
  Bill Kuebler, Director, Tower District Marketing Committee, interview, February 4, 1998.
  Felix Muzquiz, Assistant Director, Tower District Marketing Committee, interview, February 2, 1998.
  The Fresno Bee, "Talk of the Tower, February, 1998.
BULLDOG BACKERS
  "All Fired Up!" Bulldog Foundation fortieth anniversary brochure, provided by Bulldog Foundation Office, California State University Fresno.
  Pat Ogle, interview, May 19, 1998.
  Pat Ogle, written material on Bulldog Foundation fund raising drive results.
  Pat Ogle, written material on results of Bulldog Foundation fund raising drive, update, May 28, 1999.
THE BRICK MAKER & MAYOR
  Columbus Joel Craycroft, unpublished autobiography, courtesy of Joyce Gibson.
  Fresno Morning Republican, November 18, 1915.
AN OLYMPIC ATHLETE EXTRAORDINAIRE
  Omer Crane, "Tulare Gives Hero's Welcome to Bob Mathias," *The Fresno Bee,* August 28, 1948.
  Ed Rosenthal, "Bob Mathias Is Acclaimed For Victory," *The Fresno Bee,* August 7, 1948.
TIDBITS FROM 1885
  Fresno Evening Democrat, November 16, 1885.
FRESNO COUNTY TURNS 100
  Fresno County Centennial Committee, *Fresno County Centennial Almanac,* Fresno County Centennial Committee, Fresno, 1956, pp. 5, 9.
  Robert M. Wash, interview and assistance in preparation of manuscript.
A COMMEMORATIVE COMMUNION SERVICE
  Charles W. Clough and William B. Secrest, Jr., *Fresno County—The Pioneer Years,* p. 75.
  L. A. Winchell Papers, Ms.3, Chapter 22, pp. 16, 17.
  William Patterson, "Fresno Marks Centennial of First Religious Service," *The Fresno Bee,* October 21, 1955.
  The Fresno Bee, October 22, 1955.
A FARM BOY FROM CARUTHERS
  Dale L. Morgan, et al., *GPH An Informal Record of George P. Hammond and His Era in the Bancroft Library,* The Friends of the Bancroft Library, University of California, Berkeley, 1965, pp. 1-12.
  Robert M. Wash, interview and assistance in preparation of manuscript.
JIM SAVAGE'S MONUMENT
  Visit to monument site, April 19, 1998.
  The Fresno Bee, August 17, 1971.
MR. BULLDOG
  Dennis Woods, interview, May 19, 1998.
  Pat Ogle, interview, May 19, 1998.
  Pat Ogle, press release with Biography of Dennis Woods, May 19, 1998.
  Pat Ogle, written material on Bulldog Foundation fund raising drive results.
  Pat Ogle, written material on results of Bulldog Foundation fund raising drive, update, May 28, 1999.
THE CITY OF SELMA
  J. Randall McFarland, *Centennial Selma,* J. Randall McFarland, in association with *The Selma Enterprise,* Selma, California, 1980, pp. 13, 14, 17, 29-33.
  J. Randall McFarland, interview and driving tour of Selma, May 7, 1998.

HOW SELMA GOT ITS NAME
J. Randall McFarland, *Centennial Selma,* J. Randall McFarland, in association with *The Selma Enterprise*, Selma, California, 1980, pp. 37-40.

A SANDLAPPER NAMED WHITSON
J. Randall McFarland, *Centennial Selma,* J. Randall McFarland, in association with *The Selma Enterprise*, Selma, California, 1980, pp. 15, 23-25.

UNGER & HIS OPERA HOUSES
J. Randall McFarland, *Centennial Selma,* J. Randall McFarland, in association with *The Selma Enterprise*, Selma, California, 1980, pp. 84, 85.
J. Randall McFarland, interview and driving tour of Selma, May 7, 1998.
Dennis Adkins and J. Randall McFarland, playbill for the Unger Opera House's Farewell Performances, July 11, 12 and 13, 1996. Pioneer Village, Selma, California. pp. 2, 3.

THE FINAL CURTAIN
J. Randall McFarland, interview and tour of Unger Opera House, May 7, 1998.
J. Randall McFarland, *Thanks for the Memory*, script of final performance, Unger Opera House, July 13, 1996.

FIFTY YEARS OF YOUTH CLUBS
Ken Quenzer, Executive Director, Boys & Girls Clubs of Fresno County, interview, April 28, 1998.
Corinne H. Martin, Director, Resource Development, Boys & Girls Clubs of Fresno County, interview, April 28, 1998.
Boys & Girls Clubs of Fresno County, history & information packet.

COATS IN THE COURTROOM
The Honorable Stephen Henry, "Old Times in the Fresno Courthouse," *The Bar Bulletin*, Fresno County Bar Association. May, 1998, Vol. 21, No. 5, p. 12.
Robert M. Wash, interview, May 17, 1998.

A WALK THROUGH THE PARK
Robert M. Wash and the author. From observations and notes taken during a walk through Courthouse Park, May 24, 1998.

THE OLDEST ARMENIAN CONGREGATION
Centennial Commemorative Committee, *First Armenian Presbyterian Church 1897-1997,* Fresno, 1997.
Centennial Committee, *The First Congregational Church of Fresno The First One Hundred Years,* Pioneer Publishing Company, Fresno, 1984, p. 17.
Zabelle Melkonian, grandniece of Seropian brothers, information given by telephone message received through the First Armenian Presbyterian Church.
Philip Tavlian, Chairman of Centennial Commemorative Committee, First Armenian Presbyterian Church, interview and tour of church and adjacent buildings, April 20, 1998.

THE REVEREND LYSANDER TOWER BURBANK
Centennial Commemorative Committee, *First Armenian Presbyterian Church 1897-1997,* Fresno, 1997.

THE RAISIN DRIVE
Robert M. Wash, "Turbulent Year in the Raisin Industry," *Fresno County in the 20th Century: from 1900 to the 1980s,* Panorama West Books, Fresno, 1986, pp. 178-180.
Robert M. Wash, interview and assistance in preparation of manuscript.

NIGHT RIDERS IN THE VALLEY
Robert M. Wash, "Turbulent Year in the Raisin Industry," *Fresno County in the 20th Century: from 1900 to the 1980s,* Panorama West Books, Fresno, 1986, pp. 178-180.
Robert M. Wash, interview and assistance in preparation of manuscript.

JUDGE J.W. NORTH
The Fresno Bee, date not available.

THE ALABAMA COLONY
Charles Clough, *Madera,* Madera County History, Madera, 1968, p. 23.
William S. Coate, interview, July 2, 1998.
Wallace W. Elliot, *History of Fresno County,* reprinted by Valley Publishers, Fresno, 1973, pp. 118, 119.
Mordecai Scholars, *The Mordecai Memoirs,* Classroom Chronicles Press, p. 1.

THE REFUGE
William S. Coate, interview, July 2, 1998.

Notes

Wallace W. Elliot, *History of Fresno County,* reprinted by Valley Publishers, Fresno, 1973, pp. 118, 119.

Robert J. Long, "William S. Chapman: The Unknown Builder of Fresno County," *Fresno Past & Present,* quarterly journal, Fresno Historical Society, Vol. 39., No. 3, p. 3.

Mordecai Scholars, *The Mordecai Memoirs,* Classroom Chronicles Press, p. 1.

Brooke Wissler, interview at the Refuge Ranch, June 7, 1998.

THE FOUNDER OF MADERA COUNTY

William S. Coate, interview, July 2, 1998.

Wallace W. Elliot, *History of Fresno County,* reprinted by Valley Publishers, Fresno, 1973, pp. 118, 119, 226, 227.

Mordecai Historians, *Refuge,* introduction by William S. Coate, The Classroom Chronicles Press, Madera, 1988, pp. xi-xv.

Brooke Wissler, interview at the Refuge Ranch, June 7, 1998.

HIDDEN DAM

Charles Clough, *Madera,* Madera County History, Madera, 1968, pp. 78, 79, 83, 84.

Richard Grahlman, Supervisory Ranger, U.S. Army Corps of Engineers, Hensley Lake, Hidden Dam, interview May 6, 1978.

Hidden Reservoir Fresno River, California, Master Plan & Recreational Facilities, Department of the Army, Sacramento District, Sacramento, California, 1968, p. iv.

STRING TOWN & POISON SWITCH

Charles Clough, *Madera,* Madera County History, Madera, 1968, pp. 79, 80.

A GRUBSTAKER'S PARADISE

Charles Clough, *Madera,* Madera County History, Madera, 1968, pp. 43, 44, 83-85.

Betty E. Linn, *Madera County 1893-1993*, Madera Newspapers, Inc., Madera, 1993, pp. 14, 15.

A COMMUNITY ON THE FLATS

Charles Clough, *Madera,* Madera County History, Madera, 1968, pp. 81, 82.

Betty E. Linn, *Madera County 1893-1993*, Madera Newspapers, Inc., Madera, 1993, pp. 24-28.

Ruth and Bill Mason, *History of Fresno Flats,* 1997 edition, pp. 2- 8.

HOW OAKHURST GOT ITS NAME

Betty E. Linn, *Madera County 1893-1993*, Madera Newspapers, Inc., Madera, 1993, pp. 26, 27.

Ruth and Bill Mason, *History of Fresno Flats,* 1997 edition, pp. 8, 9.

FRESNO FLATS HISTORICAL PARK

Dwight Barnes, President, Sierra Sites Historical Association, interview and guided tour of Fresno Flats Historical Park, June 28, 1998.

Fresno Flats Historical Park, Brochure, Sierra Sites Historical Association.

COARSE GOLD GULCH

Charles Clough, *Madera,* Madera County History, Madera, 1968, pp. 78, 79.

Wallace W. Elliot, *History of Fresno County,* reprinted by Valley Publishers, Fresno, 1973, p. 87.

David W. Kean, *Wide Places in California Roads,* Vol. 4, The Concord Press, Sunnyvale, California, 1996, pp. 51, 52.

Betty E. Linn, *Madera County 1893-1993*, Madera Newspapers, Inc., Madera, 1993, pp. 22-24.

WARRIORS FOR ALL SEASONS

Nelson Tennis, "Forty Years Ago in Fresno," *Student Sports*, Vol. 20, No. 4, April, 1998, pp. 21, 22.

Virginia Bitters, editor, *Owl*, Fresno High School Student Body, Fresno, 1958, pp. 184-187.

James Maloney, interview, July 14, 1998.

REACH FOR THE STARS

James Maloney, interview, July 14, 1998.

Richard Ellsworth, interview, July 27, 1998.

WHERE WILDFLOWERS FLOURISHED

Wallace W. Elliot, *History of Fresno County,* reprinted by Valley Publishers, Fresno, 1973, pp. 201, 215.

Felipe Maria Errecart, "The Wildflowers of My Memories," footnote to the poem, 1973 First Place Winner Members Writing Contest, California Writers and Artists of the San Joaquin Valley.

Notes

J. Randall McFarland, *Water For a Thirsty Land,* Consolidated Irrigation District, Selma, 1996, p. 108.

Harold Salley, *History of California Post Offices 1849-1990,* 2nd edition edited by Edward L. Patera, The Depot, La Mesa, California, 1991.

Mart and Oliva Raven, interview, October 19, 1997.

Leonard Frame, interview, April 5, 1998.

DR. VINCENT HOLDS COURT

June Muller, "Finding of 1893 Invitation Recalls Only County Hanging," *The Fresno Bee.*

GEORGE DUNLAP MOSS

Helen and Forest Clingan, *Oak to Pine to Timberline,* Word Dancer Press, Clovis, 1995, p. 49.

"Sands Baker and the Dunlap Area," Clamproclamation, Jim Savage Chapter 1852, E Clampus Vitus, July, 1989.

MILLWOOD

Charles W. Clough, et al., *Fresno County in the 20th Century, from 1900 to the 1980s,* Panorama West Books, Fresno, 1986, pp. 144, 145.

Helen and Forest Clingan, *Oak to Pine to Timberline,* Word Dancer Press, Clovis, 1995, pp. 70, 71.

HAUNTINGS IN THE HIGH COUNTRY

Heyward Moore, "High Sierra Lake and Stream Names," *Fresno Past & Present,* Vol. 25, No. 4, pp. 1-8.

ROSES IN THE DESERT

Wasco Chamber of Commerce, *Welcome to Wasco,* informational brochure.

Wasco's 30th Annual Festival of Roses, Wasco Festival of Roses, Inc., Promotional brochure.

A PRIZE-WINNING VINTNER

Edwin M. Eaton, *Vintage Fresno,* The Huntington Press, Fresno, 1965, p. 78.

J. M. Guinn, *History of the State of California and Biographical Record of the San Joaquin Valley, California,* The Chapman Publishing Company, Chicago, 1905, p. 607.

Paul Vandor, *History of Fresno County,* Historic Record Company, Los Angeles, 1919, p. 937.

THE HONORABLE CHARLES A. HART

Fresno County Centennial Committee, *Fresno County Centennial Almanac,* Fresno County Centennial Committee, Fresno, 1956, p. 14.

J. M. Guinn, *History of the State of California and Biographical Record of the San Joaquin Valley, California,* The Chapman Publishing Company, Chicago, 1905, pp. 490, 491.

Paul Vandor, *History of Fresno County,* Historic Record Company, Los Angeles, 1919, pp. 124, 646-648.

A FLUME & A TOWN

Charles Clough, *Madera,* Madera County History, Madera, 1968, pp. 86-88.

Betty E. Linn, *Madera County 1893-1993,* Madera Newspapers, Inc., Madera, 1993, pp. 73, 74.

CAPTAIN RUSSEL PERRY MACE

William S. Coate, *Pieces of the Past: Madera County Vignettes,* The Classroom Chronicles Press, Madera, 1992, pp. 3, 4.

MODESTY IMMORTALIZED

Harold Salley, *History of California Post Offices 1849-1990,* 2nd edition edited by Edward L. Patera, The Depot, La Mesa, California, 1991.

Robert M. Wash, interview, August 27, 1998.

THE EISEN BROTHERS

Charles W. Clough and William B. Secrest, Jr., *Fresno County—The Pioneer Years,* pp. 147, 148.

Fresno County Centennial Committee, *Fresno County Centennial Almanac,* Fresno County Centennial Committee, Fresno, 1956, p. 36.

Robert M. Wash, "The History of Sunnyside: A Place With Space," Vol. IV, Chapter 5.

"Eisen Vineyard; Queen Among Early Ranches of Sunnyside," *Sunnyside Up,* May, 1991.

PROFESSOR GUSTAV EISEN

Charles W. Clough and William B. Secrest, Jr., *Fresno County—The Pioneer Years,* pp. 193, 339.

Charles W. Clough, et al., *Fresno County in the 20th Century, from 1900 to the 1980s,* Panorama West Books, Fresno, 1986, pp. 171, 172.

Fresno County Centennial Committee, *Fresno County Centennial Almanac,* Fresno County Centennial Committee, Fresno, 1956, p. 23.

Notes

Francis P. Farquhar, *History of the Sierra Nevada,* University of California Press, Berkeley and Los Angeles, 1965, p. 202.

Robert M. Wash, "The History of Sunnyside: A Place With Space," Vol. IV. Chapter 9.

"Roeding Family Leaves Rich Legacy In Sunnyside," *Sunnyside Up*, September, 1991.

Robert M. Wash, "The History of Sunnyside: A Place With Space," Vol. IV, Chapter 5.

"Eisen Vineyard; Queen Among Early Ranches of Sunnyside," *Sunnyside Up*, May, 1991.

THE REUNION THAT NEVER ENDS

Dennis Pollock, "The Never-Ending Reunion," *The Fresno Bee,* March 15, 1994.

Woody Laughnan, "Reunion Planners Keep on Meeting," *The Fresno Bee,* date unknown.

WHERE ANTELOPE PLAYED

Charles Clough, *Madera,* Madera County History, Madera, 1968, p. 77.

David W. Kean, *Wide Places in California Roads,* Vol. 4, The Concord Press, Sunnyvale, California, 1996, pp. 22, 23.

Betty E. Linn, *Madera County 1893-1993*, Madera Newspapers, Inc., Madera, 1993, p. 106.

NEWCOMERS FROM AN ANCIENT LAND

George Gianopulos, interview, October 22, 1998.

Dr. Helen Rockas, *History of the Greek Community of Fresno.*

A CHURCH FOR ST. GEORGE

George Gianopulos, interview, October 22, 1998.

Dr. Helen Rockas, *History of the Greek Community of Fresno.*

A SETTLEMENT NAMED LIBERTY

Wallace W. Elliot, *History of Fresno County,* reprinted by Valley Publishers, Fresno, 1973, p. 199.

Bob & Frances Henson, *Bits & Pieces of Riverdale's History*, Riverdale, 1996, pp. 3, 4, 13, 14, 15, 29, 29A.

Linda Renn, "Riverdale to celebrate 100th birthday, *Twin City Times*, Vol. XXII, No. 4, January 28, 1998.

THE CREAM CITY

Charles W.Clough, et al., *Fresno County in the 20th Century, from 1900 to the 1980s,* Panorama West Books, Fresno, 1986, p. 110.

Jim Gomes, President and Chief Executive Officer, Danish Creamery Association, interview, November 12, 1998.

Bob & Frances Henson, *Bits & Pieces of Riverdale's History*, Riverdale, 1996, pp. 4, 6, 23, 25, 46, 47.

Sharlene Gomes, *Danish Creamery Association 1895-1995,* Fresno, 1995, p. 119.

THE HARLANS OF RIVERDALE

Wallace W. Elliot, *History of Fresno County,* reprinted by Valley Publishers, Fresno, 1973, p. 215.

J. M. Guinn, *History of the State of California and Biographical Record of the San Joaquin Valley, California,* The Chapman Publishing Company, Chicago, 1905, p. 1430.

Brad Harlan, interview, November 18, 1998.

Bob & Frances Henson, *Bits & Pieces of Riverdale's History*, Riverdale, 1996, pp. 3, 27.

Linda Renn, "Harlan family is rooted in earliest Riverdale history, *Twin City Times,* Vol. XXII, No. 34, August 26, 1998.

A COURTHOUSE FOR MADERA

Charles Clough, *Madera,* Madera County History, Madera, 1968, pp. 16-18.

William S. Coate, *Pieces of the Past: Madera County Vignettes,* The Classroom Chronicles Press, Madera, 1992, p. 108.

Betty E. Linn, *Madera County 1893-1993*, Madera Newspapers, Inc., Madera, 1993, p. 84.

NIGHT DOESN'T BECOME A NAKED LADY

Mary Helen McKay, interview, October 12, 1998.

A STAGECOACH & TWO ROBBERS

William S. Coate, *Pieces of the Past: Madera County Vignettes,* The Classroom Chronicles Press, Madera, 1992, p. 88.

THE SOLDIERS & THE BARLEY SACK

William S. Coate, *Pieces of the Past: Madera County Vignettes,* The Classroom Chronicles Press, Madera, 1992, p. 190.

A TOWN NAMED BORDEN

Charles Clough, *Madera,* Madera County History, Madera, 1968, p. 78.

William S. Coate, *Pieces of the Past: Madera County Vignettes,* The Classroom Chronicles

Notes

Press, Madera, 1992, p. 78.

Wallace W. Elliot, *History of Fresno County,* reprinted by Valley Publishers, Fresno, 1973, p. 199.

A FRENCH MINING TOWN

Charles Clough, *Madera,* Madera County History, Madera, 1968, pp. 89, 90.

William S. Coate, *Pieces of the Past: Madera County Vignettes,* The Classroom Chronicles Press, Madera, 1992, p. 178.

Betty E. Linn, *Madera County 1893-1993*, Madera Newspapers, Inc., Madera, 1993, pp. 15, 16.

HILDRETH

Charles Clough, *Madera,* Madera County History, Madera, 1968, p. 83.

William S. Coate, *Pieces of the Past: Madera County Vignettes,* The Classroom Chronicles Press, Madera, 1992, pp. 83, 84.

Betty E. Linn, *Madera County 1893-1993*, Madera Newspapers, Inc., Madera, 1993, p. 16.

Harold Salley, *History of California Post Offices 1849-1990,* 2nd edition edited by Edward L. Patera, The Depot, La Mesa, California, 1991.

THE LOST HORDE OF GOLD

Betty E. Linn, *Madera County 1893-1993*, Madera Newspapers, Inc., Madera, 1993, p. 16.

WILDCAT STATION

Charles Clough, *Madera,* Madera County History, Madera, 1968, p. 91.

Betty E. Linn, *Madera County 1893-1993*, Madera Newspapers, Inc., Madera, 1993, pp. 15, 16.

RAYMOND GRANITE

Charles Clough, *Madera,* Madera County History, Madera, 1968, pp. 54, 55.

Betty E. Linn, *Madera County 1893-1993*, Madera Newspapers, Inc., Madera, 1993, pp. 35, 36.

A RIDE THROUGH GOLD COUNTRY

Trip taken by the author and Robert Wash, October 30, 1998.

Mary Dunn, interview in Raymond, October 30, 1998.

Jeannie Mason, interview in Raymond, October 30, 1998 and phone interview, November 4, 1998.

Marva Padgett, interview in Raymond, October 30, 1998.

A RACING LEGEND

Omer Crane, "Going high on the turn 25 years ago fatal move for Vukovich, Sr.," *The Fresno Bee,* May 25, 1980.

The Fresno Bee, May, 5, 1941.

Ed Orman, "Sport Thinks," *The Fresno Bee,* date not available.

John Rich; "Crash kills Fresno racer Billy Vukovich 27-year old second in family to die racing," *The Fresno Bee,* November 26, 1990.

Robert M. Wash, interview, November 18, 1998.

A LEGENDARY FAMILY OF RACERS

Charles W. Clough, et al., *Fresno County in the 20th Century, from 1900 to the 1980s,* Panorama West Books, Fresno, 1986, pp. 470-1.

The Fresno Bee, "Vukovich legacy: glorious, tragic Indy success spans 3 generations," November 26, 1990.

Bill McEwen and John Rich, "Tragedy Strikes Vukovich again. Fatal accident ends Billy's promising career," *The Fresno Bee,* November 26, 1990.

Robert M. Wash, interview and assistance in preparation of manuscript.

THE VETERANS MEMORIAL AUDITORIUM

"Remember When?" *The Fresno Bee,* August 4, 1963.

Mabelle Selland, interview, September 29, 1998.

Mabelle Selland, speech given to the Garden of the Sun Corral of the Westerners, October 21, 1998.

Roger Taylor, "Veterans Memorial Auditorium, Summary of Statement for Historical and Architectural Significance, National Register Nomination," May 10, 1994, Fresno City Hall, Housing and Development Department.

THE AUDITORIUM'S MEMORIAL TREES

Roger Taylor, "Veterans Memorial Auditorium, Summary of Statement for Historical and Architectural Significance, National Register Nomination," May 10, 1994, Fresno City Hall, Housing and Development Department.

Notes

THE AFRICAN AMERICAN LEGACY
    Jack A. Kelley, President, African American Historical and Cultural Museum, interview
    and tour of museum, November 23, 1998.
    African American Historical and Cultural Museum, brochure.
CECIL C. HINTON
    Jack A. Kelley, President, African American Historical and Cultural Museum, interview
    and tour of museum, November 23, 1998.
    Angela Valdivia, "Community Leader Hinton Dies," *The Fresno Bee*, August 26, 1987.
AN HONORED CITIZEN
    Jack A. Kelley, President, African American Historical and Cultural Museum, interview
    and tour of museum, November 23, 1998.
    Walt Porter, "Bigby Villa—Fulfillment of Many Dreams," *The Fresno Bee*, April 8, 1972.
    The Fresno Bee, April 25, 1970.
    The Fresno Bee, November 21, 1971.
    The Fresno Bee, April 7, 1972.
    The Fresno Bee, April 23, 1981.
JACK A. KELLEY
    Jack A. Kelley, President, African American Historical and Cultural Museum, interview
    and tour of museum, November 23, 1998.
    "Jack A. Kelley," biographical material provided by the African American Historical and
    Cultural Museum.
A MOUNTAIN PASS CALLED PACHECO
    Brenda Burnett Preston, *Andrew Davidson Firebaugh & Susan Burgess Firebaugh, California
    Pioneers*, Rio Del Mar Press, Rio Del Mar, California, 1995, pp. 83-89.
    Albert Shumate, PhD., *Francisco Pacheco of Pacheco Pass*, University of the Pacific, Stockton,
    1977, pp. 1-4, 11-14, 32.
BELL'S STATION
    Brenda Burnett Preston, *Andrew Davidson Firebaugh & Susan Burgess Firebaugh, California
    Pioneers*, Rio Del Mar Press, Rio Del Mar, California, 1995, pp. 91-101.
FRANCISCO PACHECO
    Albert Shumate, PhD., *Francisco Pacheco of Pacheco Pass*, University of the Pacific, Stockton,
    1977, pp. 5-14, 20-24, 31-33.
ANDREW DAVIDSON FIREBAUGH
    Brenda Burnett Preston, *Andrew Davidson Firebaugh & Susan Burgess Firebaugh, California
    Pioneers*, Rio Del Mar Press, Rio Del Mar, California, 1995, pp. 19-22, 61, 76-80.
    Andrew Davidson Firebaugh, Clamproclamation, Jim Savage Chapter No. 1852, E Clampus
    Vitus, November 17, 1968.
THE CHIEF OF THE YOSEMITE
    Lafayette Houghton Bunnell, M.D., *Discovery of the Yosemite*, G.W. Gerlicher, Los Angeles,
    1911, pp. 36, 41-50.
    Brenda Burnett Preston, *Andrew Davidson Firebaugh & Susan Burgess Firebaugh, California
    Pioneers*, Rio Del Mar Press, Rio Del Mar, California, 1995, pp. 55-58.
TENAYA'S TRAGEDY
    Lafayette Houghton Bunnell, M.D., *Discovery of the Yosemite*, G.W. Gerlicher, Los Angeles,
    1911, pp. 48-56; 125-158.
    Brenda Burnett Preston, *Andrew Davidson Firebaugh & Susan Burgess Firebaugh, California
    Pioneers*, Rio Del Mar Press, Rio Del Mar, California, 1995, pp. 58-73.
A VALLEY DISCOVERED
    Lafayette Houghton Bunnell, M.D., *Discovery of the Yosemite*, G.W. Gerlicher, Los Angeles,
    1911, pp. 52-69.
    Robert Eccleston, *The Mariposa Indian War 1850-1851*, ed. C. Gregory Crampton,
    University of Utah Press, Salt Lake City, 1957, p. 59.
    Brenda Burnett Preston, *Andrew Davidson Firebaugh & Susan Burgess Firebaugh, California
    Pioneers*, Rio Del Mar Press, Rio Del Mar, California, 1995, pp. 60, 61.
A SURVEYOR FOR FRESNO COUNTY
    American Association of University Women, *Heritage Fresno Homes and People*, Pioneer
    Publishing Company, 1975, p. 57.
    William Patnaude, Historic Resources Inventory, City of Fresno, The McKay Home, June
    27, 1978.

Notes

Paul Vandor, *History of Fresno County,* Historic Record Company, Los Angeles, 1919, pp. 723-4.

THE HARLOW HOME
Gretchen Smith Mui, *Arts & Crafts Design in America*, Chronicle Books, San Francisco, 1998, pp. 7-8.
John Panter, Historic Resources Inventory, City of Fresno, The Harlow Home, May 20, 1989.

A HOUSE BUILT WITH WHIMSY
William Patnaude, Historic Resources Inventory, City of Fresno, The Shuttera Home, June 23, 1978.

THE HOUSE ON CLARK STREET
William Patnaude, Historic Resources Inventory, City of Fresno, The Shipp Home, June 27, 1978.
Paul Vandor, *History of Fresno County,* Historic Record Company, Los Angeles, 1919, pp. 1417-8.

THE GREAT ROUGH RIDER
William S. Coate, *Pieces of the Past: Madera County Vignettes,* The Classroom Chronicles Press, Madera, 1992, p. 20.
Shirley Sargent, *Enchanted Childhoods,* Flying Spur Press, Yosemite, 1993, pp. 31-33.

THE PLEASANTON CAFE
Evelyn Sterios Fiorani, interview, January 6, 1999.

A YOUNG LADY'S LAMENT
Fresno Evening Democrat, November 20, 1885.

JAMES PHELAN'S BUILDING
Paul Vandor, *History of Fresno County,* Historic Record Company, Los Angeles, 1919, pp. 1307-8.
William Patnaude, Historic Resources Inventory, City of Fresno, James Phelan Building, June 30, 1978.

THE GREAT WHITE WAY
Charles W. Clough and William B. Secrest, Jr., *Fresno County—The Pioneer Years,* pp. 308-9.
Charles W. Clough, et al., *Fresno County in the 20th Century, from 1900 to the 1980s,* Panorama West Books, Fresno, 1986, pp. 63-4.
Evelyn Sterios Fiorani, interview, January 6, 1999.
Ken Hohmann, interview, January 9, 1999.
Schyler Rehart, interview, January 9, 1999.
The Fresno Bee, date not available.
Woodward Map, Fresno City, Nirenstein's National Map Co, Springfield, Massachusetts, 1950. Courtesy John Edward Powell.

ASA S. EDGERLY
Edwin M. Eaton, *Vintage Fresno,* The Huntington Press, Fresno, 1965, pp. 68-9.
Paul Vandor, *History of Fresno County,* Historic Record Company, Los Angeles, 1919, pp. 988-91.

THE WOMEN OF MILLERTON
Paul Vandor, *History of Fresno County,* Historic Record Company, Los Angeles, 1919, pp. 110, 128-9.

A WHISKEY A DAY
Fresno Evening Democrat, September 5, 1885.

A PIECE OF GERMAN HISTORY
American Association of University Women, *Heritage Fresno Homes and People,* Pioneer Publishing Company, 1975, p. 37.
Charles W. Clough, et al., *Fresno County in the 20th Century, from 1900 to the 1980s,* Panorama West Books, Fresno, 1986, p. 7.
William Patnaude, Historic Resources Inventory, City of Fresno, The Legler Residence, June 26, 1978.

THE MARSHAL & THE SMOKING GUN
Fresno Evening Democrat, October 31, 1885.

GOLDEN ANNIVERSARY TIMES FOUR
Daniel K. Sniffin, Documents relating to Sniffin Family genealogy.

THE LAST STRAW

Notes

Charles W. Clough and William B. Secrest, Jr., *Fresno County—The Pioneer Years,* p. 141.
Fresno Evening Democrat, September 7, 1885.
JESSE AUGUST BLASINGAME
    Charles W. Clough and William B. Secrest, Jr., *Fresno County—The Pioneer Years,* p. 94.
    Paul Vandor, *History of Fresno County,* Historic Record Company, Los Angeles, 1919, pp. 1406-9.
CHILDBIRTH AMID THE TUMULT
    Schyler Rehart, interview, January 16, 1999.
    Fresno Morning Republican, July 7, 1898.
JULY 4, 1898
    Fresno Morning Republican, July 3, 1898.
    Fresno Morning Republican, July 4, 1898.
A DOG NAMED BABE
    David H. Redinger, *The Story of Big Creek*, Angelus Press, Los Angeles, 1949, pp. xiv, xv, 105-110.
    The Fresno Bee, "Remember When?" No date available.
THE LYNCHING THAT WASN'T
    Daily Evening Expositor, July 16, 1892. Courtesy William B. Secrest, Sr.
    Fresno Morning Republican, July 17, 1892. Courtesy William B. Secrest, Sr.
    San Francisco Examiner, July 24, 1892. Courtesy William B. Secrest, Sr.
RED LIGHTS & A SENATOR
    William S. Coate, *Pieces of the Past: Madera County Vignettes, Second Edition,* The Classroom Chronicles Press, Madera, 1994, pp. 267-8.
THE MAN WITH THREE WIVES
    William S. Coate, *Pieces of the Past: Madera County Vignettes, Second Edition,* The Classroom Chronicles Press, Madera, 1994, pp. 243-4.
MADERA'S TRIUMPH OVER THE RAILROAD
    William S. Coate, *Pieces of the Past: Madera County Vignettes, Second Edition,* The Classroom Chronicles Press, Madera, 1994, pp. 297-8.
HAMPTON'S VILLAGE
    Paul Vandor, *History of Fresno County,* Historic Record Company, Los Angeles, 1919, p. 258.
THE SHELBYVILLE SWINDLE
    Charles W. Clough and William B. Secrest, Jr., *Fresno County—The Pioneer Years,* p. 160.
    Paul Vandor, *History of Fresno County,* Historic Record Company, Los Angeles, 1919, pp. 279-80.
THE SENATOR'S SWITCH
    Jon R. McFarland, *Village on the Prairie*, Fowler Mother's Club, The Ensign Publishing Company, Fowler, 1972, pp. 3-5.
MR. GENTRY OF FOWLER
    Jon R. McFarland, *Village on the Prairie*, Fowler Mother's Club, The Ensign Publishing Company, Fowler, 1972, pp. 6,7.
FOWLER PIONEERS
    Jon R. McFarland, *Village on the Prairie*, Fowler Mother's Club, The Ensign Publishing Company, Fowler, 1972, pp. 8,9.
    Paul Vandor, *History of Fresno County,* Historic Record Company, Los Angeles, 1919, pp. 660-3.
THE DRY CITY OF FOWLER
    Jon R. McFarland, *Village on the Prairie*, Fowler Mother's Club, The Ensign Publishing Company, Fowler, 1972, pp. 27, 28.
FOWLER'S FIRST MAYOR
    Jon R. McFarland, *Village on the Prairie*, Fowler Mother's Club, The Ensign Publishing Company, Fowler, 1972, pp. 28.
    Paul Vandor, *History of Fresno County,* Historic Record Company, Los Angeles, 1919, pp. 2515-6.
A BRAVE DOG NAMED DINKEY
    Wallace W. Elliot, *History of Fresno County,* reprinted by Valley Publishers, Fresno, 1973, p. 232.
    Joe Smith, *From the Valley to the High Sierra,* ed. by Dwight H. Barnes and Ray Nish, The Fresno Bee, p. 39.

Notes

THE MASON BUILDING
Charles W. Clough, et al., *Fresno County in the 20th Century, from 1900 to the 1980s,* Panorama West Books, Fresno, 1986, p. 50.
Fresno Morning Republican, October 22, 1916.
Fresno Morning Republican, July 21, 1917.
Fresno Morning Republican, March 1, 1918.
William Patnaude, Historic Resources Inventory, City of Fresno, The Mason Building, June 29, 1978.

A CALABOOSE FOR GRUB GULCH
Joe Smith, *From the Valley to the High Sierra,* ed. by Dwight H. Barnes and Ray Nish, The Fresno Bee, p. 114.

A PLACE CALLED BOOTJACK
David L. Durham, *California Geographic Names,* Word Dancer Press, Clovis, 1998, pp. 770, 805, 841.
Joe Smith, *From the Valley to the High Sierra,* ed. by Dwight H. Barnes and Ray Nish, The Fresno Bee, p. 26.

COMMON THREADS
American Association of University Women, *Heritage Fresno Women and Their Contributions,* Pioneer Publishing Company, 1987, pp. 14, 56, 90-1.
Charles W. Clough and William B. Secrest, Jr., *Fresno County—The Pioneer Years,* pp. 341-2.
Doris Halemeier, Common Threads Committee, interview, February 13, 1999.

JACOB FRANKLIN NISWANDER
Paul Vandor, *History of Fresno County,* Historic Record Company, Vol. I, Los Angeles, 1919, pp. 763-4.

JAMES CASH PENNEY COMES TO TOWN
J. C. Penney, *Lines of a Layman*, Wm. B. Eerdmans Publishing Co., Grand Rapids, 1956, p. 146.
"J. C. Penney Meets Paul P. Harris," The Rotarian, October, 1994.
The Fresno Bee, March 17, 1952.

BILLY CARUTHERS
Laura Wickham Sinclair, "Early History of Caruthers," *The History of Caruthers*, 2nd edition, Caruthers High Future Business Leaders of America, Caruthers, 1976, pp. 1-7, 54.
Charles W. Clough and William B. Secrest, Jr., *Fresno County—The Pioneer Years,* p. 170.

A RICH LINEAGE OF SPANISH CALIFORNIA
Susanna Bryant Dakin, *Rose, or Rose Thorn?* The Friends of the Bancroft Library, University of California, Berkeley, 1963, pp. 1-11.
Ron Goble, "Emparan looks back on 25 years as farm official," *The Fresno Bee*, March 1, 1986, p. D3.
Myrtle M. McKittrich, *Vallejo, Son of California*, Binfords & Mort, Portland, 1944, pp. 1, 18.
Robert M. Wash, notes for speech for Fowler Friday Evening Club, genealogy of Robert V. Emparan, unpublished manuscript.

A VISIONARY PROJECT
Robert Pennell, Cultural Resources Manager, Table Mountain Rancheria, interview and tour of project, February 23, 1999.

A RESTORATION MIRACLE IN THE FOOTHILLS
Robert Pennell, Cultural Resources Manager, Table Mountain Rancheria, interview and tour of project, February 23, 1999.

A PRE-ELECTION CELEBRATION
William S. Coate, *Pieces of the Past: Madera County Vignettes,* The Classroom Chronicles Press, Madera, 1992, pp. 143-4.

THE FOOTHILL TOWN OF O'NEALS
Charles Clough, *Madera,* Madera County History, Madera, 1968, p. 82.
William S. Coate, *Pieces of the Past: Madera County Vignettes,* The Classroom Chronicles Press, Madera, 1992, pp. 4, 44.
David W. Kean, *Wide Places in California Roads,* Vol. 4, The Concord Press, Sunnyvale, California, 1996, p. 154.
Betty E. Linn, *Madera County 1893-1993*, Madera Newspapers, Inc., Madera, 1993, pp. 34-5.

A GATEWAY TO THE SIERRA
Charles Clough, *Madera,* Madera County History, Madera, 1968, pp. 80-1.

Notes

David W. Kean, *Wide Places in California Roads,* Vol. 4, The Concord Press, Sunnyvale, CA, 1996, p. 151.

Betty E. Linn, *Madera County 1893-1993,* Madera Newspapers, Inc., Madera, 1993, pp. 29-31.

A STAGE BOUND FOR YOSEMITE

William S. Coate, *Pieces of the Past: Madera County Vignettes, Second Edition,* The Classroom Chronicles Press, Madera, 1994, p. 237-8.

FRED M. ROESSLER

American Association of University Women, *Heritage Fresno Homes and People,* Pioneer Publishing Company, 1975, p. 77.

Paul Vandor, *History of Fresno County,* Vol. II, Historic Record Company, Los Angeles, 1919, pp. 2523-4.

Ben R. Walker, *The Fresno County Blue Book,* Arthur J. Cawston, managing editor and publisher, Fresno, 1941, pp. 524, 527.

PAYMASTER HANFORD PICKS A TOWN'S LOCATION

Kim German, ed., "Hanford A Step Into History," The Hanford Visitor Agency, Hanford, 1999, p. 9.

"Hanford Visitor's Guide," Hanford Visitor Agency, Hanford, p. 29.

HANFORD'S CHINA ALLEY

Camille Wing, interview and tour of China Alley and Taoist Temple, Hanford, March 12, 1999.

HANFORD'S TAOIST TEMPLE

Hanford Visitor's Guide, Hanford Visitor Agency, Hanford, p. 16.

"The Historic Taoist Temple," pamphlet, Taoist Temple Preservation Society, Hanford.

Camille Wing, interview and tour of China Alley and Taoist Temple, Hanford, March 12, 1999.

CHINESE CENTER OF KNOWLEDGE

"Hanford Visitor's Guide," Hanford Visitor Agency, Hanford, p. 31.

Camille Wing, interview and tour of China Alley and Taoist Temple, Hanford, March 12, 1999.

THE WASHINGTON IRRIGATED COLONY

Rachel A. Dack, "Portraits of Easton—Its Early History," *Washington Union High School Centennial 1882-1982,* Easton Historical Society, 1992, pp. 54-8.

Charles W. Clough and William B. Secrest, Jr., *Fresno County—The Pioneer Years,* p. 144.

Wallace W. Elliot, *History of Fresno County,* reprinted by Valley Publishers, Fresno, 1973, p. 114-5.

Fresno County Centennial Committee, *Fresno County Centennial Almanac,* Fresno County Centennial Committee, Fresno, 1956, pp. 95.

THE VALLEY'S PREMIER SHEEPMAN

J. M. Guinn, *History of the State of California and Biographical Record of the San Joaquin Valley, California,* The Chapman Publishing Company, Chicago, 1905, pp. 669-70.

Paul Vandor, *History of Fresno County, Vol. II,* Historic Record Company, Los Angeles, 1919, pp. 1547-8.

Rob Walrond, "Fresno Pioneer William Helm Had Strong Influence on Growth, Prosperity of San Joaquin Valley," *Fresno Past & Present,* quarterly journal, Fresno Historical Society, Vol. 29, No. 3, pp. 1-6.

EL CAMINO VIEJO

Charles W. Clough and William B. Secrest, Jr., *Fresno County—The Pioneer Years,* pp. 39-43.

Fresno County Centennial Committee, *Fresno County Centennial Almanac,* Fresno County Centennial Committee, Fresno, 1956, pp. 119-20.

F. F. Latta, *El Camino Viejo a Los Angeles,* Kern County Historical Society, Bakersfield, 1936, p. 3.

Earl E. Williams, *El Camino Viejo,* Oakland National Horse Show, Concord, 1970, Foreword.

TRAVELERS ALONG THE CAMINO

Fresno County Centennial Committee, *Fresno County Centennial Almanac,* Fresno County Centennial Committee, Fresno, 1956, pp. 119-20.

F. F. Latta, *El Camino Viejo a Los Angeles,* Kern County Historical Society, Bakersfield, 1936, pp. 3-25.

Notes

Earl E. Williams, *El Camino Viejo*, Oakland National Horse Show, Concord, 1970, pp. 1-9, 22.

TWO WILD TOWNS IN THE WEST
Charles W. Clough and William B. Secrest, Jr., *Fresno County—The Pioneer Years,* pp. 39, 42-3.
F. F. Latta, *El Camino Viejo a Los Angeles*, Kern County Historical Society, Bakersfield, 1936, pp. 12-3.
Linda Sitterding, California History Librarian, Fresno County Free Library, California History Room, interview, April 20, 1999.
Earl E. Williams, *El Camino Viejo*, Oakland National Horse Show, Concord, 1970, pp. 19-20.

THE WELLS OF THE CHANE INDIANS
Charles W. Clough and William B. Secrest, Jr., *Fresno County—The Pioneer Years,* pp. 39-41.
Earl E. Williams, *El Camino Viejo*, Oakland National Horse Show, Concord, 1970, p. 22.

SPANISH PLACE NAMES
F. F. Latta, *El Camino Viejo a Los Angeles*, Kern County Historical Society, Bakersfield, 1936, pp. 6-14.
Albert Shumate, PhD., *Francisco Pacheco of Pacheco Pass*, University of the Pacific, Stockton, 1977, pp. 15-6.
Earl E. Williams, *El Camino Viejo*, Oakland National Horse Show, Concord, 1970, pp. 16-30.

FRESNO'S FIRST CONGREGATIONAL CHURCH
Charles W. Clough and William B. Secrest, Jr., *Fresno County—The Pioneer Years,* p. 135.
First Congregational Church of Fresno, "Save the Big Red Church," brochure.
First Congregational Church of Fresno Centennial Committee, *The First Congregational Church of Fresno*, Pioneer Publishing, Fresno, 1984, pp. 7-9, 13, 20, 30.

WORLD WAR II COMES TO FRESNO
Based on the author's memories.

THE YEAR 1945 IN FRESNO
Charles W. Clough, et al., *Fresno County in the 20th Century, from 1900 to the 1980s,* Panorama West Books, Fresno, 1986, pp. 290-1.

THE MARCH AGAINST "DEMON RUM"
Charles W. Clough, et al., *Fresno County in the 20th Century, from 1900 to the 1980s,* Panorama West Books, Fresno, 1986, pp. 92-3.
Jon R. McFarland, *Village on the Prairie*, Fowler Mother's Club, The Ensign Publishing Company, Fowler, 1972, pp. 27-8.
Samuel Elliot Morison, *The Oxford History of the American People*, Oxford University Press, New York, 1965, pp. 899-900.

HANFORD'S CARNEGIE MUSEUM
"Facts About the Hanford Carnegie Museum," provided by Pamela Stoddard, Director/Curator, Hanford Carnegie Museum.
Hanford Carnegie Museum, brochure.
Pamela Stoddard, Director/Curator, Hanford Carnegie Museum, interview and tour, March 12, 1999.

THE CHAUTAUQUA COMES TO FOWLER
Charles W. Clough, et al., *Fresno County in the 20th Century, from 1900 to the 1980s,* Panorama West Books, Fresno, 1986, pp. 89-91.

FRESNO'S FIRST BAPTIST CHURCH
Brief History of First Baptist Church, provided by First Baptist Church of Fresno.
First Baptist Church of Fresno Centennial Committee, *First Baptist Church Centennial History*, First Baptist Church, Fresno, 1982, pp. 5-11, 18-20.
Fresno First Baptist Church, *Ministry 2000.*

FROM COLLIS TO KERMAN
Charles W. Clough, et al., *Fresno County in the 20th Century, from 1900 to the 1980s,* Panorama West Books, Fresno, 1986, pp. 130-2.
Fresno County Centennial Committee, *Fresno County Centennial Almanac,* Fresno County Centennial Committee, Fresno, 1956, p. 100.
Linda Geringer, Executive Director, Kerman Chamber of Commerce, interview, April 1, 1999.

GUSTAV KREYENHAGEN
Charles W. Clough and William B. Secrest, Jr., *Fresno County—The Pioneer Years,* p. 263, 266.

Notes

Paul Vandor, *History of Fresno County,* Vol. I, Historic Record Company, Los Angeles, 1919, p. 1246.

Paul Vandor, *History of Fresno County,* Vol. II, Historic Record Company, Los Angeles, 1919, p. 1671.

Edward L. Kreyenhagen, Historic Resources Inventory Nomination Form, Fresno County Landmarks Records & Advisory Commission, January 1999.

THE KREYENHAGEN BROTHERS

Charles W. Clough and William B. Secrest, Jr., *Fresno County—The Pioneer Years,* pp. 263, 266.

Paul Vandor, *History of Fresno County,* Vol. I, Historic Record Company, Los Angeles, 1919, pp. 1246, 1251.

Paul Vandor, *History of Fresno County,* Vol. II, Historic Record Company, Los Angeles, 1919, p. 1671.

Edward L. Kreyenhagen, Historic Resources Inventory Nomination Form, Fresno County Landmarks Records & Advisory Commission, January 1999.

A HOME FOR LATINO ARTS

Arte Americas, promotional material.

Nancy Marcus, Director, interview and tour of Arte Americas, October 2, 1998.

ADOLPH DOMENGINE

Charles W. Clough and William B. Secrest, Jr., *Fresno County—The Pioneer Years,* p. 267.

John Harris, President, Harris Farms, Inc., interview, May 7, 1999.

Paul Vandor, *History of Fresno County,* Vol. II, Historic Record Company, Los Angeles, 1919, pp. 2181-2.

ARTHUR G. WAHLBERG

Charles W. Clough, et al., *Fresno County in the 20th Century, from 1900 to the 1980s,* Panorama West Books, Fresno, 1986, pp. 382-4.

Edwin M. Eaton, *Vintage Fresno,* The Huntington Press, Fresno, 1965, pp. 97-8.

Paul Vandor, *History of Fresno County,* Vol. II, Historic Record Company, Los Angeles, 1919, pp. 1691-2.

THE FIRST MAYOR OF FRESNO

Wallace W. Elliot, *History of Fresno County,* reprinted by Valley Publishers, Fresno, 1973, pp. 129-30.

Paul Vandor, *History of Fresno County,* Vol. I, Historic Record Company, Los Angeles, 1919, pp. 415.

A PRESERVATIONIST'S DREAM

Steve Bannister, member Historic Preservation Commission, City of Hanford, interview, April 5, 1999.

Jim Beath, Community Development Director, City of Hanford, interview, April 5, 1999.

Vince Peterson, Retired City Manager, City of Hanford, interview, April 5, 1999.

John Edward Powell, interview, April 5, 1999.

HANFORD'S HISTORIC CENTRAL PLAZA

City of Hanford, historic building information, provided by office of Community Development Director, April 7, 1999.

Kim German, ed., "Hanford: A Step Into History," The Hanford Visitors Agency, Hanford, 1999, pp. 22-5.

Hanford Visitors Agency, historic building information, web pages.

Kings County Centennial Committee, *Kings County, a Pictorial History*, County Government Center, Hanford, 1992, p. 49.

Delores Terrell, "Gems in the Treasure-trove of the Kings: Hanford's Historic Civic Center Park and Its Surroundings," internet.

FROM CRANES TO BASS

David W. Kean, *Wide Places in California Roads,* Vol. 4, The Concord Press, Sunnyvale, CA, 1996, pp. 18-9.

Betty E. Linn, *Madera County 1893-1993*, Madera Newspapers, Inc., Madera, 1993, pp. 19-22.

A VISIT TO A MOUNTAIN HIDEAWAY

Helen and Forest Clingan, interview and visit to their home, April 11, 1998.

THE BLACK KID

Charles Clough, *Madera,* Madera County History, Madera, 1968, p. 96.

CLINGAN'S JUNCTION

Notes

Helen and Forest Clingan, interview, April 11, 1998.
Helen and Forest Clingan, *Oak to Pine to Timberline*, Word Dancer Press, Clovis, 1995, pp. 64-6.
SMOKE SIGNALS IN THE VALLEY
Frank F. Latta, *Handbook of Yokuts Indians*, 50th Anniversary Commemorative Issue, Coyote Press, Salinas, 1999, pp. 336-9.
Helen and Forest Clingan, *Oak to Pine to Timberline*, Word Dancer Press, Clovis, 1995, pp. 7-9.
REUBEN CARLTON BAKER
Reuben Albaugh, "Cattle, Country and Champions," Archives of the R. C. Baker Museum.
Paul Vandor, *History of Fresno County,* Vol. I, Historic Record Company, Los Angeles, 1919, pp. 1254-7.
BAKER'S SHOE CASING COMPANY
R. C. Baker, letter written to stockholders of Baker Oil Tools, Inc., April 10, 1957, Archives of the R. C. Baker Museum.
Paul Vandor, *History of Fresno County,* Vol. I, Historic Record Company, Los Angeles, 1919, p. 1257.
A TRIP TO THE BIG BLUE HILLS
Charles W. Clough and William B. Secrest, Jr., *Fresno County—The Pioneer Years,* p. 224.
Fresno County Centennial Committee, *Fresno County Centennial Almanac,* Fresno County Centennial Committee, Fresno, 1956, p. 112.
COALING STATION A
Charles W. Clough and William B. Secrest, Jr., *Fresno County—The Pioneer Years,* p. 277-9.
Charles W. Clough, et al., *Fresno County in the 20th Century, from 1900 to the 1980s,* Panorama West Books, Fresno, 1986, pp. 115-20.
"Coalinga and the Pleasant Valley…Its History," brochure, R.C. Baker Memorial Museum.
Fresno County Centennial Committee, *Fresno County Centennial Almanac,* Fresno County Centennial Committee, Fresno, 1956, p. 90.
R. C. BAKER MEMORIAL MUSEUM
Charles W. Clough, et al., *Fresno County in the 20th Century, from 1900 to the 1980s,* Panorama West Books, Fresno, 1986, pp. 119.
"Coalinga and the Pleasant Valley…Its History," brochure, R.C. Baker Memorial Museum.
Tour of the R. C. Baker Memorial Museum, April 14, 1999.
HURON
Charles W. Clough, et al., *Fresno County in the 20th Century, from 1900 to the 1980s,* Panorama West Books, Fresno, 1986, pp. 114-5.
Charles W. Clough and William B. Secrest, Jr., *Fresno County—The Pioneer Years,* pp. 258-9, 262-3.
Fresno County Centennial Committee, *Fresno County Centennial Almanac,* Fresno County Centennial Committee, Fresno, 1956, p. 99.
Jim Doughty, Community Development Director, City of Huron, interview, April 19, 1999.
A SETTLEMENT NAMED ALCALDE
John Walton Caughey, *California,* Prentice-Hall, Inc., Englewood, Cliffs, New Jersey, 1953. pp. 275-6.
Charles W. Clough and William B. Secrest, Jr., *Fresno County—The Pioneer Years,* pp. 278-9.
Helen F. Cowan, Curator, R.C. Baker Memorial Museum, interview, April 19, 1999.
Wallace W. Elliot, *History of Fresno County,* reprinted by Valley Publishers, Fresno, 1973, p. 86.
EDNA DOMENGINE'S KIDNAPPING
William B. Secrest Sr., "The Kidnapping of Edna Domengine," *Fresno Past & Present*, Fresno City and County Historical Society, quarterly journal, Vol. 34, No. 2, pp. 2-5.
Paul Vandor, *History of Fresno County,* Vol. I, Historic Record Company, Los Angeles, 1919, pp. 387-8.
ARTHUR P. MAY
"A. P. May, Inc., Celebrates Its 25th Anniversary," *Coalinga Daily Record*, December 9, 1932. Archives of R. C. Baker Memorial Museum, Coalinga.
"A. P. May, Identified With Growth of Coalinga," *Coalinga Daily Record*, November 28, 1940. Archives of R. C. Baker Memorial Museum, Coalinga.

Notes

"Arthur P. May Center Figure in Early Days," *Coalinga Daily Record*, December 9, 1932. Archives of R. C. Baker Memorial Museum, Coalinga.

"Arthur P. May, Coalinga's First Mayor Is Called," *Coalinga Daily Record*, November 27, 1940. Archives of R. C. Baker Memorial Museum, Coalinga.

Arthur P. May Collection, letters and biographical material, Archives of R. C. Baker Memorial Museum, Coalinga.

MUIR'S LOOK AT THE VALLEY

John Muir, *The Treasures of the Yosemite*, Lewis Osborne, Ashland, 1970, pp. 15-6.

CHASING A KIDNAPPER

William B. Secrest Sr., "The Kidnapping of Edna Domengine," *Fresno Past & Present*, Fresno City and County Historical Society, quarterly journal, Vol. 34, No. 2, pp. 6-8.

Paul Vandor, *History of Fresno County*, Vol. I, Historic Record Company, Los Angeles, 1919, pp. 387-8.

POPE TIRE COMPANY

Charles W. Clough, et al., *Fresno County in the 20th Century, from 1900 to the 1980s*, Panorama West Books, Fresno, 1986, p. 272.

George "Bud" and Grace Pope, interview, April 26, 1999.

ICE CREAM WITH YOUR COFFEE

John Edward Powell, "Benham Ice Cream Building, Historic Resources Inventory Nomination Form," City of Fresno, August 31, 1994.

THE ELLA HOXIE HOME

Charles W. Clough, et al., *Fresno County in the 20th Century, from 1900 to the 1980s*, Panorama West Books, Fresno, 1986, pp. 52-3.

John Edward Powell, "The Ella Hoxie Home, Historic Resources Inventory Nomination Form, City of Fresno," August 31, 1994.

Paul Vandor, *History of Fresno County*, Vol. I, Historic Record Company, Los Angeles, 1919, pp. 609-11; 647; 648-51.

THE PICKFORD FAMILY OF FRESNO

Joel Pickford, interview, April 30, 1999.

Ben R. Walker, *The Fresno County Blue Book*, Arthur J. Cawston, managing editor and publisher, Fresno, 1941, pp. 139, 145.

GEORGE PICKFORD

"George Pickford, Pioneer Resident of Fresno, Dies," *The Fresno Bee*, December 21, 1941.

Joel Pickford, interview, April 30, 1999.

Ben R. Walker, *The Fresno County Blue Book*, Arthur J. Cawston, managing editor and publisher, Fresno, 1941, p. 376.

ROLLIN PICKFORD

Joel Pickford, *California Light, the Watercolors of Rollin Pickford*, The Press at California State University, Fresno, Fresno, 1998, pp. 231-258.

Joel Pickford, interview, April 30, 1999.

THE HOME OF INGVART TEILMAN

American Association of University Women, *Heritage Fresno Homes and People*, Pioneer Publishing Company, 1975, p. 70.

John Edward Powell, interview and tour of Teilman Home, May 7, 1999.

EMMANUEL LUTHERAN CHURCH

John Edward Powell, "Emmanuel Lutheran Church, Historic Resources Inventory Nomination Form," City of Fresno, August 31, 1994.

L. C. WESLEY SUPER GARAGE

John Edward Powell, interview, May 12, 1999.

John Edward Powell, "L. C. Wesley Super Garage, Historic Resources Inventory Nomination Form," City of Fresno, August 31, 1994.

MARGARET HUDSON

Margaret Hudson, interview and tour of her gardens and studios, May 10, 1999.

FRESNO BETSUIN BUDDHIST TEMPLE

Rev. William T. Masuda, Rinban of Fresno Betsuin Buddhist Temple, interview, May 12, 1999.

Ryo Munekata, Chairman, BCA 75th Anniversary History Project, *Buddhist Churches of America, Vol. I*, Nobart, Inc. Chicago, 1974, pp. 53; 156-8.

85th Anniversary Committee, *85th Anniversary of the Fresno Betsuin Buddhist Temple 1901-1986*, pp. 17-21.

Notes

IN THE TEMPLE GARDEN
  Toyoko Arakawa, editor, "Fresno Betsuin Buddhist Temple," informational pamphlet, revised edition, 1992.
  Rev. William T. Masuda, Rinban of Fresno Betsuin Buddhist Temple, interview, May 12, 1999.
  Ryo Munekata, Chairman, BCA 75th Anniversary History Project, *Buddhist Churches of America, Vol. I*, Nobart, Inc. Chicago, 1974, p. 161.
  85th Anniversary Committee, *85th Anniversary of the Fresno Betsuin Buddhist Temple 1901-1986*, p. 22.
TWO ARCHITECTS NAMED SWARTZ
  John Edward Powell, "Parker Nash Building, Historic Resources Inventory Nomination Form," City of Fresno, August 31, 1994, Sheet 2.
  Ben R. Walker, *The Fresno County Blue Book,* Arthur J. Cawston, managing editor and publisher, Fresno, 1941, pp. 406-7.
HOBART PARK
  John Edward Powell, "Hobart Park, Historic Resources Inventory Nomination Form," City of Fresno, August 31, 1994.
A WOMAN NAMED MARJAREE
  Building Trust, Quarterly Newsletter of the Marjaree Mason Center, December, 1999, p. 1.
  Building Trust, Quarterly Newsletter of the Marjaree Mason Center, March, 1999, p. 1.
  Tim F. Reese, Executive Director, Marjaree Mason Center, Inc., interview, May 20, 1999.
JUDGE ERNEST KLETTE
  Ernest Klette, unpublished autobiography, pp. 23-6, 29, 39, 86-88, 91-2.
  "Resolution of the Fresno County Bar Association With Respect to the Memory of the Late Ernest Klette," December 8, 1950.
  Paul Vandor, *History of Fresno County,* Vol. I, Historic Record Company, Los Angeles, 1919, pp. 924, 929.

Bibliography

Adkins, Dennis and J. Randall McFarland. Playbill for the Unger Opera House's Farewell Performances. July 11, 12 and 13, 1996. Pioneer Village, Selma, California.

African American Historical and Cultural Museum. Brochure.

Albaugh, Reuben. "Cattle, Country and Champions." Archives of the R. C. Baker Museum.

"All Fired Up!" Bulldog Foundation fortieth anniversary brochure. Provided by Bulldog Foundation Office, California State University, Fresno.

American Association of University Women. *Heritage Fresno: Homes and People.* Fresno: Pioneer Publishing Company, 1975.

-----. *Heritage Fresno: Women and Their Contributions.* Fresno: Pioneer Publishing Company, 1987.

Andrew Davidson Firebaugh. Clamproclamation. Jim Savage Chapter No. 1852. E Clampus Vitus. November 17, 1968.

"A. P. May, Inc., Celebrates Its 25th Anniversary." *Coalinga Daily Record*, December 9, 1932. Archives of R. C. Baker Memorial Museum, Coalinga.

"A.P. May, Identified With Growth of Coalinga." *Coalinga Daily Record*, November 28, 1940. Archives of R. C. Baker Memorial Museum, Coalinga.

Arakawa, Toyoko, editor. "Fresno Betsuin Buddhist Temple." Informational pamphlet. Revised edition, 1992.

Arte Americas. Promotional material.

"Arthur P. May Center Figure in Early Days." *Coalinga Daily Record,* December 9, 1932. Archives of R.C. Baker Memorial Museum, Coalinga.

"Arthur P. May, Coalinga's First Mayor Is Called." *Coalinga Daily Record*, November 27, 1940. Archives of R. C. Baker Memorial Museum, Coalinga.

Arthur P. May Collection. Letters and biographical material. Archives of R. C. Baker Memorial Museum, Coalinga.

Aspetitia, Captain Raewyn. Salvation Army, Fresno Corps. Interview, December 2, 1998.

Baker, R. C. Letter written to stockholders of Baker Oil Tools, Inc., April 10, 1957. Archives of R. C. Baker Museum, Coalinga.

Bancroft, Hubert Howe. *History of California.* Printed in facsimile from the first American edition. Santa Barbara, California, 1963.

Bannister, Steve. Member of Historic Preservation Commission, City of Hanford. Interview, April 5, 1999.

Barnes, Dwight. President, Sierra Sites Historical Association. Interview and guided tour of Fresno Flats Historical Park, June 28, 1998.

Beath, Jim. Community development director, City of Hanford. Interview, April 5, 1999.

Behind-the-Scenes Facts. Brochure. Santa Cruz Seaside Company.

Bingham, Paul O. and Beverly Bubar Denenberg. "Maynard Dixon as Muralist: Sketches for the Mark Hopkins Hotel Mural." *California History*, California Historical Society, Vol. LXIX, No. 1, Spring 1990.

Bitters, Virginia, editor. *Owl.* Fresno High School Student Body. Fresno, 1958.

Boyd, William Harland and Glendon J. Rodgers. *San Joaquin Vignettes, The Reminiscences of Captain John Barker.* Bakersfield: Kern County Historical Society, Merchants Printing and Lithographing Co., Inc., 1955, pp. vii, 99-105.

Boys & Girls Clubs of Fresno County. History & information packet.

Brief History of First Baptist Church. Provided by First Baptist Church of Fresno.

Broeske, John. Program director, KMJ Radio. Interview, August 4, 1998.

Building Trust. Quarterly newsletter of the Marjaree Mason Center, December, 1998, and March 1999.

Bunnell, Lafayette Houghton, M.D. *Discovery of the Yosemite.* Los Angeles: G. W. Gerlicher, 1911.

Bursik, George. The Hoonanian Home. Historic Resources Inventory, City of Fresno, 1993.

California Dried Fig Advisory Board. *48 family favorites with California Figs*.

Caughey, John Walton. *California*. Englewood Cliffs, NJ: Prentice-Hall, Inc., 1953.

Centennial Commemorative Committee. *First Armenian Presbyterian Church 1897-1997*. Fresno, 1997.

Centennial Committee. *The First Congregational Church of Fresno: The First One Hundred Years*. Fresno: Pioneer Publishing Company, 1984.

City of Hanford. Historic building information. Provided by office of Community Development Director, April 7, 1999.

Clingan, Helen and Forest. Interview, April 11, 1998.

-----. *Oak to Pine to Timberline*. Fresno: Word Dancer Press, Fresno, 1985.

Clough, Charles W. and William B. Secrest, Jr. *Fresno County: The Pioneer Years*. Fresno: Panorama West Books, 1984.

Clough, Charles W. et al. *Fresno County in the 20th Century, from 1900 to the 1980s*. Fresno: Panorama West Books, 1986.

Clough, Charles. *Madera*. Madera County History, Madera, 1968.

"Coalinga and the Pleasant Valley...Its History." Brochure. R. C. Baker Memorial Museum.

Coate, William S. Interview, July 2, 1998.

-----. *Pieces of the Past: Madera County Vignettes*. Madera: The Classroom Chronicles Press, 1992.

-----. *Pieces of the Past: Madera County Vignettes*. 2nd edition. Madera: The Classroom Chronicles Press, 1994.

Cowan, Helen F. Curator, R. C. Baker Memorial Museum. Interview, April 19, 1999.

Coy, Owen C., Ph.D. *California County Boundaries*. Berkeley: California Historical Survey Commission, 1923. Revised edition. Fresno: Valley Publishers, 1973.

Crampton, Bucher. *Grasses In California*. Berkeley and Los Angeles: University of California Press, 1974.

Crane, Omer. "Going high on the turn 25 years ago fatal move for Vukovich, Sr." *Fresno Bee*, May 25, 1980.

-----. "Tulare Gives Hero's Welcome to Bob Mathias." *Fresno Bee,* August 28, 1948.

Craycroft, Columbus Joel. Unpublished autobiography. Courtesy of Joyce Gibson.

Dack, Rachel A. "Portraits of Easton: Its Early History." *Washington Union High School Centennial 1882-1982*. Easton Historical Society, 1982.

Dakin, Susanna Bryant. *Rose, or Rose Thorn?* Berkeley: The Friends of the Bancroft Library, University of California, 1963.

Department of the Army. *Hidden Reservoir Fresno River, California*. Master Plan & Recreational Facilities, Sacramento District. Sacramento, California, 1968.

Dingman, Frances, the Salvation Army Western Territory Museum. Interview, December 2, 1998.

Dixon, Charles E. *Rancho Laguna De Tache*. April 9, 1961.

Dixon, Maynard. *Rim-Rock and Sage*. San Francisco: The California Historical Society, 1977.

"Donations to Mariposa County Courthouse - 1957." Collections of Scott Pinkerton.

Doughty, Jim. Community development director, City of Huron. Interview, April 19, 1999.

Dunn, Mary. Interview in Raymond, October 30, 1998.

Durham, David L. *California Geographic Names*. Clovis: Word Dancer Press, 1998.

Eaton, Edwin M. *Vintage Fresno*. Fresno: Huntington Press, 1965.

Eccleston, Robert. *The Mariposa Indian War 1850-1851*. C. Gregory Crampton, ed. Salt Lake City: University of Utah Press, 1957.

Ellena, Raymond. "Burell." *Fresno County Centennial Almanac*. Fresno: Fresno County

Centennial Committee, 1956.

Elliot, Wallace W. *History of Fresno County.* Reprint. Fresno: Valley Publishers, 1973.

Ellsworth, Richard. Interview, July 27, 1998.

Errecart, Felipe Maria. "The Wildflowers of My Memories." Footnote to the poem. First place winner in 1973 members' writing contest, California Writers and Artists of the San Joaquin Valley.

"Facts About the Hanford Carnegie Museum." Provided by Pamela Stoddard, director/curator, Hanford Carnegie Museum.

Farquhar, Francis P. *History of the Sierra Nevada.* Berkeley and Los Angeles: University of California Press, 1965.

Fiorani, Evelyn Sterios. Interview, January 6, 1999.

Fiore, Nicholas. Ski school director, Badger Pass. Interview, January 22, 1998.

First Baptist Church of Fresno Centennial Committee. *First Baptist Church Centennial History.* Fresno: First Baptist Church, 1982.

First Congregational Church of Fresno. "Save the Big Red Church." Brochure.

First Congregational Church of Fresno Centennial Committee. *The First Congregational Church of Fresno.* Fresno: Pioneer Publishing, 1984.

Frame, Leonard. Interview, April 5, 1998.

Fresno Business Journal. Frank J. Sanders: Duke of Tulare Street is back. March 21, 1994.

Fresno County Abstract Company. *Abstract of the Title to Rancho Laguna De Tache.* Fresno, California, no date.

Fresno County Centennial Almanac. Fresno: Fresno County Centennial Committee, 1956.

Fresno First Baptist Church. *Ministry 2000.*

Fresno Flats Historical Park. Brochure. Sierra Sites Historical Association.

Geringer, Linda. Executive director, Kerman Chamber of Commerce. Interview, April 1, 1999.

German, Kim, ed. "Hanford, A Step Into History." Hanford: Hanford Visitor Agency, 1999.

Gianopulos, George. Interview, October 22, 1998.

Goble, Ron. "Emparan looks back on 25 years as farm official." *Fresno Bee,* March 1, 1986.

Gomes, Jim. President and chief executive officer, Danish Creamery Association. Interview, November 12, 1998.

Gomes, Sharlene. *Danish Creamery Association 1895-1995.* Fresno, 1995.

Grahlman, Richard. Supervisory ranger, U.S. Army Corps of Engineers, Hensley Lake, Hidden Dam. Interview, May 6, 1978.

Greenwood, Gina. Director of marketing and public relations for Storyland. Interview, August 27, 1998.

Gudde, Erwin G. *California Place Names.* Berkeley and Los Angeles: University of California Press, 1949.

Guinn, J. M. *History of the State of California and Biographical Record of the San Joaquin Valley, California.* Chicago: Chapman Publishing Company, 1905.

Haak, Dr. Harold. "CSUF's Past, Present and Future." Annual address to the Academic Assembly of California State University, Fresno, August, 1986.

Hagerty, Donald J. *Desert Dreams.* Layton, Utah: Peregrine Smith Books, 1993.

Halemeier, Doris. Common Threads Committee. Interview, February 13, 1999.

Hanford Carnegie Museum. Brochure.

Hanford Visitors Agency. Historic building information. Web pages.

"Hanford Visitor's Guide." Hanford: Hanford Visitor Agency.

Harlan, Brad. Interview, November 18, 1998.

Harris, John. President, Harris Farms, Inc. Interview, May 7, 1999.

Bibliography

Henry, Stephen, the Honorable. "Old Times in the Fresno Courthouse," *The Bar Bulletin.* Fresno County Bar Association, May, 1998, Vol. 21, No. 5.

Henson, Bob & Frances. *Bits & Pieces of Riverdale's History.* Riverdale, 1996.

Hohmann, Ken. Interview, January 9, 1999.

Hudelson, Nancy. *Meux Home News,* Vol. V, No. IV.

Hudson, Margaret. Interview and tour of her gardens and studios, May 10, 1999.

"Jack A. Kelley." Biographical material provided by the African American Historical and Cultural Museum.

"J. C. Penney Meets Paul P. Harris," *The Rotarian,* October, 1994.

Kean, David W. *Wide Places in California Roads.* Vol. 4. Sunnyvale, CA: Concord Press, 1996.

Keeler, Guy. "A last alas for a study club unparallel'd." *Fresno Bee,* May 27, 1983.

Kelley, Jack A. President, African American Historical and Cultural Museum. Interview and tour of museum, November 23, 1998.

Kings County Centennial Committee. *Kings County: A Pictorial History.* Hanford: County Government Center, 1992.

Klette, Ernest. Unpublished autobiography.

Kreyenhagen, Edward L. Historic Resources Inventory nomination form. Fresno County Landmarks Records & Advisory Commission, January, 1999.

Kubiak, Rick. "A History of the San Joaquin Valley Civil War Round Table."

Kuebler, Bill. Director, Tower District Marketing Committee. Interviews, February 4, 1998, and August 5, 1998.

Latta, F. F. *El Camino Viejo a Los Angeles.* Bakersfield: Kern County Historical Society, 1936.

-----. *Dalton Gang Days.* Santa Cruz: Bear State Books, 1976.

-----. *Handbook of Yokuts Indians.* 2nd edition. Santa Cruz: Bear State Books, 1977.

-----. *Handbook of Yokuts Indians.* 50th Anniversary Commemorative Issue. Salinas: Coyote Press, 1999.

Linn, Betty E. *Madera County 1893-1993.* Madera: Madera Newspapers, Inc., 1993.

Long, Robert J. "William S. Chapman: The Unknown Builder of Fresno County," *Fresno Past & Present,* quarterly journal, Fresno City and County Historical Society. Vol. 39, No. 3.

Laughnan, Woody. "Reunion Planners Keep on Meeting." *Fresno Bee,* date unknown.

Maloney, James. Interview, July 14, 1998.

Marcus, Nancy. Interview and tour of Arte Americas, October 2, 1998.

Martin, Corinne H. Director, resource development, Boys and Girls Clubs of Fresno County. Interview, April 28, 1998.

Mason, Jeannie. Interview in Raymond, October 30, 1998. Phone interview, November 4, 1998.

Mason, Ruth and Bill. *History of Fresno Flats.* 1997 edition.

Masuda, the Rev. William T. Rinban of Fresno Betsuin Buddhist Temple. Interview, May 12, 1999.

Melkonian, Zabelle. Grandniece of Seropian brothers. Information given by telephone message received through the First Armenian Presbyterian Church.

McEwen, Bill and John Rich. "Tragedy strikes Vukovich again." "Fatal accident ends Billy's promising career." *Fresno Bee,* November 26, 1990.

McFarland, J. Randall. *Centennial Selma.* Selma: J. Randall McFarland, in association with the *Selma Enterprise,* 1980.

-----. Interview and driving tour of Selma. May 7, 1998.

-----. *Thanks for the Memory.* Script of final performance, Unger Opera House, July 13, 1996.

-----. *Water For a Thirsty Land.* Selma: Consolidated Irrigation District, 1996.

Bibliography

McFarland, Jon R. *Village on the Prairie*. Fowler: Fowler Mother's Club, the Ensign Publishing Company, 1972.

McGrath, Matthew M. and John Edward Powell. "The Architect." Promotional brochure provided by Manning Properties, 1997.

McKay, Mary Helen. Interview, October 12, 1998.

McKittrich, Myrtle M. *Vallejo, Son of California*. Portland, OR: Binfords & Mort, 1944.

Moore, Heyward. "High Sierra Lake and Stream Names." *Fresno Past & Present,* quarterly journal, Fresno City and County Historical Society. Vol. 25, No. 4.

Mordecai Historians. *Refuge*. Introduction by William S. Coate. Madera: Classroom Chronicles Press, 1988.

Mordecai Scholars. *The Mordecai Memoirs*. Madera: Classroom Chronicles Press.

Morgan, Dale L. et al. *GPH An Informal Record of George P. Hammond and His Era in the Bancroft Library*. The Friends of the Bancroft Library, University of California, Berkeley, 1965.

Morison, Samuel Elliot. *The Oxford History of the American People*. New York: Oxford University Press, 1965.

Mui, Gretchen Smith. *Arts & Crafts Design in America*. San Francisco: Chronicle Books, 1998.

Muir, John. *The Treasures of the Yosemite*. Ashland, OR: Lewis Osborne, 1970.

Muller, June. "Finding of 1893 Invitation Recalls Only County Hanging." *Fresno Bee.*

Munekata, Ryo. Chairman, BCA 75th Anniversary History Project. *Buddhist Churches of America, Vol. I*. Chicago: Nobart, Inc., 1974.

Muzquiz, Felix. Assistant director, Tower District Marketing Committee. Interview, February 2, 1998.

Nielsen, Ernest. *Boundary Tree: Laguna De Tache Spanish Land Grant*. February 11, 1961.

Ogle, Pat. Interview, May 19, 1998.

-----. Press release with biography of Dennis Woods, May 19, 1998.

-----. Written material on results of Bulldog Foundation fund raising drive.

-----. Written material on results of Bulldog Foundation fund raising drive, update, May 28, 1999.

Orman, Ed. "Sport Thinks." *Fresno Bee,* date not available.

Padgett, Marva. Interview in Raymond, October 30, 1998.

Panter, John. The Harlow Home. Historic Resources Inventory, City of Fresno, May 20, 1989.

Patnaude, William. James Phelan Building. Historic Resources Inventory, City of Fresno, June 30, 1978.

-----. The Hewitt Home. Historic Resources Inventory, City of Fresno, June 26, 1978.

-----. The Legler Residence. Historic Resources Inventory, City of Fresno, June 26, 1978.

-----. The Mason Building. Historic Resources Inventory. City of Fresno, June 29, 1978.

-----. The McKay Home. Historic Resources Inventory. City of Fresno, June 27, 1978.

-----. The Shipp Home. Historic Resources Inventory. City of Fresno, June 27, 1978.

-----. The Shuttera Home. Historic Resources Inventory. City of Fresno, June 23, 1978.

Patterson, William K. "Fresno Marks Centennial of First Religious Service." *Fresno Bee,* October 21, 1955.

-----. "Latta, authority on valley Indians, dead at 90." *Fresno Bee*, May 17, 1983.

Pennell, Robert. Cultural resources manager, Table Mountain Rancheria. Interview and tour of project, February 23, 1999.

Penney, J. C. *Lines of a Layman*. Grand Rapids, MI: Wm. B. Eerdmans Publishing Co., 1956.

Peterson, Vince. Retired city manager, City of Hanford. Interview, April 5, 1999.

Bibliography

Pickford, Joel. *California Light, the Watercolors of Rollin Pickford*. Fresno: The Press at California State University, Fresno, 1998.

-----. Interview, April 30, 1999.

Pinkerton, Scott. *History and Description of Mariposa County Courthouse 1854*. Brochure. Mariposa County Chamber of Commerce.

-----. Interviews, November 7, 1989, and November 10, 1989.

-----. *Mariposa County Courthouse*. Mariposa: Mariposa Heritage Press, 1989.

Pollock, Dennis. "The Never-Ending Reunion." *Fresno Bee,* March 15, 1994.

Pope, George "Bud" and Grace. Interview, April 26, 1999.

Porter, Walt. "Bigby Villa—Fulfillment of Many Dreams." *Fresno Bee,* April 8, 1972.

Powell, John Edward. "Charles Franklin." Unpublished biographical sketch.

-----. "Benham Ice Cream Building." Historic Resources Inventory nomination form. City of Fresno, August 31, 1994.

-----. "The Ella Hoxie Home." Historic Resources Inventory nomination form. City of Fresno, August 31, 1994.

-----. "Emmanuel Lutheran Church." Historic Resources Inventory nomination form. City of Fresno, August 31, 1994.

-----. "Hobart Park." Historic Resources Inventory nomination form. City of Fresno, August 31, 1994.

-----. "L. C. Wesley Super Garage." Historic Resources Inventory nomination form. City of Fresno, August 31, 1994.

-----. "Parker Nash Building." Historic Resources Inventory nomination form. City of Fresno, August 31, 1994.

-----. Interviews, November 8, 1997; December 27, 1997; April 5, 1999; May 12, 1999; November 8

-----. Interview and tour of Teilman Home, May 7, 1999.

Powers, Muriel. Interview, November 6, 1989.

Preston, Brenda Burnett. *Andrew Davidson Firebaugh & Susan Burgess Firebaugh, California Pioneers*. Rio Del Mar: Rio Del Mar Press, 1995.

Quenzer, Ken. Executive director, Boys and Girls Clubs of Fresno County. Interview, April 28, 1998.

Radanovich, Leroy. *Mariposa Gazette*, May 25, 1995.

Raven, Mart and Oliva. Interview, October 19, 1997.

Rawls, Bill. Assistant manager, International Agri-Center, Inc. Interviews, January 12, 1998, and January 15, 1998.

Redinger, David H. *The Story of Big Creek*. Los Angeles: Angelus Press, 1949.

Reese, Tim F. Executive director, Marjaree Mason Center, Inc. Interview, May 20, 1999.

Rehart, Schyler. Interviews, August 7, 1998; January 9, 1999; January 16, 1999.

Renn, Linda. "Harlan family is rooted in earliest Riverdale history." *Twin City Times,* Vol. XXII, No. 34, August 26, 1998.

-----. "Riverdale to celebrate 100th birthday." *Twin City Times*, Vol. XXII. No. 4, January 28, 1998.

"Resolution of the Fresno County Bar Association With Respect to the Memory of the Late Ernest Klette." December 8, 1950.

Rich, John. "Crash kills Fresno racer Billy Vukovich, 27-year old second in family to die racing." *Fresno Bee*, November 26, 1990.

Rising, Maria. International Agri-Center, Inc. Web pages for the California Farm Equipment Show and International Exposition.

Robbins, Wilfred William, Margaret K. Bellure and Walter S. Ball. *Weeds of California*.

Sacramento: State Department of Agriculture, 1941.

Rockas, Dr. Helen. *History of the Greek Community of Fresno.*

Rogers, Richard. Interview, January 16, 1998.

Roscoe, Theodore. *The Web of Conspiracy.* Englewood Cliffs, NJ: Prentice-Hall, 1959.

Rosenthal, Ed. "Bob Mathias Is Acclaimed For Victory." *Fresno Bee,* August 7, 1948.

Rotary Kids Country. Promotional brochure.

Rotary Storyland and Playland. Promotional brochure.

Rowell, Chester H. *A Brief Account of the Life of Chester H. Rowell.* Unpublished manuscript.

Salley, Harold. *History of California Post Offices 1849-1990.* 2nd edition edited by Edward L. Patera. La Mesa: The Depot, 1991.

"Sands Baker and the Dunlap Area." Clamproclamation. Jim Savage Chapter 1852, E Clampus Vitus, July, 1989.

Sanders, Frank J. Biographical notes and history.

Sargent, Shirley. *Enchanted Childhoods.* Yosemite: Flying Spur Press, 1993.

Secrest, William B., Sr. "The Kidnapping of Edna Domengine." *Fresno Past & Present,* quarterly journal, Fresno City and County Historical Society, Vol. 34, No. 2.

Selland, Mabelle. Interview, September 29, 1998.

-----. Speech given to the Garden of the Sun Corral of the Westerners, October 21, 1998.

Sinclair, Laura Wickham. "Early History of Caruthers," *The History of Caruthers.* 2nd edition. Caruthers: Caruthers High Future Business Leaders of America, 1976.

Shelton, G.M. "Buel, Veteran Bee Cartoonist, Soon Will Retire, Go Fishing." *Fresno Bee,* June 27, 1948.

Shumate, Albert, Ph.D. *Francisco Pacheco of Pacheco Pass.* Stockton: University of the Pacific, 1977.

Sitterding, Linda. California history librarian, Fresno County Free Library California History Room. Interview, April 20, 1999.

Smith, Joe. *From the Valley to the High Sierra.* Ed. by Dwight H. Barnes and Ray Nish. *Fresno Bee.*

Smith, Wallace. *Garden of the Sun.* Los Angeles: Lymanhouse, 1939.

-----. *Prodigal Sons.* Boston: Christopher Publishing House, 1951.

Sniffin, Daniel K. Documents relating to Sniffin Family genealogy.

Stagner, Clyde. Interview, January 12, 1998.

Stoddard, Pamela. Director/curator, Hanford Carnegie Museum. Interview and tour, March 12, 1999.

Streit, Edwin. "The Old Neighborhood." *Fresno Past & Present,* quarterly journal, Fresno City and County Historical Society, Vol. 28, No. 3, Fall, 1986.

Tavlian, Philip E. Chairman of First Armenian Presbyterian Church Centennial Commemorative Committee. Interview and tour of church and adjacent buildings, April 20, 1998.

Taylor, Roger. "Summary of Statement for Historical and Architectural Significance" of Veterans Memorial Auditorium. National Register nomination, May 10, 1994. Fresno City Hall, Housing and Development Department.

Tennis, Nelson. "Forty Years Ago in Fresno." *Student Sports.* Vol. 20, No. 4, April, 1998.

Terrell, Delores. "Gems in the Treasure-trove of the Kings: Hanford's Historic Civic Center Park and Its Surroundings." Internet.

"The Historic Taoist Temple. Pamphlet. Hanford: Taoist Temple Preservation Society.

"The Origin of Christmas Kettles." Provided by Captain Raewyn Aspetitia, Salvation Army, Fresno Citadel.

Valdivia, Angela. "Community Leader Hinton Dies." *Fresno Bee*, August 26, 1987.

Vandor, Paul. *History of Fresno County,* Vols. I & II. Los Angeles: Historic Record Company, 1919.

Walker, Ben R. *The Fresno County Blue Book.* Fresno: Arthur J. Cawston, managing editor and publisher, 1941.

Walrond, Rob. "Fresno Pioneer William Helm Had Strong Influence on Growth, Prosperity of San Joaquin Valley." *Fresno Past & Present*, quarterly journal, Fresno City and County Historical Society, Vol. 29, No. 3.

Wasco Chamber of Commerce. *Welcome to Wasco*. Informational brochure.

Wasco's 30th Annual Festival of Roses. Wasco Festival of Roses, Inc. Promotional brochure.

Wash, Robert M. "After the Assassination of Lincoln did John Wilkes Booth escape and use Fresno as a hide-out??!" *Fresno County Sun*, May 19, 1995.

-----. *The Dalton Gang.* Unpublished paper presented to the Fowler Friday Evening Club.

-----. "The History of Sunnyside: A Place With Space," chapter 5, "Eisen Vineyard; Queen Among Early Ranches of Sunnyside." *Sunnyside Up*, Vol. IV, Issue 5, May 1991.

-----. "The History of Sunnyside: A Place With Space," chapter 9, "Roeding Family Leaves Rich Legacy In Sunnyside." *Sunnyside Up*, Vol. IV, Issue 9, September 1991.

-----. Interviews. November 6, 1997; November 19, 1997; April 10, 1998; May 17, 1998; November 18, 1998.

-----. Notes for speech for Fowler Friday Evening Club, "Genealogy of Robert V. Emparan." Unpublished manuscript.

-----. *The Rancho Laguna De Tache Mexican Land Grant and the "Witness Tree."* Unpublished manuscript.

-----. "Turbulent Year in the Raisin Industry." *Fresno County in the 20th Century, from 1900 to the 1980s*. Fresno: Panorama West Books, 1986.

Washington Union High School Centennial 1892-1992. Fresno: Easton Historical Society, 1992.

Williams, Earl E. *El Camino Viejo.* Oakland National Horse Show, Concord, 1970. Foreword.

Winchell, L. A. Papers. Ms. 3. Chapter 22.

Wing, Camille. Interview and tour of China Alley and Taoist Temple, Hanford, March 12, 1999.

Wissler, Brooke. Interview, June 7, 1998.

Wood, Raymond F. *The Early History of Mariposa County.* Fresno: Academy Library Guild, 1954.

Woodward map, Fresno City. Springfield, MA: Nirenstein's National Map Co., 1950. Courtesy John Edward Powell.

Woods, Dennis. Interview, May 19, 1998.

85th Anniversary Committee. *85th Anniversary of the Fresno Betsuin Buddhist Temple 1901-1986*

Daily Evening Expositor. July 16, 1892. Courtesy William B. Secrest, Sr.

The Fresno Bee. April 5, 1926. Obituary.

-----. June 2, 1933. p. 7-B. Files of John Edward Powell.

-----. January 1, 1937.

-----. May 5, 1941.

-----. "George Pickford, Pioneer Resident of Fresno, Dies." December 21, 1941.

-----. August 19, 1943.

-----. August 21, 1951.

-----. March 17, 1952.

-----. May 2, 1952.

-----. May 5, 1952.

-----. November 11, 1952. Obituary.

-----. January 25, 1955.

-----. October 22, 1955.

-----. November 10, 1957.

-----. "Remember When?" August 4, 1963.

-----. November 5, 1967.

-----. April 25, 1970.

-----. August 17, 1971.

-----. November 21, 1971.

-----. April 7, 1972.

-----. December 30, 1973.

-----. April 23, 1981.

-----. February 7, 1982.

-----. "Vukovich legacy: glorious, tragic Indy success spans 3 generations." November 26, 1990.

-----. "Booth To Stay Buried." May 27, 1995.

-----. "Talk of the Tower." February 1998.

-----. "Remember When?" No date available.

-----. "Prior, Shelton Sell Auto Agency to Frank J. Sanders." No date available.

Fresno Evening Democrat. October 31, 1885.

-----. September 5, 1885.

-----. September 7, 1885.

-----. November 16, 1885.

-----. November 20, 1885.

Fresno Morning Republican. July 17, 1892. Courtesy William B. Secrest, Sr.

-----. July 3, 1898.

-----. July 4, 1898.

-----. July 7, 1898.

-----. December 23, 1899.

-----. November 18, 1915.

-----. October 22, 1916.

-----. July 21, 1917.

-----. March 1, 1918.

San Francisco Examiner, July 24, 1892. Courtesy William B. Secrest, Sr.

The Selma Enterprise, August 21, 1941.

Index

Index

Index

About the Author

Cathy Rehart's mother's family arrived in Fresno Station in 1873, the year after the town was founded. She was born in the Sample Sanitarium on Fulton Street, is a third generation graduate of Fresno High School and a second generation graduate of Fresno State College with a BA in English and history. She is the mother of three grown children.

During the years her children were in school, her involvement in their activities resulted in service on several PTA boards, the Fresno High School Site Council and the Cub Scouts. Later she served as first Vice-Chairwoman for the Historic Preservation Commission for the City of Fresno; as a member of the Board of Directors of the Fresno City and County Historical Society; as chair of the Preservation Committee of the FCCHS; and a President of the La Paloma Guild, the FCCH's auxiliary.

From 1986 to 1994, she held the position of Education/Information Director for the FCCHS.

Her work as a freelance writer includes writing the KMJ Radio scripts for "The Valley's Legends and Legacies" —from which this book is derived—and other writing projects on local history.